China's Road to Greater Financial Stability

Some Policy Perspectives

EDITORS

Udaibir S. Das, Jonathan Fiechter, and Tao Sun

INTERNATIONAL MONETARY FUND

Cataloging-in-Publication Data
Joint Bank-Fund Library

China's road to greater financial stability : some policy perspectives /
editors Udaibir S. Das, Jonathan Fiechter and Tao Sun.—Washington,
D.C. : International Monetary Fund, 2013.
p. : ill. ; cm.

Includes bibliographical references.

1. Finance—China   2. Financial institutions—China.   3. Banks and
banking—China.   4. Economic development—China.   5. Macroeconomics.
I. Das, Udaibir S.   II. Fiechter, Jonathan.   III. Sun, Tao, 1970–
IV. International Monetary Fund.

HG187.C6C55 2013

ISBN: 978-1-61635-406-0 (paper)
ISBN: 978-1-48431-534-7 (ePub)
ISBN: 978-1-47552-373-7 (Mobi pocket)
ISBN: 978-1-47553-321-7 (Web PDF)

Please send orders to:
International Monetary Fund, Publication Services
P.O. Box 92780, Washington, DC 20090, U.S.A.
Tel.: (202) 623-7430   Fax: (202) 623-7201
E-mail: publications@imf.org
Internet: www.elibrary.imf.org
www.imfbookstore.org

Contents

Acknowledgments

The last four years have been a roller-coaster ride for global financial stability. As China transforms its economic and financial future, a key lesson from the crisis is to put in place financial stability safeguards. This book was born of that realization. It is a culmination of the efforts of many people in China, staff of the International Monetary Fund (IMF), and select policy-focused China watchers. The diversity of contributors ensures that we set out issues across different perspectives. Several of the contributors are senior-level practitioners with knowledge and years of experience on China matters. We thank them for their contributions despite their busy schedules.

We would like to extend our special thanks to Deputy Managing Director Min Zhu, who was instrumental in this book coming together. We discussed the original idea with him at the "High-Level Regional Symposium on Monitoring and Managing Financial Stability: Lessons from and for the FSAP" in Shanghai in December 2011, and greatly benefited from his support and guidance for this book.

We would like to pay a special tribute to the staff of the Financial Stability Bureau and the International Department of the People's Bank of China, who contributed in several different ways during the course of the 2010–11 China Financial Sector Assessment Program to deepening our understanding of the financial stability challenges confronting China. The underlying logic in putting the book together stems from the partnership we developed during those years. We are also grateful for the encouragement provided by José Viñals, Financial Counsellor and Director of the IMF Monetary and Capital Markets Department, who believed in the need for a book such as this.

We would also like to thank Nirmaleen Jayawardane of the IMF Monetary and Capital Markets Department for formatting support, and Patricia Loo and Joanne Johnson of the IMF External Relations Department for coordinating the production of the book.

Last, but not least, we would like to thank a large number of colleagues at the IMF, including those from the Asia and Pacific Department, for their support.

Udaibir S. Das
Jonathan Fiechter
Tao Sun

Foreword

"They must often change, who would be constant in happiness or wisdom."
—*Confucius*

The vast economic and financial transition currently under way in China surely has no precedent in modern economic times. We are indeed witnessing a fascinating and exciting period of economic history. China's economic ascendancy, which has generated immense opportunities for wealth creation and redistribution, has also been accompanied by a significant expansion in the financial services sector. Not surprisingly, this scale and pace of change is posing some complex financial stability challenges.

It is thus a very great pleasure for me to introduce this impressive series of papers on China's rapidly growing financial system. This volume makes a timely and definitive contribution to the world's understanding of the Chinese financial system and its interaction with and impact on the real economy. As the financial sector matures, some of the inherent risks and stress points embedded in the "old" financial system have started to emerge. Fortunately, policy efforts have continued to focus on what is needed to maintain stability while gradually pursuing structural change and financial sector deepening. It is fitting then that this volume focuses on financial system stability—crucial for continued economic progress in China, and also for the functioning of the global monetary and financial system.

The breadth of issues and proposals raised in this book highlights both the considerable ground covered in China in recent years as well as the challenges that lie ahead. The volume brings together contributions from a broad range of world-class experts, including Chinese policymakers, academic leaders, private market participants, and IMF staff. The book reflects the IMF's ongoing commitment to promote worldwide financial stability and to work closely with the Chinese authorities in support of their financial reform agenda.

Policymakers today are still in a firefighting mode. A key lesson emerging from this long global crisis is that issues of financial soundness that might arise in a single financial firm or in a segment of a country's financial market can quickly turn into a full-fledged nationwide crisis of confidence. To quote a Chinese proverb: "A spark can start a fire that burns the entire prairie." If not addressed promptly and effectively, issues regarding the soundness of the financial system may quickly morph into a macroeconomic crisis, with adverse effects on output, trade, and employment. Given the interconnectedness of financial systems and markets, problems in one country may be rapidly transmitted across borders.

A second key lesson from this crisis has been the persistence of the poisonous adverse feedback loop between macrosovereign risk and financial sector weaknesses. In addition to the primacy of strengthening public balance sheets and lowering public debt in key advanced economies, increased efforts are being marshalled by global leaders to strengthen the robustness of financial systems, including supervisory and regulatory frameworks. Some of these initiatives require bold political decisions related to these frameworks. In this respect, the IMF's increased focus on financial sector surveillance and the effective integration of financial stability analysis in our Financial Sector Assessment Programs (FSAPs) are timely and will help our members better identify risks to financial stability and address those risks through enhanced policy and structural changes.

Financial reforms in China have been a priority for over a decade and the authorities are fully aware of the challenges ahead. They should be commended for the patience and skill with which they have deftly handled the process thus far, and for their intellectual objectivity and openness to learning from outside experience. The first independent assessment of the Chinese financial system was carried out by the IMF and World Bank during 2010–11 as part of the FSAP. The assessment lauded the progress that had been made over the past decade and also confirmed what senior Chinese officials had already been highlighting: there are important gaps in the regulatory and supervisory system, and China needs to broaden and deepen its financial markets and services in order to create a more diversified sector that operates on commercial principles. While the banking system will continue to play a dominant role, other elements of the financial sector will need to assume a larger share of the intermediation role.

At the same time, reforms in China should seek to modernize the monetary policy framework so that the central bank can respond and adapt to the opening of the financial and capital accounts and help sustain China's economic growth and development goals. Despite the remarkable improvement in China's ability to transform savings into productive investments, a consistent macroeconomic policy framework is intrinsic to financial stability.

The increasingly complex global environment will not make life any easier for China's policymakers. First, Asia remains vulnerable to external shocks through the trade channel and from shifting tides of investor sentiment. As we have seen during the crisis, this has strongly affected international financial flows and the functioning of capital markets. On the corporate side, major international firms are restructuring and choosing to disengage from some business lines and market segments altogether, which is affecting the availability of credit. Second, the agenda for globally agreed-upon regulatory reforms is ambitious and the impact of these reforms on markets and financial intermediation has yet to play out. These factors have implications for financial stability in China and will require careful thought, monitoring, and action.

On the bright side, China stands to benefit from the mistakes and lessons of others that have come to light during this crisis. Of particular significance for China is the importance of gathering and analyzing relevant data and information, complying with internationally agreed-upon regulatory norms, implementing robust disclosure practices that act as a buffer against excessive risk-taking, and strengthening monitoring and supervision of nonbank financial institutions. In addition, China needs to develop a clear and accountable institutional framework for financial stability in which the roles and responsibilities of the relevant government institutions are clearly specified.

As the financial crisis recedes and the global economy mends, the appropriate set of financial stability policies will need ongoing attention. This vigilance is the new normal for all policymakers, regulators, and supervisors around the world given the rapid pace of innovation and technological change in financial markets. Even if one subscribes to Hyman Minsky's "financial instability hypothesis" that the financial system is inherently prone to swings between robustness and fragility, policymakers have no choice but to do everything within their power to strive for stability in order to reduce the severity of boom-bust cycles and the burden of distress on the general public.

In this spirit, it is reassuring to know that China will continue on its path of reform and sustain its important contribution to global financial stability. The experience of other IMF member countries suggests that the appropriate sequencing, quality, and timely implementation of financial reforms will decisively influence the financial stability outcome. In China's case, continued coordinated interagency efforts will also be needed to build a comprehensive macroprudential framework for measuring and managing systemic risks. All of this will support China's efforts to rebalance its economy while building a safe and strong financial system that contributes to sustainable growth and employment.

Finally, I would like to extend my thanks to the contributors to this volume. Their essays will contribute richly to the development of the ideas and policies best suited to supporting China's unique reform path. China has been steadily building the foundation for the future and is well aware of the journey ahead. There will be bumps and bends in the road that will force China's policymakers to frequently adapt plans and sometimes change course. But with their commitment to the importance of financial stability, I am confident they will succeed in their quest for durable, broad-based economic growth.

Christine Lagarde
Managing Director
International Monetary Fund

Introduction

Continued reform of China's financial sector is essential. As the financial sector becomes more complex and domestic and cross-border interconnections expand, the preservation of financial stability in China, a high policy priority, becomes even more of a challenge. The years 2010–11, therefore, were quite significant because China participated for the first time in an external assessment of its financial system, an in-depth analysis undertaken as part of the joint IMF-World Bank Financial Sector Assessment Program (FSAP). China published the resulting financial stability assessment along with detailed reports on its observations of five international financial sector standards. For China, it was a big step forward to allow an independent set of experts to have access to its data and information, to work with these experts to determine risks and gaps in the system, and then to agree to publish the findings.

The results and conclusions of the financial stability analysis were by no means the end of the process, but rather the start of a deeper engagement on financial stability issues. This book focuses on some of the major financial stability issues that came up during the course of the FSAP. It documents what China is already working on to enhance its financial stability monitoring capabilities, while seeking to highlight areas where ongoing policy efforts might focus. It also provides a perspective on shifts taking place in the manner in which China views its financial sector policies and oversees the stability of the financial system. The topics cover issues such as the financial stability framework, risk and vulnerability analysis, systemic linkages, liquidity management, and sequencing financial reforms. These are examined in a forward-looking manner, consistent with China's objective of strong, sustained, and balanced growth.

China today has become an important global player in financial markets, and a comprehensive approach to the maintenance of financial stability is essential. As China examines policy options for transitioning from its earlier role as a processor of tradable goods for external markets to becoming a source of final demand growth, the financial system needs to adapt. A balance will need to be maintained between domestic considerations and the international implications of the evolving economy. A roadmap for reform should include strengthening the monetary policy framework, continuing to improve the regulatory, supervisory, and financial stability framework, deepening and developing financial markets, and eventually moving toward the longer-term goal of an open capital account with the renminbi as a fully convertible currency. It is for this reason that I believe the FSAP in 2010–11 was so important. A strengthened Chinese financial system will not only help transform China's growth model toward a more inclusive economy but it will also facilitate the maintenance of stable financial conditions.

The Chinese authorities responsible for financial stability acknowledge the importance of these issues. The challenge facing China will be the sequence, design, and proper implementation of the reforms. There is little doubt that important progress has been made in moving to a more market-based financial system. But China will need to address the buildup of financial sector vulnerabilities as a consequence of the rapid expansion of credit in recent years. The macrofinancial interconnections are deepening and the structural complexity of the financial system is growing.

There are legal and institutional limitations in terms of data collection, monitoring of systemic issues, and information exchange. Systemic risk monitoring and identification requires access to and continuous monitoring of data on business and financial cycles; credit quantity and quality; systemically important institutions, markets, and instruments; and firms and activities that might be outside the perimeter of regulation. There are well-known near-term risks arising primarily from crisis-related credit expansion, the increase in off-balance-sheet exposures, the rapid increase in real estate prices, and potential external spillovers. Given these pressures, preserving financial stability is a huge task. A systematic and steady approach to strengthening the financial infrastructure will have significant benefits for China's long-term economic growth and performance.

The ongoing global economic and financial crisis has reshaped the focus of the FSAP product. The China FSAP emphasized the importance of a sound financial stability framework. It aimed to help national authorities identify the source, probability, and potential impact of key risks to macrofinancial stability, assess China's ability to manage and resolve financial crises, and design longer-term policies and reforms. The IMF has sought to recognize—and learn from—the shortcomings of precrisis FSAPs, which may have underappreciated idiosyncratic and systemic liquidity risks and cross-border or cross-market interconnections. More focus is now being placed on country-specific circumstances. The FSAP has also benefited from an improved analytical toolkit covering a wider range of risks, cross-border spillovers, and interactions between the financial sector and the broader economy. We have also sought to make our assessments more candid and transparent.

In 2010, the FSAP was made a mandatory part of Article IV surveillance for jurisdictions with systemically important financial sectors. For all other jurisdictions, participation in the FSAP is voluntary. Key considerations in making the FSAP mandatory included the important spillovers that can stem from disruptions in financial centers that are highly interconnected with those in the rest of the world, and the need to make financial sector surveillance more risk-based by focusing on jurisdictions with the greatest impact on the global financial system.

This landmark decision has formally brought financial sector issues to the core of the IMF's bilateral surveillance. For both advanced and emerging economies, FSAPs represent a unique opportunity to obtain an external assessment of their financial sectors, while taking advantage of lessons arising from the current crisis. Although FSAPs cannot prevent future crises, they can help national authorities assess the quality and preparedness of their financial infrastructures to deal with major strains in their financial sectors. The improved FSAP is playing a particularly important role in the Asia Pacific region, where we have seen a significant increase in demand since the onset of the financial crisis. Most Asian members with large financial sectors have now undertaken one or more FSAPs.

The three questions arising out of the FSAPs that have become central to financial stability framework are:

- *How prepared are systemic countries to assess the adequacy of their financial stability policy framework and implement tougher regulatory supervisory standards?* The global crisis has underscored the need to evaluate the effectiveness of financial supervision, the quality of financial stability analysis and reports, the role of and coordination between the various institutions involved in financial stability policy, and the effectiveness of monetary policy. Addressing these issues presents challenges for national authorities and the international community.

- *Are countries adequately assessing the source, probability, and potential impact of key risks to macrofinancial stability?* The FSAP makes a comprehensive assessment of the financial system and its linkages with the real economy. This involves, in particular, investigating the features of the overall policy framework that may attenuate or amplify financial stability risks (e.g., the exchange rate regime). It also involves quantitative stress testing of banks and the broader financial system, and a qualitative assessment of the authorities' ability to monitor and identify systemic risks.

- *What systems are in place to manage and resolve financial crises?* The adequacy of contingency planning, financial safety nets, and resolution regimes that provide for the orderly restructuring or liquidation of financial institutions has become essential today. Resolutions of cross-border institutions and insolvencies in the nonbank sector make this more complicated. Effective coordination of policies across key agencies is crucial to reduce gaps and ensure consistent communications.

There are still many questions regarding financial stability that have yet to be fully addressed. For instance, how prepared are countries to implement major regulatory changes, including Basel III, and will that be enough to address systemic risks or is more required? How do we ensure that regulatory reforms and higher prudential standards are applied consistently across countries and without undue disruption to the ability of the financial system to support growth? Are we adequately covering the "nonsystemic" institutions and markets in our financial stability monitoring? Can we design a financial safety net that helps mitigate the need for "excess" reserve accumulation? How can we ensure consistency in the quantitative risk analysis to improve cross-country comparability and go beyond bank-centric risks to include sovereign risks, asset price shocks, and spillovers? Hopefully this book on China's financial stability issues will contribute to a dynamic discussion of these important questions.

José Viñals
Financial Counsellor and Director
International Monetary Fund

Overview: China's Road to Greater Financial Stability

UDAIBIR S. DAS, JONATHAN FIECHTER, AND TAO SUN

China's economic ascendency is generating both positive financial sector developments as well as complex financial stability challenges. With rapid growth has come a substantial expansion of the financial services sector and a marked improvement in China's ability to transform its savings into productive and growth-inducing investments. The interconnections between macroeconomic outcomes and the financial sector are deepening. And while the banking system is likely to continue to play a dominant role, conditions are falling into place for the rest of the financial sector to assume a larger share of the intermediation function. Even as these positive changes are unfolding, however, the steady maturation of China's financial system is also bringing to the fore risks embedded in the structure of its financial industry, capital markets, and the limitations of ad hoc policy responses.

China has made it clear in several official statements that preserving financial stability is a major economic policy priority. There is a consensus that a consistent macroeconomic policy framework is intrinsic to the country's financial stability. So even though the financial system may appear stable in prudential terms, China acknowledges that much more needs to be done to make the financial sector more viable by improving incentive structures, institutions, and allocation processes. The contingent risks from the financial system to the state exchequer also need to be contained. Although ongoing improvements in risk management, prudential regulation, and supervision remain critical, further deepening and maturation of the financial system will be influenced in large part by the process by which the macroeconomic policy framework evolves.

This book is about some of these financial stability challenges facing China. It seeks to improve understanding of the financial sector policy processes under way and the shifts in China's financial stability priorities. The book has two central messages. The first is that the design, pace, and quality of implementation of financial reform and ensuing economic growth will heavily influence financial stability outcomes. The second is that continued and coordinated interagency efforts are needed to build a comprehensive macroprudential framework to measure and manage systemic risks. Reactive and piecemeal approaches to reform and to addressing gaps are risky because the different reform measures are interrelated. The experience of other countries suggests the need for an overarching approach to reform with a well-reasoned sequencing of actions. Furthering commercially oriented market reform may be the least-risky way to support the potential growth of China's financial sector. Such an approach might also help influence the role of the state in the financial services sector in a way that creates an environment conducive to China's pursuit of sustainable, balanced, and inclusive growth. At the same time, such an approach could better equip the government to handle China-specific sources of financial stability risk.

As noted in this volume, China is moving toward a more integrated macrofinancial approach to financial stability. It is looking to learn from the reform experiences of other countries and to adapt modern and internationally acceptable financial and prudential know-how to China's particular circumstances. The country's awareness of risk surveillance and financial stability monitoring at the technical level is growing impressively. The need for institutional changes in the regulatory setup is being given careful thought, and some reforms are being considered. China already has several prudential tools that may be used to address financial risks, including dynamic provisioning, variable capital requirements, reserve requirements, and rules related to loan-to-value and loan-to-deposit ratios. Further efforts are needed to assess the effectiveness and use of these tools and to refine policies in terms of how and when these buffers and requirements will be applied as China's reforms progress. Among the key challenges in this regard will be the resources, capacity, and interagency collaboration necessary to monitor financial stability and integrate the findings in other policy areas.

The task ahead for China on the financial stability agenda is thus significant. A transition from a planned to a market-based financial system on a scale as vast as that of China has no precedent in the history of modern policymaking. Chinese financial firms face credit, market, operational, and liquidity risks, and economic cycles are inevitable, as evidenced by the 2008 global financial crisis. Moving along the reform path will pose additional risks and new challenges. Hence, priority must be given to establishing the institutional and operational preconditions that are crucial to successfully manage a wide-ranging financial reform agenda and the objectives outlined in China's Twelfth Five-Year Plan. The official agencies, as well as the financial industry, need to build economic forecasting skills and the capacity to make timely judgments in response to changing economic conditions and to mitigate adverse spillovers.

From the macroadjustment viewpoint, implementing effective policy instruments to dampen sharp swings in the economy is very important. Given the structural features in China, industries with excess capacity and asset bubbles in the real estate sector are a constant vulnerability. Effective macroeconomic management and aggregate analysis could contribute to reducing sharp fluctuations in the economy, reducing the risk of nonperforming assets building up in the financial system, and, hence, preserving financial stability. Data collection should be enhanced to facilitate a better understanding of financial institutions' balance sheets and their interconnections, and to develop a forward-looking early warning system to identify trends and activities that have the potential to threaten financial stability.

Against this backdrop, this volume brings together expert perspectives on what would contribute to financial stability in China. The book is set up in four parts: the financial policy context, the key macroeconomic factors affecting financial stability, the critical role of financial system oversight, and the future outlook for the financial system, with final comments from the governor of the People's Bank of China.

PART I: REFORMING THE FINANCIAL SYSTEM AND ENSURING FINANCIAL STABILITY

The book starts by setting the policy context and overall intent of financial policy reforms in China. In Chapter 1 ("Reform and Development of China's Financial Sector"), Shiyu Liu outlines China's major financial reforms over the last decade and how they have been fundamental to maintaining the country's financial stability. He summarizes the major changes that have occurred in China's financial industry and emphasizes that the country's financial institutions have been quick to adopt modern corporate governance practices. The chapter also discusses how financial markets today play an important role in helping China rebalance consumption and investment patterns as well as the policy thinking behind exchange rate and interest rate liberalization by way of developing a long-term mechanism to strengthen financial stability.

With the process of financial reform and liberalization ongoing, reform initiatives will need to be carefully crafted to the risks to financial stability. Country experiences have shown that although financial liberalization may spur growth and development, it also often entails risks if not properly designed and sequenced. A flexible strategy is required that anticipates the complications and disruptions that may arise and provides guidance on how best to arrange the policy measures without delaying necessary changes. In Chapter 2 ("Financial Reform: An Essential Ingredient in Transforming China's Economic Development Model"), Nigel Chalk and Murtaza Syed discuss the rationale for reform and the risks of maintaining the status quo. Anchored against the lessons learned from international experiences, the chapter stresses that reform without the necessary preconditions in place can be extremely perilous for financial stability. Summarizing the benefits of financial reform, the authors outline a roadmap that could be considered in the next phase and suggest establishing a new framework for monetary policy, developing broader channels for intermediation, and dismantling repressive financial policies and practices.

Chapter 3 ("Strengthening the Financial Stability Framework in China") by Keith Hall and Tao Sun discusses global trends in financial stability and the macroprudential policy framework, and how China's institutional arrangements measure up. The authors investigate China's endeavor to promote financial stability through three broad streams: *surveillance*, the early identification of potential threats to financial stability; *mitigation*, the measures that need to be taken to make the financial system more resilient to shocks; and *crisis management*, the principles and procedures for responding to distress or failures in the financial system. The chapter provides policy suggestions that include preparation of a data set that might provide the authorities with some early warning of systemic risks and the formalization of the shared responsibilities on financial stability matters among official agencies and industry associations. The chapter also discusses contingency plans for responding promptly to a crisis involving one or more systemically important financial institutions and striking the right balance between "open" and "closed" resolution outcomes.

PART II: MACROECONOMIC FACTORS AFFECTING FINANCIAL STABILITY

The second part of the book includes three chapters on macroeconomic factors affecting financial stability. In Chapter 4 ("China's Sovereign Balance Sheet Risks and Implications for Financial Stability"), Yang Li and Xiaojing Zhang compile a first-time-ever sovereign balance sheet for China from 2000 to 2010 to analyze structural changes and institutional developments. They show that the short-term sovereign risk mainly arises from housing credit and local government debts, while medium- to long-run vulnerabilities are due to risks in the external balance sheet, corporate debt, and underfunded social security liabilities. They also simulate China's debt dynamics and highlight the importance of maintaining higher GDP growth, and thus a positive gap between the GDP growth rate and interest rates. The authors argue that transforming the development model to sustain higher growth is the fundamental approach to managing risks to China's sovereign balance sheet and preserving financial stability.

Chapter 5 ("Systemic Liquidity, Monetary Operations, and Financial Stability in China") by Nuno Cassola and Nathan Porter sets out ways in which domestic liquidity and monetary policy operations intersect with financial stability in China. It highlights how central bank operations and facilities influence liquidity and financial prices and the role these factors play in mitigating a crisis. The chapter also discusses liquidity management in China and some of the key implications of financial liberalization. The authors argue that future financial stability would benefit from further reforming standing liquidity facilities, developing the ability over time to undertake daily open-market operations, and introducing reserve averaging. Further adaption of liquidity management objectives and active use of indirect liquidity management instruments should help ease the task of monetary management in China as the money multiplier becomes less stable. Moreover, the efficiency of financial prices should improve as the financial sector is further liberalized and market liquidity grows, ultimately strengthening the interest rate transmission channel.

China has made significant progress toward liberalizing capital flows and taking measured moves toward the international use of the renminbi. In Chapter 6 ("Capital Flows, International Use of the Renminbi, and Implications for Financial Stability"), Shaun K. Roache and Samar Maziad review recent progress in these areas and assess how this process may evolve in the future and the implications for domestic financial stability. The experiences of other countries demonstrate that the appropriate sequencing of reforms is critical for full international financial integration. Financial market deepening and a robust macroeconomic and regulatory framework provide the necessary preconditions for full capital account liberalization. Moreover, as interest rates are liberalized and quantitative restrictions lifted, there may be a need to absorb liquidity from the financial system, adjust relative prices, and place increased reliance on indirect monetary tools.

PART III: STRENGTHENING FINANCIAL SYSTEM OVERSIGHT

The theme of the five chapters that make up the third part of the book is financial system oversight. China has made impressive strides in the regulation and supervision of its financial system. There have also been marked improvements in risk management, backed by a regulatory system that demands high-quality capital and liquidity, often through simple and basic regulatory requirements. As further reform and broadening of the financial service sector takes place, however, complexity and risks will increase. Consistent implementation of global regulatory standards and improvements in supervisory effectiveness become the two essential components of financial sector reform and the management of financial stability. Inconsistencies or laxity in application run the risk of misaligning incentives and distorting expected reform outcomes. As liberalization progresses, China must balance calls for local concessions while creating a level and even-handed playing field for all. It will also have to manage gaps in the global regulatory framework that could impact financial stability in China, such as the absence of a global loss-sharing arrangement for troubled internationally active banks.

In Chapter 7 ("Structure of the Banking Sector and Implications for Financial Stability"), Silvia Iorgova and Yinqiu Lu analyze the structure of China's banking system and its relevance for financial stability. They argue that it is vital to keep the structural factors in mind as reform unfolds in order to avert the potential undesirable accumulation of credit risks and internal macroeconomic imbalances. More broadly, policies should seek to reduce moral hazard and improve banks' credit risk management and corporate governance. Moreover, to curb the incentive to excessively use the banking system for fiscal policy purposes—such as for funding local infrastructure projects—future reforms should reduce fiscal revenue-expenditure mismatches faced by local governments. The chapter makes the point that such reforms are a complex undertaking that go beyond the remit of financial sector policies.

In Chapter 8 ("Practical Experiences in Strengthening Banking Supervision and Regulation"), Huaqing Wang outlines the seven areas of supervisory policy that have been the focus of the China Banking Regulatory Commission in recent years. These policies are helping strengthen the financial condition of banks active in the securities markets and improving the level of disclosure and transparency. The chapter summarizes specific steps related to improving banks' capital, liquidity, leverage, and risk management; implementing the Basel III regulatory framework;

strengthening the supervision of systemically important financial institutions; addressing shadow banking; and managing cross-border financial risks.

As it continues to strengthen its supervisory system, China confronts a choice. Should it follow the mainstream supervisory model of allowing banks to independently determine their business models and lending strategies? Or should China continue to closely control and oversee the operations of banks, giving them relatively limited discretion in terms of the choice of business models? The financial infrastructure within China remains underdeveloped, with the need to improve credit risk management, including the management of nonperforming loans, and reduce loan concentrations. Intermediaries such as accounting firms, law firms, assessment agencies, rating agencies, and credit reporting agencies are still in the early stages of development. In Chapter 9 ("Seeking the Middle Ground for Supervision), Jonathan Fiechter and Aditya Narain take a look at the strengths of the current system and the challenges it needs to navigate. They recommend priorities to help China transition to a supervisory regime that can effectively oversee a commercially driven financial system that can meet the needs of a growing Chinese economy and the varied needs of Chinese savers and borrowers. There is an urgent need for forward resource planning and for a government-backed strategy to upgrade the skills of supervisors by making financial supervision a sought-after career stream. The authors recommend that China aim to meet the mainstream model halfway by retaining some of the elements of its current regime, including the focus on simplicity and conservatism, while at the same time embracing the lessons that came out of the 2008 financial crisis regarding the risks of not holding bank management accountable, including the importance of making bank management more accountable for building their own risk management systems.

In Chapter 10 ("Strengthening Macroprudential Management"), Changneng Xuan discusses the recent development of macroprudential regulatory policies and measures taken by the central bank. He examines in detail the approaches China is considering in terms of enhancing monitoring and the management of systemic risks. He also discusses the institutional setup and stresses the need for accountability and coordination. The chapter touches on the challenges to implementing macroprudential policy in China given that systemic risk is multidimensional and often difficult to identify and measure owing to data gaps and structural complexities. Xuan highlights that effective macroprudential policymaking depends on its effective coordination with other public policies and on filling information gaps. In addition, the growing importance of cross-border systemic risks and regulatory arbitrage underscores the critical importance of effective domestic and international coordination.

An effective financial market infrastructure is a necessary though insufficient (as the recent global financial crisis demonstrated) condition for a safe transition to a more market-based financial system. As Chinese banks and financial firms broadly become more commercially oriented, financial market deepening could help avoid some of the risks of disorderly disintermediation in times of stress and macroeconomic uncertainty. China's capital markets have experienced rapid development in the last two decades. Shuqing Guo in Chapter 11 ("Capital Markets and Financial Stability") examines China's capital markets and the implication for financial stability. Specifically, the chapter summarizes the development of China's capital markets as well as current issues and recent reforms. Guo then explains the low level of systemic risk in China's capital markets and why now is an opportune time to push forward bolder securities market reforms. The author argues that developed capital markets in China would help promote financial stability through multiple channels, including risk distribution, availability of hedging instruments, direct small and medium-sized enterprise financing, lower risk concentrations in trust companies, and avoidance of a real estate bubble, by broadening the investment channels.

PART IV: OUTLOOK FOR THE FUTURE

The global financial crisis has heightened risks to financial stability in China. Adversely affected by the crisis, the country had to implement policy and support measures to maintain banking and market activities. The crisis forced policymakers and agencies involved with financial stability to reexamine their goals, parameter assumptions, and risk thresholds related to financial stability. Against this challenging backdrop, the final part of the book focuses on the future outlook for financial stability in China.

In Chapter 12 ("China's Road to Sustainable Growth and Financial Stability: A Systemic Perspective"), Andrew Sheng and Geng Xiao explore from a systemic perspective a feasible path for China to achieve sustainable growth alongside financial stability. As it assumes a larger global role in areas such as social, ecological, and global stability, China needs to adopt key reforms to enable the financial sector to develop on a stable footing. The authors argue that to maintain system stability, China must not only strengthen institutional infrastructure and the span of policy tools but also rebalance credit access to the private sector and increase competition. Improving social inclusion would require removing financial repression and paying labor a fair share of total factor income, while exercising discipline on the efficiency of investment.

Joseph Yam then discusses how to strike a balance between attaining market freedom in finance and addressing market failure. In Chapter 13 ("Delivering Financial Stability in China"), he argues that it is necessary for China to place greater emphasis on arrangements that allow the potency of financial markets to be harnessed in the public interest. Delivering stability, integrity, diversity, and efficiency in financial intermediation is important to promote economic growth and development. The chapter concludes that maintaining financial stability is not an academic issue. While difficult to achieve, financial stability is easier to maintain in a culture where the basic function of the financial system is viewed as supporting the economy and not as "a playground for money making." Yam calls for a "cultural revolution" in the world of finance so that stable conditions can be maintained at a low social cost.

In Chapter 14 ("The Impact of Financial Liberalization on China's Financial Sector"), Jun Ma and Hui Miao discuss the implications of the financial liberalization program on China's financial sector. Assuming that these reforms will be largely completed within the coming three to five years, the authors' impact analysis shows that nonbank financing will gain market share from banks, and banks' net interest margins will contract and be replaced by fee income. Global expansion by Chinese financial firms will be a double-edged sword. While brokerage and asset management sectors will benefit, and the insurance sector will likely see improved return on investment, this may be offset by a rise in domestic deposit rates and the rebalancing of global business opportunities, with further liberalization of the financial sector.

Victor Shih, in Chapter 15 ("This Time Is Different: The Domestic Financial Impact of Global Rebalancing"), compares the 1998–2002 financial reform with the current situation. During the period reviewed, Shih argues that the Chinese authorities successfully brought the country through a difficult period with sweeping financial reform. Today, however, China is facing financial and macroeconomic stress and has fewer policy options and a narrower financial space to buffer a significant worsening of the financial sector balance sheet. Shih argues that going forward the central bank will need to be much more aggressive in releasing sufficient liquidity into the economy to address any imminent risks, especially if significant financial reforms are carried out at the same time.

The future of the international monetary system has seen heated debate since 2007. Drawing on extensive data and international experiences, Eswar Prasad and Lei Ye in Chapter 16 ("The Renminbi's Prospects as a Global Reserve Currency") review recent steps toward the international use of the renminbi and evaluate its prospects as a global reserve currency. The chapter argues that China's low level of financial market development remains a major constraint to the likelihood of the renminbi attaining reserve currency status. Moreover, in the absence of an open capital account and free convertibility of the currency, it is unlikely that the renminbi will become a prominent reserve currency. However, on the basis of the anticipated pace of reforms, the authors believe that the renminbi will become a competitive reserve currency over the next decade and in some measure become a substitute for the U.S. dollar, although the dollar will retain its dominance.

CONCLUSIONS

We hope that this collection of papers will help improve understanding of the various paradoxes China confronts as it pursues financial sector reform. It is intended to provide some new perspectives while reaffirming the validity of many of the ideas already echoed by Chinese policymakers, academics, and capital market participants. The overall objective is to complement existing work while emphasizing the need for China to place a sharper focus on financial stability issues. To the extent that the book is informative regarding the source and potential impact of risks to macrofinancial stability in China, we view it as a small contribution to a large and evolving policy topic. The global financial crisis has clearly demonstrated the important domestic and cross-border spillovers that stem from disruptions in domestic financial systems that are interconnected. Proper institutional arrangements, a risk-based system of monitoring financial markets, and appropriate prudential tools (both micro and macro) are a must if China is to maintain financial stability as it moves forward to liberalize and open up its financial markets and continues to make the needed macroeconomic adjustments.

PART I

Reforming the Financial System and Ensuring Financial Stability

CHAPTER 1

Reform and Development of China's Financial Sector

Shiyu Liu

Since the onset of the new millennium, China has clearly put forward the strategic objective to build a market-oriented and more open economic system. Deepening financial reform and expanding openness to foreigners have become important goals. Guided by this objective, the key tasks include deepening financial institutional reform, developing financial markets, encouraging financial innovation, and advancing reform of price formation mechanisms for interest rates and exchange rates.

Financial market efficiency has continued to improve in terms of resource allocation, and the capacity of financial institutions to guard against risk has been considerably strengthened. Macroprudential regulation has also been continually strengthened, which has effectively guarded against financial risks and realistically helped China preserve financial stability. Thus, through a series of major financial reforms, historic changes have occurred in China's financial industry.

ESTABLISHMENT OF CORPORATE GOVERNANCE SYSTEMS

The health of financial institutions is the microfoundation of financial stability. After the Asian financial crisis, Chinese authorities realized the urgency and importance of deepening financial reform. Under the unified leadership of the State Council, the authorities initiated the financial restructuring of all types of large financial institutions in 2003 and have essentially completed the restructuring. Substantial progress has been achieved with respect to the reform and development of other types of financial institutions.

Advances have been made in the shareholding reform of the wholly state-owned commercial banks. In 2003, the Chinese authorities used the Bank of China (BOC) and China Construction Bank (CCB) as pilots to launch a joint stock reform of wholly state-owned commercial banks. The reform was carried out by disposing of nonperforming assets, bolstering capital, establishing modern corporate governance frameworks, introducing strategic investors, and conducting public offerings domestically and abroad. The Central Huijin Investment Company was established to serve as the investor on behalf of the state. A market-based approach was adopted to dispose of nonperforming assets in order to reduce losses and best protect against ethical risks. When joint stock companies were incorporated, importance was attached to setting up uniform corporate governance frameworks, and the role of strategic investors was fully developed in such areas as improving corporate governance, introducing international standards and practices, and promoting technical and operational cooperation. With respect to specific operations, the reform employed the principle of gradual progression in proper sequence, with pilot trials first, followed gradually by other steps after experience was obtained.

Based on the preliminary success of the pilot projects, the shareholding reform was then implemented for the Industrial and Commercial Bank of China (ICBC) and Agricultural Bank of China (ABC). Since 2005, the four large commercial banks noted above have successively launched initial public offerings, and all have successively completed dual listings of A shares and H shares. Through these reforms, corporate governance of large commercial banks has been standardized, risk management mechanisms have been upgraded, and asset quality and profitability have improved year by year, underpinning financial health and promoting market competition (Figures 1.1 and 1.2). The reform also played an

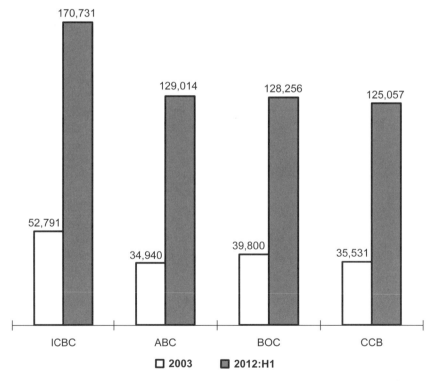

Source: Based on data from annual reports of the large commercial banks.
Note: ABC = Agricultural Bank of China; BOC = Bank of China; CCB = China Construction Bank; ICBC = Industrial and Commercial Bank of China.

Figure 1.1 Total Assets of Large Commercial Banks
(Hundreds of millions of renminbi)

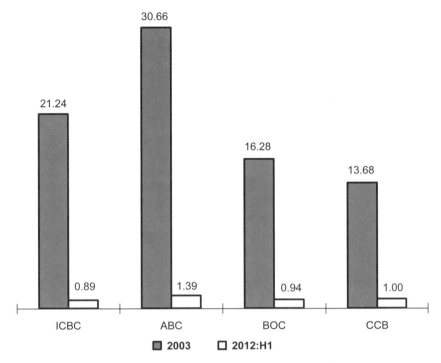

Source: Compiled based on data from annual reports of the large commercial banks.
Note: ABC = Agricultural Bank of China; BOC = Bank of China; CCB = China Construction Bank; ICBC = Industrial and Commercial Bank of China.

Figure 1.2 Nonperforming Loan Ratios of Large Commercial Banks
(In percent)

important role underpinning China's resilience to shocks during the recent global financial crisis.

In terms of rural financial reform, China began to implement a pilot reform program for rural credit cooperatives in June 2003, and gradually expanded the scope of the program nationwide. During the reform process, positive incentive mechanisms for funding support were designed and implemented, and efforts were undertaken to mobilize the participation and support of local governments and rural credit cooperatives. Through the reform, the governance structure of the cooperatives has been continuously optimized, risk control capabilities have improved markedly, and operating performance has continuously improved. As of end-June 2012, 1,858 county-level (municipal) rural credit cooperatives, 247 rural commercial banks, and 173 rural cooperative banks had been set up nationwide. The nonperforming-loan (NPL) ratio of rural credit cooperatives fell to 4.7 percent, while the capital adequacy ratio increased to 10.8 percent (Figures 1.3–1.6). Additionally, reforms were undertaken of the three rural financial business departments of the ABC and the Postal Savings Bank of China. Finally, the program promoted new rural financial institutions such as town and village

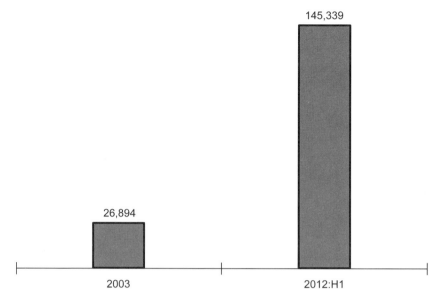

Source: The People's Bank of China.

Figure 1.3 Total Assets of Rural Credit Cooperatives
(Hundreds of millions of renminbi)

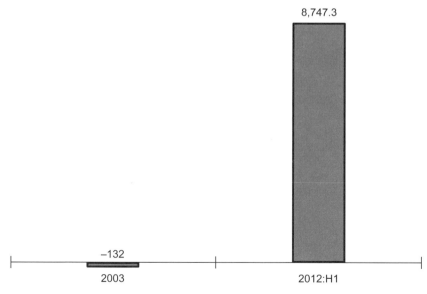

Source: The People's Bank of China.

Figure 1.4 Owners' Equity of Rural Credit Cooperatives
(Hundreds of millions of renminbi)

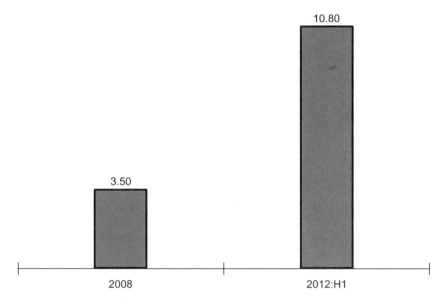

Source: The People's Bank of China.

Figure 1.5   Capital Adequacy Ratio of Rural Credit Cooperatives
(In percent)

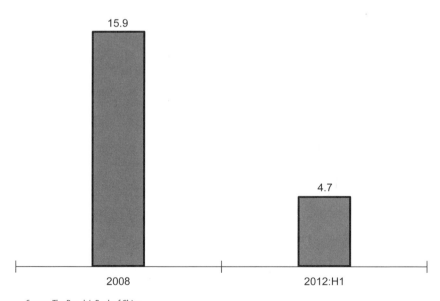

Source: The People's Bank of China.

Figure 1.6   Nonperforming Loan Ratios of Rural Credit Cooperatives
(In percent)

banks, and put in place a series of support policies that collectively have played an important role in improving rural financial services.

Progress has also been achieved in reforming other financial institutions. While reforms of large commercial banks and rural credit cooperatives were being carried out, other financial institutions were also encouraged to reform on their own and with external support. A group of small and medium-sized commercial banks, including China Everbright Bank, China CITIC Bank, and Bank of Beijing, have gradually established modern corporate governance frameworks through financial restructuring, introduction of domestic and foreign strategic investors, and initial public offerings. Reforms of policy banks have also advanced steadily. Breakthroughs were achieved with respect to the reform of the four asset management companies, with the completion of shareholding reform of both China Cinda Asset Management and China Huarong Asset Management.

In the securities industry, comprehensive regulation resulted in the shutting down of a group of illegally operating securities dealers, and another group of securities dealers was restructured according to market principles. The capital adequacy ratios, management standards, and service capabilities of the industry as a whole have been substantially upgraded. Two large insurance companies, the People's Insurance Company of China and China Life Insurance, took the lead in listing their stocks on international capital markets. Some insurance companies, including China Reinsurance Group and New China Life Insurance, have successfully completed capital infusion and ownership reform work.

The results of China's financial reforms over the past decade have been positive and the overall strength of the financial industry has improved markedly. As of June 2012, banking industry assets totaled 128.6 trillion renminbi, representing growth of 3.8 times over year-end 2002, with an average capital adequacy ratio of 12.3 percent and a provision coverage ratio of 175 percent. The assets

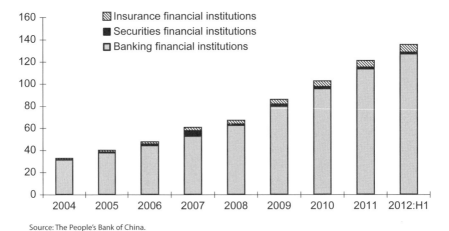

Source: The People's Bank of China.

Figure 1.7 Total Assets in the Financial Sector
(Trillions of renminbi)

of securities companies totaled 1.6 trillion renminbi and assets under management by fund management companies totaled 2.4 trillion renminbi, representing growth of two times and 19.3 times, respectively, over year-end 2002. Insurance industry assets totaled 6 trillion renminbi, an increase of 9.4 times over year-end 2002 (Figure 1.7).

DEEPENING OF DOMESTIC FINANCIAL MARKETS

Since 2002, market-oriented reforms have greatly encouraged financial innovation and improved market outcomes. Efforts have focused on increasing market transparency and establishing a system in which the market segments operate in a complementary manner. This has played an important role in supporting economic development, optimizing social financing needs, and maintaining financial stability.

Great strides have been made in developing securities markets. Prior to that, for a variety of reasons, the development of China's securities markets, and in particular its corporate bond market, had been very slow. Based on an earnest review of experiences and lessons, several series of measures were adopted in 2004 to promote financial market reform and development. The first series involved continued development of the over-the-counter market. On the interbank market, institutional investors were positioned as the investment principals to gradually form a hierarchically ordered investor structure with market makers at the core, financial institutions as the principals, and the joint participation of other investors. A second series of measures aimed to reduce unnecessary administrative approvals. In order to conform to the market-oriented financing requirements of enterprises, innovations in the bond market system were encouraged, a registration system was implemented for corporate short-term financing bills and medium-term notes, and an approval system was put in place for corporate bonds and bonds of publicly traded companies. The third series of measures involved fully developing the right set of market incentive and market discipline mechanisms, such as disclosure and credit ratings. These measures played a prominent role in promoting the rapid development of the financial markets, and particularly the bond market. The outstanding bond balances increased from 2.8 trillion renminbi at the end of 2002 to 22.1 trillion renminbi at the end of 2011. As a proportion of GDP, outstanding bonds increased from 24 to 47 percent in the same period (Figures 1.8 and 1.9). According to Bank for International Settlements statistics, in terms of size, China's bond market ranked third in the world and second in Asia at the end of 2011.

Chinese authorities have continuously promoted the innovation of products and instruments in bond markets. In recent years, based on market demand, products including short-term financing bills, ultra-short-term financing bills, medium-term notes, and aggregate products have been successively introduced on the interbank market, thus increasing direct financing channels for enterprises and improving the financing structure. The financial derivatives market came into being and experienced marked development with the successive introduction

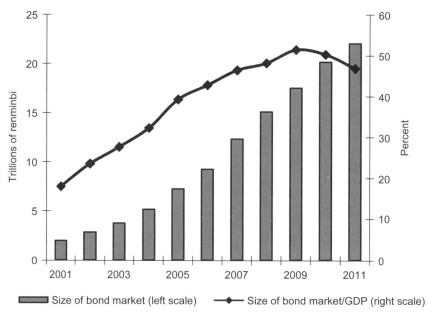

Source: The People's Bank of China.

Figure 1.8   Outstanding Bond Balances and Their Ratios to GDP
(In trillions of renminbi and percent)

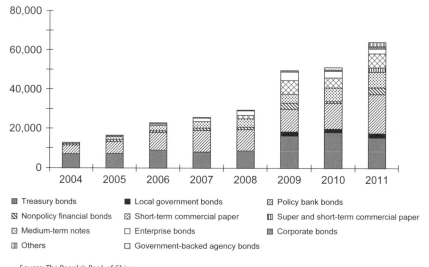

Source: The People's Bank of China.

Figure 1.9   Bond Issuance
(In trillions of renminbi)

of forward bond trading, renminbi interest rate swaps, securities lending, credit risk mitigation instruments, stock index futures, and securities margin trading operations, thus enriching risk management mechanisms for investors and for the sharing of credit risk. In 2005, a pilot project on credit asset securitization was launched. As of the end of June 2012, 11 financial institutions had issued a cumulative total of 66.78 billion renminbi in securitized products. The securitization of credit assets helps to mitigate capital adequacy pressures on banks as a result of growth in credit assets and strengthens the risk management capabilities of financial institutions.

The authorities have also worked continuously to improve the money, gold, foreign exchange, and stock markets. The pricing function of the money market has been continuously strengthened. Since 2003, an interest rate system has been established in which the Shanghai Interbank Offer Rate (SHIBOR) serves as the benchmark rate, and interest rates for interbank borrowings and repurchases are decided by buyers and sellers. The number of market participants has increased continuously, and transaction volume has increased substantially. In 2002, China instituted reform of the gold market and established the Shanghai Gold Exchange. At present, the early stages of a multilayered gold market combine spot and derivatives trading and exchange and off-exchange trading, catering to institutions as well as individuals. Since 2005, in order to coordinate with reform of the exchange rate formation mechanism, the over-the-counter trading mechanism and market-maker system have been introduced on the interbank foreign exchange market. A price transmission mechanism for the foreign exchange market has gradually taken shape, and the elasticity of the renminbi exchange rate has increased markedly. Progress has been achieved in the reform of the initial public offering system, and the financing function of the equity markets has improved substantially.

Market infrastructure is increasingly sound. Based on market development needs, the National Association of Financial Market Institutional Investors was established to bring into full play the self-regulatory organizational advantages of proximity to the market and a better capability to enhance innovation based on market demand. Infrastructure facilities, including a uniform central clearing system, centralized trading information platform, and secure and stable funds settlement system, were established. To continuously enhance transparency and strengthen market discipline, sound systems were also established, including a market-maker system, settlement agent system, money broker system, disclosure system, and credit rating system.

ADVANCING THE FLEXIBILITY OF RENMINBI AND INTEREST RATE LIBERALIZATION

China has made a major breakthrough in advancing the flexibility of the renminbi exchange rate. In July 2005, China instituted a reform of the renminbi exchange rate formation mechanism, establishing a managed floating exchange rate regime based on market supply and demand and adjusted with reference to a basket of currencies. At a time when the impact of the global financial crisis was quite severe, the renminbi exchange rate remained essentially stable, which helped China weather the crisis and promoted global financial stability and rebalancing of the global economy. At present, there is a notable bidirectional floating characteristic of the renminbi exchange rate and a marked increase in exchange rate flexibility. Market mechanisms now play a fundamental role in determining renminbi exchange rate levels (Figures 1.10 and 1.11).

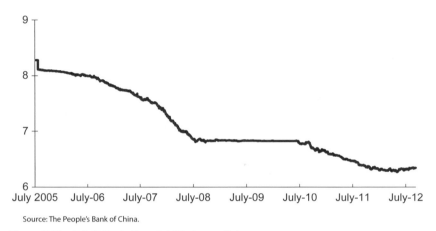

Source: The People's Bank of China.

Figure 1.10 U.S. Dollar to Renminbi Exchange Rate

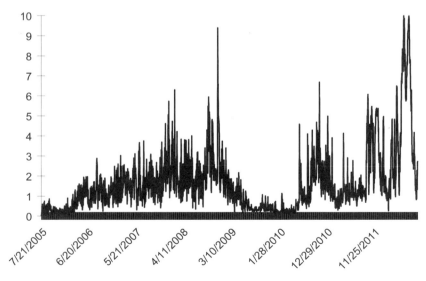

Sources: State Administration of Foreign Exchange; and Bloomberg.

Figure 1.11 Daily Fluctuation Range of the Renminbi to U.S. Dollar Exchange Rate
(In percent)

The authorities have advanced interest rate liberalization in an orderly manner. At present, market reforms of the money market and bond market have been fully realized, and the SHIBOR is gradually becoming the pricing benchmark for the money market, bills markets, and derivatives market. Since 2004, China has successively lifted controls on the renminbi lending ceiling rate and deposit floor rate. Currently, interest rates on financial institution deposits are permitted to float up to 1.1 times the deposit benchmark interest rate, and interest rates on loans are permitted to float downward to 0.7 of the lending benchmark interest rate. The role of the market mechanism in the formation of interest rates has thus strengthened markedly.

INCREASING THE DEGREE OF OPENNESS OF THE FINANCIAL INDUSTRY

Since 2006, China has fulfilled its World Trade Organization commitments by affording national treatment to foreign-owned financial institutions, lifting restrictions on market access in the breadth and scope of renminbi operations, and pressing ahead with renminbi capital account convertibility, which has greatly increased the level of financial market openness. As of end-June 2012, banks from 15 countries and regions had established 37 wholly foreign-owned banks (with 254 subordinate branches) and two joint venture banks (with seven subordinate branches and one affiliate institution) in China; 76 foreign banks from 26 countries and regions had established 95 branches in China; and another 175 banks from 45 countries and regions had established 204 representative offices in China. The number of joint-venture securities companies and joint-venture fund management companies totaled 12 and 41, respectively, and insurance companies from 16 countries and regions established 55 foreign-owned insurance companies in China, with a total of nearly 1,400 branch and affiliate institutions at various levels. As of end-August 2012, China had approved Qualified Foreign Institutional Investor (QFII) quotas totaling US$80 billion, and 152 foreign institutions possessed QFII qualifications. There is now financial openness characterized by mutual benefit and joint development.

China actively participates in international organizations concerned with international financial industry reforms, standards, and systems such as the Financial Stability Board and the Basel Committee on Banking Supervision in order to promote international financial regulatory reform. China attaches importance to the introduction and implementation of international standards, best practices, and methods. Since the early 2000s, China has given priority to implementing the Basel Accord, with particular emphasis on raising capital adequacy ratios and asset quality. Since 2003, an important component of financial industry reform has been to recognize international standards or make reference to international standards to increase transparency and increase capital requirements, disclosure requirements, and accounting and external audit standards.

DEVELOPING MECHANISMS FOR LONG-RUN FINANCIAL STABILITY

Against a backdrop of increasingly severe volatility in international financial markets in recent years, Chinese authorities have consistently attached importance to maintaining monetary and financial stability. They began studying the macroprudential policy framework and the proper handling of relationships between economic growth and price stability, and guarding against financial risk early on. At the same time, China has attached importance to the development of systems and mechanisms to maintain financial stability.

The authorities have also strengthened and improved macroprudential management. After the international financial crisis erupted in 2008, China began studying ways to strengthen the macroprudential policy framework. The dynamic adjustment of differentiated reserve measures in place since 2010 combines the aggregate adjustment tools of monetary credit and liquidity management with the strengthening of macroprudential management. This plays an important role in enhancing the ability of financial institutions to guard against risk, guiding and providing incentives for financial institutions to take the initiative to preserve financial health, and adjusting the supply of monetary credit. Drawing on international experiences and adapting them to national conditions, China has begun to implement countercyclical capital buffers, excess capital requirements, and forward-looking provision requirements, and has preliminarily established a countercyclical macroprudential management framework. China is now in the process of exploring the establishment of systems for systemic financial risk monitoring and evaluation of correlations within the financial system, as well as those between the financial system and the shadow banking system, and between the financial system and the real economy. The aim is to guard against financial risk across industries, markets, and borders.

The authorities have also promoted financial safety net development. In order to strengthen mechanisms for cooperation and information sharing between the People's Bank of China (PBC) and the China Banking Regulatory Commission (CBRC), Securities Regulatory Commission, and Insurance Regulatory Commission, a national centralized financial statistics information system has been established. This has strengthened cooperation and the regulation of new cross-sector products. Early warning systems and correction mechanisms have been strengthened, grounded in early detection and early correction to prevent the transmission and spread of financial risk. In the process of risk correction, the emphasis is on strengthening the tools available to the central bank as lender of last resort and effectively reducing ethical risk and the cost of financial assistance. In order to promote the establishment of a market-oriented risk correction arrangement, the Securities Investor Protection Fund, Futures Investor Safeguard Fund, and Insurance Protection Fund were successively established. A third-party custodian system for the trading and settlement of client securities was implemented to prevent securities companies from engaging in illegal acts such as misappropriation of client settlement funds. After in-depth study and discussion, there has been progress with respect to the deposit insurance program, and efforts are currently focused on refining and implementing the program in a push to establish this system as quickly as possible.

The authorities have established a system to protect the interests of financial consumers. With the rapid development of financial markets and the increasing variety of financial products, the proper handling of the relationship between developing the industry and protecting the interests of financial consumers has become increasingly important. The 2012 National Financial Work Conference proposed giving higher priority to protecting the interests of financial consumers. Drawing on international experience, special financial consumer protection entities have been established at the PBC and regulatory agencies. These entities are responsible for studying financial consumer protection policies, establishing and refining financial consumer interest protection mechanisms and protective measures, and receiving, investigating, and handling financial consumer complaints.

COMPLETION OF THE FIRST IMF FINANCIAL SECTOR ASSESSMENT PROGRAM

The current global financial crisis demonstrated the importance of comprehensively evaluating financial systems. As early as 2003, China conducted a self-assessment of financial sector stability in accordance with the IMF's Financial Sector Assessment Program (FSAP) framework and the relevant international standards. At the G20 summits held in Washington and London in November 2008 and March 2009, all member countries committed to submitting to FSAP assessments by the IMF and the World Bank. In order to fulfill its commitment, China formally launched its first FSAP assessment in August 2009. Through the joint efforts and close cooperation of Chinese and foreign parties, the assessment concluded successfully in November 2011. The relevant assessment reports— *People's Republic of China: Financial System Stability Assessment* (FSSA), *China: Financial Sector Assessment* (FSA), and *People's Republic of China: Detailed Assessment Report of China's Implementation of International Standards and Principles in the Financial Field* (DAR)—have already been published.[1]

The assessments found that China's financial system has achieved marked progress with respect to commercial transition and financial health, and that the health of the financial system has continually strengthened. The assessments pointed out the need for China to accelerate the commercialization of the financial system in order to continue to improve financial regulation, establish sound and mechanized frameworks for financial stability and crisis management, further perfect the financial infrastructure, and expand financial coverage. Undertaking

---

[1] The FSSA is available at www.imf.org/external/pubs/cat/longres.aspx?sk=25350.0; the FSA is available at www.worldbank.org/content/dam/Worldbank/document/WB-Chinas-Financial-Sector-Assessment-Report.pdf; and the DAR is available at www.imf.org/external/pubs/cat/longres .aspx?sk=25350.0.

the FSAP assessment was an important test of the outcomes of China's financial system development in recent years. It has aided in the integration of international experience into an examination of financial institution health, and it has afforded China's financial sector a more sober awareness of the risks and challenges it faces.

Although notable results have been achieved through China's financial reforms, the country's financial system will face new challenges as the economic development model shifts and structural adjustments proceed, particularly amid continuing economic and financial globalization. The government's recently published *Twelfth Five-Year Plan for Financial Industry Development and Reform* addressed the need to comprehensively promote financial reform, openness, and development, and to significantly strengthen the financial industry's overall position, international competitiveness, and risk-resistance capacity.[2]

Looking forward, China will continue to deepen financial reforms and expand financial openness in order to increase market orientation and globalization and to build a modern financial system that is structurally sound, secure, and efficient, thus markedly increasing its level of service to the real economy.

---

[2]The plan is available at www.csrc.gov.cn/pub/csrc_en/newsfacts/release/201210/W0201210106313 55001488.pdf.

CHAPTER 2

Financial Reform: An Essential Ingredient in Transforming China's Economic Development Model

NIGEL CHALK AND MURTAZA SYED

Managed well, financial reform in China will generate significant benefits to the Chinese economy in terms of growth, employment, and improved standards of living that will help sustain the country's spectacular growth performance and accelerate the ongoing rebalancing of its growth model. Done right, it could be as significant as the state-owned enterprise reform of the 1990s. Conversely, a prolonged delay in financial liberalization, or implementing it in a poorly designed or badly executed manner, would pose substantial risks for China. It would also have important negative spillovers for an already-fragile global economy. This chapter discusses the rationale for reform and outlines a roadmap that could be implemented over the next five years.

THE STATUS QUO: CHINA'S FINANCIAL SYSTEM

Two words immediately come to mind when defining China's financial system as it stands today: liquidity and control. The system is flush with liquidity, both because of a high stock of savings that is held domestically by China's closed capital account (Figure 2.1) and large inflows associated with the country's balance of payment surpluses (and the corresponding foreign currency intervention necessary to resist appreciation of the exchange rate). To prevent this liquidity from fueling dangerous lending booms and asset bubbles, the People's Bank of China (PBC) relies on control—predominantly direct tools such as quantitative limits on bank credit and regulations of deposit and loan rates, and indirect tools such as relatively high reserve requirements (Figure 2.2). These have proven effective in recent years, given the historically bank-based nature of China's financial system, in conducting macroeconomic management. A by-product of these policies has been to keep both loan and deposit rates artificially low, create incentives for banks to allocate much of their lending to very large, capital-intensive enterprises, and lower costs of sterilizing China's foreign currency intervention.

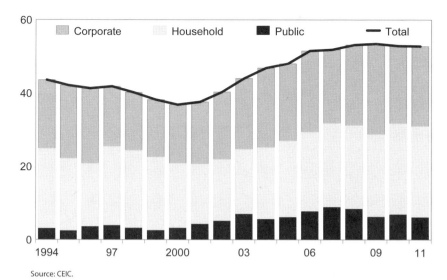

Source: CEIC.

Figure 2.1 Saving Decomposition
(In percent of GDP)

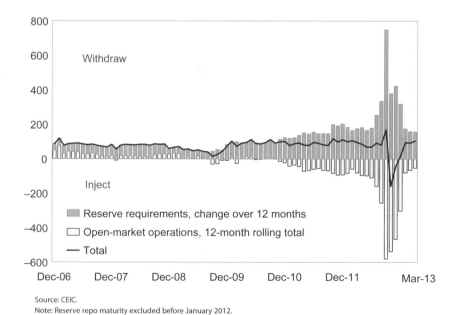

Source: CEIC.
Note: Reserve repo maturity excluded before January 2012.

Figure 2.2 Sterilization by the People's Bank of China
(Change in percent of net foreign assets change over 12 months)

WHY SHOULD WE CARE ABOUT FINANCIAL REFORM IN CHINA?

First and foremost, as China is the world's second-largest economy, it is in everyone's interest for it to have a safe, stable, well-regulated, and efficient system of financial intermediation. Over the past three years we have learned all too well of the enormous global social costs that financial instability in systemic economies can create.

Second, sustaining China's spectacular growth record will be impossible without a modern financial system that efficiently intermediates savings and allocates capital. Indeed, financial reform will be necessary to achieve many of the key themes identified in China's Twelfth Five-Year Plan, including (1) boosting household income by increasing the returns to savings; (2) increasing consumption through prudently managed household credit as well as instruments that smooth consumption and hedge risk (Figure 2.3); (3) reducing income disparities through better access to financial services, including in rural areas; (4) increasing employment through a more appropriate pricing of capital and by moving toward a more labor-intensive means of production (Figure 2.4); and (5) supporting the development of new industries by reallocating resources on market terms and making more financing available to small and medium-sized enterprises and start-ups, including in the services sector.

And third, China is, in any case, outgrowing the current system of direct government influence over the allocation and pricing of credit. This managed

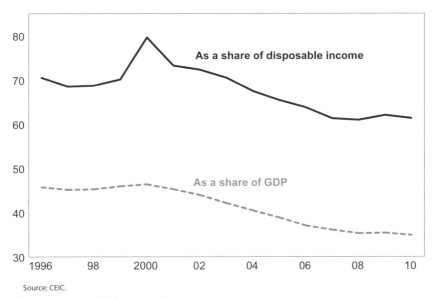

Source: CEIC.

Figure 2.3 Household Consumption
(In percent)

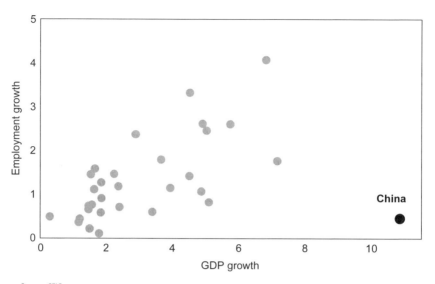

Source: CEIC.

Figure 2.4 Average Employment Growth, 2004–10
(In percent)

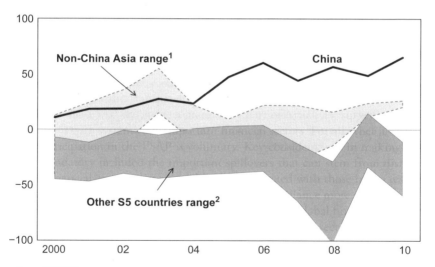

Source: IMF (2011).
[1]Includes Indonesia, Korea, Singapore, and Taiwan Province of China.
[2]Includes the euro area, Japan, United Kingdom, and United States.

Figure 2.5 Imputed "Subsidy" to Capital
(In percent of marginal product of capital)

approach certainly allowed for strong growth following the start of China's reform efforts, in part because sectors with high-growth potential were easier to identify. However, the system was not perfect and, as a side effect, this approach generated significant downsides in the form of overcapacity, capital-intensive means of production, a tendency for asset bubbles, and a periodic need for public-funded bank recapitalizations. With the Chinese economy growing in size and complexity, the ability to steer credit directly is diminishing and the costs from misallocating resources is growing (Figure 2.5).

WHAT ARE THE RISKS OF CONTINUING WITH THE CURRENT SYSTEM?

China has long been characterized by a very deep financial system, but one that has relied predominantly on banks to intermediate enormous levels of household and corporate saving. However, this bank-dominated structure is now changing. Since the global financial crisis, China has seen acceleration in the pace of financial innovation, an expansion of new ways to intermediate savings, and a migration of resources out of banks and into other forms of financial intermediation such as trusts, wealth management products, and corporate bonds (Figure 2.6).

The diversification and development of financial markets and instruments is generally healthy. It will facilitate more efficient means of allocating China's

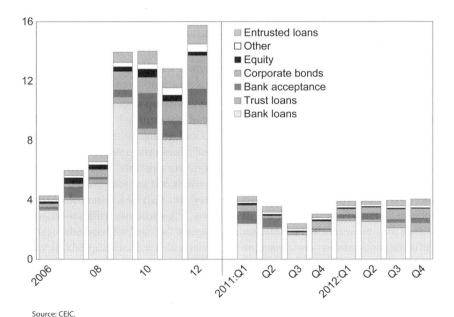

Source: CEIC.

Figure 2.6 Social Financing
(In trillions of renminbi)

capital, open up financing opportunities for companies that previously were unable to get bank loans, and increase the level of remuneration that households receive on their savings.

However, these changes also pose risks to financial and macroeconomic stability. First, regulation of the nonbank system of intermediation is weaker and less developed than that for banks. Second, care is needed to ensure the banks are healthy enough to withstand a steady loss of resources that a growing nonbank system could imply. In this regard, we are already seeing evidence of growing liquidity pressures for smaller banks in China. Third, the underlying system of macroeconomic control needs to evolve with the times. In particular, the current regulation of interest rates distorts the pricing of both deposits and loans and creates huge incentives for resources to migrate out of the banks to institutions that are not subject to such controls on the rates of return they offer. Why put your money in a bank deposit that earns less than inflation when you can choose from a convenient array of more lucrative wealth management products instead? Further, international experience tells us that the use of administrative limits on the quantity of bank lending as a means to exercise macroeconomic control is likely to become less and less effective as financial innovation takes hold and more and more intermediation takes place outside of the banks.

Financial reform is, therefore, essential to sustain the ability of Chinese policymakers to effectively guide the macroeconomy, ensure that the expansion of nonbank channels proceeds in a safe and sound way, and prevent the banking system from being undermined by a loss of deposits and funding.

WHAT LESSONS CAN BE GLEANED FROM INTERNATIONAL EXPERIENCE?

A number of China's G20 peers have reformed their financial sectors, and their experiences provide important lessons. As in China, their pre-reform financial sector landscapes were often characterized by a heavy bias toward bank intermediation, rigid segmentation across financial institutions by function, low levels of competition, regulated interest rates, a large public sector role (including directed lending and state guarantees of financial institutions), the conducting of monetary policy mainly through direct instruments, and capital controls. In addition, countries embarking on financial liberalization have encountered several challenges, and their reform efforts have often led to periods of financial volatility and crisis. Boxes 2.1 to 2.4 outline some of the major steps and mistakes made by some of the other G20 economies as they moved toward a more modern and market-based financial system. From international experience, a few broad lessons that stand out are detailed below.

Lesson 1: Financial sector weaknesses should be sought out and addressed before liberalization begins. This includes examining the ability to adequately price and manage risks, recapitalizing or restructuring systemic institutions, and enhancing corporate governance. If unaddressed, weaknesses create the potential for financial

Box 2.1   Financial Reform in Indonesia, 1982–96

Initial Conditions

Indonesia's financial sector reforms were part of a broad effort to diversify the economy and expand the role of the private sector. The economy had demonstrated robust, albeit resource-driven growth, had an open current account, and pursued a managed float. The financial sector was dominated by five large state-owned banks, government-directed lending was prevalent, interest rates were regulated (and typically negative in real terms), and the growth in bank credit was subject to administrative ceilings. On the capital account, outflows had been mostly liberalized but inflows were subject to strict controls.

Sequencing

Reforms proceeded in two broad steps:

- *Phase I (1982–86):* Indirect monetary policy instruments were introduced, interest rates were liberalized, and credit ceilings were phased out.

- *Phase II (1987–92):* Restrictions on the activities of banks were loosened, directed lending was reduced, and there was greater latitude on the operations of foreign banks. Reserve requirements were equalized across the banking industry, removing a source of preferential treatment for the state banks. Prudential regulation and supervision was enhanced. Capital account liberalization began in 1989, with controls on portfolio and bank capital inflows steadily eased.

Outcomes

During the early stages of reform, real interest rates moved higher to market clearing levels and the more efficient private banks began to build market share. Macroeconomic policies were kept restrictive, particularly with fiscal policy steadily tightening. Vulnerabilities began to build up in the second phase of reforms from 1987–92, but these risks were left largely undiagnosed. In large part, the risks were due to weak corporate governance, inadequate regulation and supervision, and a macroeconomic policy mix that encouraged large speculative capital inflows. Despite increasing competition, bank ownership remained highly concentrated, and large private banks, which were subsidiaries of politically powerful business conglomerates, were able to use their influence to circumvent regulatory limits related to connected lending. Large parts of the financial sector (and its largest corporate borrowers) were perceived to be covered by implicit public guarantees, a perception that had been strengthened by a succession of opaque bailouts. There was an absence of a clear framework to resolve failing institutions, and banks had few incentives to manage downside risks. Overcapacity in the financial sector grew over a number of years, spurring excessive lending to relatively unproductive sectors, including real estate.

The Path to Crisis

As the capital account became more open, domestic imbalances in the financial system combined with a tightly managed exchange rate gave rise to a surge in speculative capital inflows. Domestic banks borrowed heavily offshore in foreign currency to fund rapid growth in local currency loans. Regulatory efforts to dissuade such carry trades were largely too little and too late. As the Asian financial crisis unfolded in 1997, the weaknesses were exposed in the Indonesian financial sector—including currency and maturity mismatches—putting strains on corporate and bank balance sheets and, eventually, ending in a full-blown systemic banking crisis.

institutions to take growing risks to boost returns and cover up their underlying vulnerabilities. These vulnerabilities will then grow as financial reform proceeds, potentially revealing weaknesses within systemic institutions.

Lesson 2: The macroeconomic policy framework should move toward market-based monetary policy at an early stage, based on indirect instruments and with increased exchange rate flexibility. Before financial reform proceeds, the monetary authority needs to have at its disposal sufficient tools for macroeconomic control to prevent an unintended surge in lending or creating the conditions for large capital inflows.

Lesson 3: Implicit public guarantees of financial institutions should be explicitly withdrawn during the early stages of liberalization. Instead, such blanket backing should be replaced with an explicit scheme for deposit insurance. Ensuring that banks face hard budget constraints would be an important prerequisite for a more commercially oriented banking system that adequately prices risk and efficiently allocates credit. It also helps mitigate moral hazard risks and prevents banks from taking undue risks as restrictions on bank activities are eased and new markets opened.

Lesson 4: The financial, legal, and accounting framework should be revised before embarking on major reforms. The major prerequisites for an effective regulatory and supervisory framework include (1) clear objectives and mandates for the agencies; (2) regulatory independence, with appropriate accountability; (3) adequate resources (staff and funding); and (4) effective enforcement and resolution powers.

Lesson 5: The regulatory and supervisory perimeter needs to be sufficiently wide and well coordinated to prevent regulatory arbitrage and to identify emerging vulnerabilities. Virtually all post-liberalization crises can be traced to inadequate supervision or regulations not keeping up with changing financial landscapes. All potentially systemically important financial institutions, including non-bank financial institutions, need to be covered before restrictions on financial activities are significantly relaxed and new markets developed. The regulatory and supervisory framework should be empowered to limit concentration in bank ownership and clearly identify beneficial owners (to mitigate the risks of connected lending). Activities in nonbank financial institutions in particular should be monitored closely. These institutions should be prohibited from taking deposits.

Lesson 6: Measures to deepen financial and capital markets should move in parallel with reform of the banking system. Financial market development is important to improve the allocation of capital and create competition. However, lopsided sequencing can have significant effects on bank balance sheets by undermining their deposit base or by eroding their pool of corporate clients. This, in turn, can lead banks to increase risk exposures.

Lesson 7: Many of the important objectives of financial sector reform—including greater competition and efficiency, and enhanced risk management—depend on having market-determined deposit and loan rates. Interest rate liberalization facilitates the development of a market-based monetary policy framework based

Box 2.2   Financial Reform in Japan, 1975–90

Initial Conditions

The pre-reform financial sector landscape in Japan was dominated by banks with limited options for savers, low regulated interest rates, and strict limits on bond issuance. The financial sector was also characterized by rigid segmentation of financial institutions by function. Discretionary administrative guidance was the principal method of financial regulation, with "convoy regulation" aimed at ensuring financial institutions evolved at the same pace, implicitly inhibiting competition. As financial liberalization began, Japan did, however, have a largely open capital account.

Sequencing

The following key features characterized Japanese financial sector liberalization:

- *The capital account was liberalized early in the process.* In the 1980 Foreign Exchange Control Act, corporate borrowers were given greatly expanded opportunities to raise funds overseas.

- *Liberalization was asymmetric.* Corporate borrowers were provided access to a broader range of funding alternatives before savers were given choices in investment instruments. A number of new markets grew, including a commercial paper and corporate bond market, but retail investors were given only limited access.

- *Deposit rate liberalization proceeded slowly and at a slower pace than lending rates.* Indeed, it took until 1994 before deposit rates were fully market determined.

Outcomes

The lopsided pace of liberalization caused the banks to quickly lose many of their best borrowers, while savers had few choices but to remain in bank deposits. As a result, many large and medium-sized enterprises reduced their dependence on bank financing and increased their funding from bond and equity markets, where nonbank financial institutions were large investors. From 1980–90, the ratio of bank debt to total assets for large, publicly listed manufacturing firms dropped by almost 20 percentage points (to less than 15 percent). On the other hand, household deposits continued to rise as barriers to entry into the investment trust business remained high and banks were not permitted to market investment management services. The loss of corporate clients and banks' efforts to continue to build market share led them to expand their exposure to the property market and to smaller firms. Lending decisions became heavily influenced by collateral values (rather than a notion of capacity to repay), credit standards weakened, and from 1980–90, loans to the real estate industry doubled. Much of the remainder of the banks' loan book was devoted to small firms, with correspondingly higher credit risks.

The Path to Crisis

In the early 1990s, Japan's real estate bubble burst and the resulting decline in property prices, equity prices, and economic growth exposed the underlying vulnerabilities on bank balance sheets. The deceleration of economic growth impaired the capacity of small businesses to repay, nonperforming real estate loans skyrocketed as collateral values plummeted, and the fall in equity prices shrunk bank capital. The banking system became mired in a collapse from which it has yet to fully recover.

on indirect instruments with an effective transmission mechanism. This provides increased scope for macroeconomic control to mitigate the risks of instability as reforms proceed. Other goals, such as enhanced competition, allocational efficiency, and stronger risk management, all rely on allowing prices (interest rates) to provide the right market-based signals.

Lesson 8: Successful liberalization of interest rates needs several preconditions. These preconditions include a stable macroeconomic environment, absorption of excess liquidity, an interest rate structure that is not in serious disequilibrium prior to liberalization, an active and well-functioning money market, and a sound payments system. Strong supervisory policies and instruments and a flexible and effective monetary policy framework are also required. In particular, monetary policy needs to guard against an excess supply of credit as interest rate constraints are removed (Figure 2.7). In successful cases of liberalization (e.g., Australia, Canada, and Belgium), credit expansion was mitigated by a deliberate containment of liquidity and increases in real interest rates (Figure 2.8). Conversely, other countries (e.g., Argentina, Chile, and Mexico) lost control of monetary aggregates as they liberalized, injecting enormous amounts of credit and monetary stimulus into their economies that culminated in asset bubbles and banking crises.

Lesson 9: Opening to international portfolio flows should occur only after the bulk of financial sector reform has been achieved. The current scale of global capital flows and the increasing sophistication and interconnectedness of the world's financial markets create large risks for countries that open themselves up to international capital flows before the distortions and misalignments in their domestic financial systems are resolved. The early stages of capital account liberalization can open up to stable long-term sources of financing, such as direct investment inflows. However, full liberalization—including that for short-term portfolio flows—should be put in place only after the bulk of financial sector reform is in place.

WHAT ARE THE BENEFITS OF FINANCIAL LIBERALIZATION AND REFORM?

So far, we have outlined the downsides of allowing reform efforts to languish and the risks of incorrect implementation of the reform agenda, with cautionary tales from four important cases outlined in Boxes 2.1 to 2.4. But what are the benefits for China to liberalize its financial system?

First, a well-executed financial reform program will allow the Chinese economy to steadily adapt to the ongoing evolution in financial intermediation and to maximize the benefits from an increasingly diverse set of financial markets and instruments. Developing credible competition for the banks—in the form of corporate bond markets, deeper and more liquid equity markets, mutual funds, exchange-traded funds, derivatives, and other financial products—will

Box 2.3   Financial Reform in Korea, 1980–96

Initial Conditions

The Korean financial sector was largely state owned, highly regulated, and used as an allocation tool by the government to advance its economic development agenda. Monetary policy was conducted using interest rate and credit ceilings as well as reserve requirements. The government guided resources to its preferred sectors by a combination of directed credit and preferential lending rates. The capital account was largely closed.

Sequencing

- *Early reforms included bank privatization and measures to increase financial competition*, although the banking sector emerged from the privatization process with ownership concentrated among large industrial conglomerates. Nonbank institutions developed, albeit increasingly owned and controlled by these industry groups.

- *Progress was also made in developing money and interbank markets*, an important precursor for a move to a more indirect monetary policy, and the government somewhat scaled back its efforts to direct credit.

- *Interest rates remained tightly regulated* until 1993, in part to protect certain sectors.

- *Regulatory standards for loan classification, provisioning, accounting, and large exposures saw little improvement,* while supervision remained fragmented.

- *Restrictions on capital inflows began to be weakened in 1989,* largely by allowing financial institutions to borrow offshore.

Outcomes

In 1994, the ceiling on foreign currency lending by domestic banks was eliminated, but limits on banks' medium- and long-term borrowing from international markets were retained. As a result, Korean banks began to finance their domestic long-term foreign currency lending with short-term foreign currency loans. At the same time, there were large gaps in the prudential regulations relating to foreign exchange exposures in overseas branches and offshore funds, which accounted for a significant build-up in short-term external liabilities.

The Path to Crisis

From 1994–97, banks rapidly built up huge maturity mismatches on their balance sheets and the financial sector became exposed to economically nonviable projects through a complex network of cross-holdings within industrial groups and connected lending. By 1997, banks and nonbank institutions found it increasingly difficult to roll over their external short-term funding, leading to an exhaustion of official reserves and an all-out balance of payments crisis.

create incentives for the whole financial system to operate in a more effective and productive manner. Capital will be allocated more efficiently, and companies (particularly smaller enterprises) that at present are mostly denied access to bank loans will have new options to finance their operations (Geng and N'Diaye, 2012; Feyzioglu, 2009).

Second, well-designed reform, accompanied by a robust regulatory infrastructure that spans all forms of financial intermediation and guarantees seamless coordination across regulators, will help ensure that the financial system continues to develop in a robust way without excessive risktaking, lowering the possibility of future financial volatility and disruption.

Third, making a broader range of alternative investment instruments available to households will increase the return on their savings (Nabar, 2011), allow households and corporate savers to hold a more diversified portfolio of assets, and reduce the tensions that are currently evident from having housing viewed as a preferred store of value (Figure 2.9).

And finally, financial reform will facilitate China's move toward a more modern means of macroeconomic control, one that deploys market-clearing prices to determine the availability and cost of credit rather than having both the price and quantity of loans regulated by the government (Figure 2.10). This will strengthen the monetary transmission mechanism and give the central bank greater ability to fine-tune policy in response to changing economic conditions (Feyzioglu, Porter, and Takats, 2009).

These benefits are well known to China's policymakers and were highlighted in the Twelfth Five-Year Plan, which included a clear commitment to moving ahead with the reform of the country's financial system.

WHAT ARE THE MAIN ELEMENTS OF THE NEEDED REFORMS?

There is certainly no "one-size-fits-all" approach to sequencing financial sector liberalization, especially in an economy as sophisticated and complex as China's. In many cases, the appropriate pace and sequencing of reforms will involve balancing multiple trade-offs. Dynamic judgment will be required as the financial system evolves in potentially unpredictable ways and as reforms are implemented. As the situation for many comparator countries demonstrates, the agenda for financial reform is a complex, multiyear undertaking. However, starting now will ensure this process can be largely completed within the horizon of the Twelfth Five-Year Plan. A broad roadmap for reform should include adopting a new monetary policy framework; raising real interest rates; strengthening and expanding regulatory coverage of the financial system, including putting in place a broad set of tools for crisis management; developing financial markets and alternative means of intermediation; deregulating interest rates; and, eventually, opening up the capital account.

Box 2.4   Financial Reform in Mexico, 1988–93

Initial Conditions

To combat high inflation and low growth, Mexico undertook a broad set of reforms in the late 1980s to increase the role of markets in various aspects of the economy. The banking system was largely publicly held and segmented across sectors, interest rates were regulated, and supervision was generally weak.

Sequencing

Mexico pursued a rapid pace of financial reform alongside a broad effort at macroeconomic stabilization and capital account liberalization that included the following:

- *A big-bang program of sweeping reforms introduced in 1989–90,* including eliminating interest rate controls; replacing very high reserve requirements with liquidity ratios; removing restrictions on private sector lending; ending mandatory lending to the public sector; and removing sector segmentation (which allowed for the emergence of universal banks).

- *Privatization of 18 domestic banks from 1991–92.* Before the banks were sold, the government provided unlimited state-backed deposit insurance.

Outcomes

Bank balance sheets grew rapidly both before and after privatization, as banks tried to capture market share in a newly liberalized market. In response, the authorities began to tighten prudential regulations between 1991–93 by increasing minimum capital adequacy ratios (from 6 to 8 percent); strengthening loan classification and provisioning rules; and imposing stricter limits on foreign exchange positions. However, the new regulatory and supervisory framework was seriously deficient and concealed a range of increasing vulnerabilities, not least weaknesses in the Mexican accounting system. Banks were required to classify as nonperforming only that portion of the loan (or the interest payment) which was due but had not yet been repaid. Banks were also permitted to exercise significant discretion in the risk classification of their loans, which allowed them to inflate capital ratios. In addition, there was no consolidated accounting for universal banks, making it hard to judge risks at a group level. Domestic banks were able to circumvent prudential regulations designed to prevent currency mismatches, while large interest rate differentials and the exchange rate peg provided strong incentives for carry trades.

The Path to Crisis

In the wake of liberalization, the newly privatized Mexican financial institutions began to increasingly fund their operations through over-the-counter structured notes that were linked to exchange rate developments. Accounting rules allowed the banks to book these positions as claims that were not counted toward their net open foreign exchange position. The increasing bank exposures triggered a balance of payments and financial crisis in 1994, which was amplified by the balance sheet weaknesses that were hidden within the system.

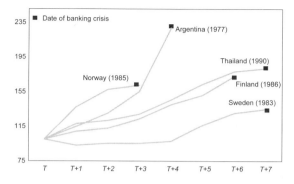

Source: CEIC.
Note: *T* = time of interest rate liberalization, normalized to equal 100.

Figure 2.7   Private Credit
(Percent of GDP)

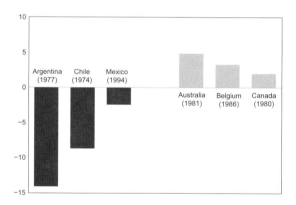

Source: CEIC.

Figure 2.8   Real Interest Rates
(In percent; three-year average post-interest-rate liberalization)

A New Framework for Monetary Policy

Financial reform should involve a reinvention of the monetary policy framework in order to move away from the current system—which is reliant on controls on deposit and loan rates, the exchange rate, and the quantity of credit—to one in which the central bank has clear objectives in terms of growth, inflation, and financial stability. In addition, the PBC should be given flexibility and control over the macroprudential and monetary tools that will be needed to achieve these goals.

As a first step, the high levels of liquidity currently residing in the financial system would need to be absorbed. Judging this liquidity absorption, however,

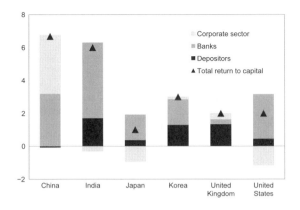

Source: CEIC.

Figure 2.9 Distribution of the Returns to Bank-Intermediated Capital
(Real returns in percent)

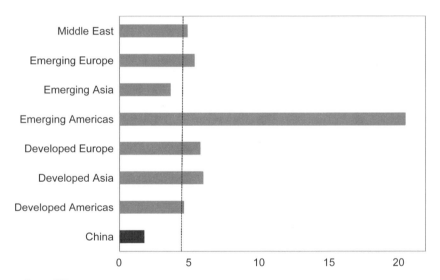

Source: CEIC.
Note: Vertical line is the global average.

Figure 2.10 Real Cost of Capital, 2005–09
(In percent)

will be complicated by the lack of reliable price signals and the fact that the "true" level of liquidity in the system is masked by the lack of fully market-determined interest rates, direct controls on credit, and administrative determination of both the price and quantity of paper issued by the central bank. Nevertheless, as a first step, open-market operations should be deployed to absorb the liquidity overhang by placing central bank paper at market-determined rates, allowing interbank rates to rise closer to the top of the regulated loan-deposit rate corridor, and moving the structure of deposit and loan rates up closer to the neutral real interest rate.

At the same time, the ongoing liquidity injection that is created by large-scale foreign currency intervention will need to be decreased by appreciating the exchange rate to a point where the currency market is more balanced and there are genuine two-way flows in the balance of payments and two-way movements in the exchange rate (Figure 2.11). This would lessen the need for monetary tools—including the use of reserve requirements and open-market operations—to be geared so much toward sterilizing foreign currency inflows and managing the currency. Instead, policies could be refocused toward a more market-based and countercyclical approach geared toward the domestic economy.

With liquidity absorbed and interest rates clearing the capital market, the central bank could then shift toward the use of more indirect monetary instruments to exercise macroeconomic control. The central bank would be able to move to using short-term rates—perhaps the seven-day repo rate—as its effective operational target for monetary policy and phase out direct influence on the growth, allocation, and pricing of credit. The PBC would be able to effectively influence short-term rates through open-market operations and to conduct those operations with quantities determined by achieving market clearing at a given target level for the policy interest rate. Reserve averaging could be introduced to decrease interest rate volatility, and reserve requirements could be remunerated at a market-determined rate (Figure 2.12).

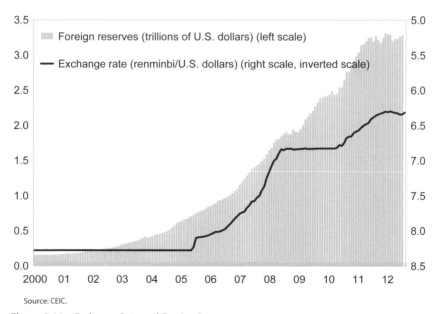

Source: CEIC.

Figure 2.11 Exchange Rate and Foreign Reserves

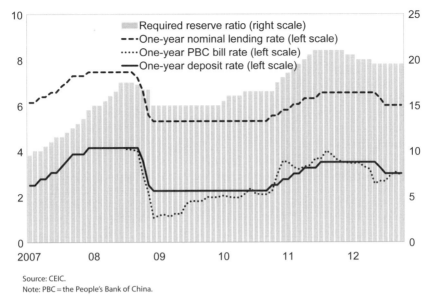

Source: CEIC.
Note: PBC = the People's Bank of China.

Figure 2.12 Short-Term Interest Rates
(In percent)

As financial innovation and development makes money demand unstable, targeting M2 would no longer be a feasible proposition and a new framework for the conduct of monetary policy would be needed. In particular, the PBC could move toward a monetary policy regime directed toward growth, inflation control, and financial stability, and achieved through a combination of interest rates and macroprudential tools.

Improving Regulation and Supervision

As the system evolves, the government will need to be nimble in adapting to the changing environment by increasing the commercial orientation of the banking system, bolstering its crisis management capabilities, and strengthening supervisory efforts to identify and manage macrofinancial vulnerabilities.

Further advances in the regulatory and supervisory regime will be needed to ensure it is sufficiently adaptable and dynamic to react in a new environment of tighter liquidity, indirect monetary control and, eventually, liberalized interest rates. In a more liberalized environment, strict supervision will be needed to prevent banks and nonbank institutions from engaging in unsafe practices to boost profitability or gain market share. Particular attention will be needed to address the supervisory and regulatory gaps that will inevitably emerge in a more dynamic and liberalized setting. To this end, investments should be made to improve stress-testing capabilities; increase oversight of the largest financial institutions; overhaul the crisis management and resolution framework; build a process for the orderly exit of weak or failing financial institutions; develop clear rules on central bank emergency liquidity support; put in place a formal deposit insurance scheme; and pursue better data quality and collection. Interagency regulatory and supervisory coordination will also need to become more ongoing and systematic, identifying and resolving regulatory gaps. A key step will be to establish a permanent, high-level interagency Financial Stability Committee to monitor and identify macrofinancial vulnerabilities and implement a macroprudential framework geared toward preventing the buildup of systemic risks (see Chapter 3 for a more detailed discussion).

Developing Broader Channels for Intermediation

Strengthening nonbank financial intermediation will be an important objective of financial reform. Such institutions will act as competition to the banking system, offer companies alternate avenues for project financing, and provide households with a broader range of financing and investment possibilities. Expansion of nonbank areas of intermediation will, however, need to largely move in tandem with reform of bank-based intermediation. Failure to do so could create incentives for faster migration of resources out of the banks (into bonds, equities, trusts, leasing, and wealth management products), with accompanying supervisory and regulatory challenges and the potential for destabilizing the banking system.

The focus should be on dismantling impediments to the development of alternate markets and instruments, but with corresponding clarity about regulations and responsibilities of those new institutions. Priorities include reducing segmentation, increasing liquidity, and simplifying regulatory requirements in equity and bond markets. In addition, efforts should be made to encourage a broad institutional investor base, including pension, insurance, and mutual fund companies.

In conjunction with developing a wider range of investment products, enhanced regulation and supervision would help ensure that risks to financial stability are well managed. In addition, a comprehensive framework for disclosure and consumer protection will be needed to ensure investors are fully aware of the risks they undertake when diversifying their assets away from bank deposits. For prudential reasons, precedence should be given to gaining experience with plain-vanilla instruments before allowing more sophisticated ones such as securitized and trust products.

Liberalizing Loan and Deposit Rates

With a robust monetary framework in place, and with interest rates rising to clear the capital market, the next step will be to move away from the regulation of loan and deposit rates by the central bank. The preferred strategy would be to gradually lift the ceiling on deposit rates and allow such rates to be determined by banks on a competitive basis. This would facilitate an increase in the cost of funding and move toward a corresponding increase in the loan rates. The lifting of the ceiling could be phased in based on the term of the deposits in order to

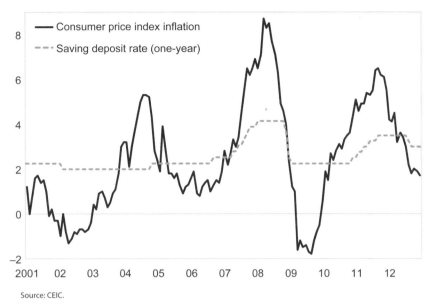

Source: CEIC.

Figure 2.13   Inflation and the Deposit Rate
(In percent)

allow banks time to adjust. As the deposit rate ceiling is raised, the floor on loan rates will become increasingly less binding and could eventually be removed (Figure 2.13).

With interest rates liberalized, financial institutions should be held accountable for managing their risks. In particular, regulated firms that are deemed by their supervisor to be well capitalized and well managed could be granted more discretion and held accountable for conducting their operations prudently and in compliance with the regulatory framework. Similarly, customers of financial products could assume greater responsibility for their own financial decisions, complemented by adequate consumer protection, disclosure, and improved financial literacy.

As this transition proceeds, it will be essential to ensure that it does not translate into an unintended loosening of monetary and credit conditions. This will be complicated by the fact that the ongoing financial reform and liberalization will make the appropriate pace of monetary growth very difficult to predict. Nevertheless, monetary policy would need to be attentive and used actively to counter the potentially unpredictable impact of interest rate liberalization on liquidity, credit growth, and monetary conditions.

The process will need to be carefully managed—through the use of both monetary policy tools to adapt liquidity conditions and the application of macroprudential restraints—in order to counter any surge in credit growth as interest rates become more market-determined. Particular attention will need to be paid to ensuring credit does not expand at a precipitous rate either in the aggregate or to particular sectors (e.g., real estate or consumer credit). It will, therefore, be important as interest rates are deregulated that regulatory and supervisory tools be used to their fullest to ensure that banks do not engage in overly aggressive competition or unsafe practices to attract deposits, expand lending, or compress margins to gain market share.

Greater freedom to set loan and deposit rates will create incentives for banks to better manage and price risk and will make money market interest rates more representative of true financial conditions. At the same time, a more market-determined system of interest rates will provide valuable price signals for macroeconomic policymaking and strengthen the transmission mechanism for monetary policy.

Opening Up the Capital Account

As the domestic financial system becomes more marketbased, with fewer distortions in the determination of market-clearing levels of credit and interest rates, China can then proceed to dismantle its extensive system of controls on capital flows.

The early stages of capital account liberalization should focus on removing restrictions on more stable, long-term sources of financing such as direct investment flows (as is already being done). As the reform process advances—with interest rates that are market-determined, a robust monetary policy and regulatory framework in place, a flexible currency, banks operating prudently, and the domestic financial system liberalized—the stage would be set to ease restrictions on short-term inflows. In doing so, the current Qualified Foreign Institutional Investor and Qualified Domestic Institutional Investor systems could be effectively used to gradually open up the account in stages and at a different pace for different forms of investments.

CONCLUDING THOUGHTS

In sum, both the rationale and the agenda for financial reform in China are clear. Prior to the global crisis, China was on a firm trajectory toward a more modern financial system capable of addressing the challenges of a more mature and complex economy. However, as financial systems across the globe suffered severe setbacks, Chinese policymakers paused. In some ways, this was natural. But over the medium term, China needs to maintain the pace of change. Thus, it is encouraging to note the prominent role assigned to financial reforms in the Twelfth Five-Year Plan. Indeed, the roadmap laid out above can be completed over a five-year horizon. Done right, financial liberalization would be the next big wave of reform that China needs. It could be as significant as the state-owned enterprise reform of the 1990s, laying the foundation for continued strong growth in China in the coming decades.

This chapter has aimed to outline a roadmap toward that end that encompasses both the key elements and sequencing of the required financial reform effort. Continuing to defer progress in this area runs the risk that the financial system might evolve in an uncoordinated and disorderly fashion, outpacing supervisory capacity and revealing regulatory gaps. Indeed, the likelihood is high that developments are already proceeding on a timetable that is being driven not by careful, preemptive, and concerted policy planning, but rather in ad hoc fashion, propelled by the accelerating pace of market disintermediation and innovation. Such a trajectory is in the interest of neither China nor the rest of the world.

REFERENCES

Feyzioglu, Tarhan, 2009, "Does Good Financial Performance Mean Good Financial Intermediation in China?" IMF Working Paper 09/170 (Washington: International Monetary Fund).

Feyzioglu, Tarhan, Nathan Porter, and Elod Takats, 2009, "Interest Rate Liberalization in China," IMF Working Paper 09/171 (Washington: International Monetary Fund).

Geng, Nan, and Papa N'Diaye, 2012, "Financial Development, Corporate Investment and Savings in China," IMF Working Paper 12/80 (Washington: International Monetary Fund).

International Monetary Fund (IMF), 2011, "People's Republic of China: Spillover Report for the 2011 Article IV Consultation and Selected Issues," Country Report 11/193 (Washington: International Monetary Fund).

Nabar, Malhar, 2011, "Targets, Interest Rates, and Household Saving in Urban China," IMF Working Paper 11/223 (Washington: International Monetary Fund).

CHAPTER 3

Strengthening the Financial Stability Framework in China

KEITH HALL AND TAO SUN

Over the past decade, China has maintained a stable financial system during a period of rapid economic expansion and significant structural change and reform. This commendable performance reflects the great strides made by the Chinese authorities in deepening financial reform, mitigating financial risks, and strengthening supervisory capabilities. But, until recently, it has also reflected a willingness by government to periodically draw on the public purse to relieve the banking system of bad debts and inject sizable amounts of capital. The authorities are fully aware of the moral hazard involved in these types of state intervention and are keen to promote a financial system that is better prepared to contain its own risks. The urgency for doing so is heightened by the knowledge that both domestic and cross-border systemic linkages in China are intensifying as the size and complexity of the financial sector expands, and as the authorities encourage further financial innovation to better service the needs of a dynamic economy.

The ultimate responsibility for promoting and maintaining financial stability in China resides with the State Council, the highest executive authority. From an operational perspective, however, this responsibility is very largely discharged by the following four agencies:

- The People's Bank of China (PBC), which as the central bank is specifically charged with guarding against financial risks and maintaining financial stability;
- China Banking Regulatory Commission, which is the prudential regulator of banks;
- China Securities Regulatory Commission, which regulates the securities market and futures markets; and
- China Insurance Regulatory Commission, which regulates the insurance industry.

Of the other government agencies, the most important from a financial stability perspective are the Ministry of Finance, whose responsibilities as fiscal agent include debt issuance and the management of state-owned assets, and the State Administration of Foreign Exchange, which has custody of foreign exchange reserves. Together these two agencies provide the government with a very substantial backstop for the financial system—the resources to intervene in times of financial stress.

The work that these agencies need to undertake jointly to promote financial stability can be broken down into three broad streams:

- *Surveillance*—the early identification of potential threats to financial stability;
- *Mitigation*—the measures that need to be taken to make the financial system more resilient to shocks; and
- *Crisis management*—the principles and procedures for responding to distress or failures in the financial system.

Each of these streams represents a significant body of work in its own right and requires a high level of interagency cooperation and coordination to be fully effective.

On *surveillance*, the main challenge is to identify the macroeconomic and financial variables that provide the most insight into the potential risks and vulnerabilities facing the financial system. This information obviously varies from country to country depending on the scope of national statistical collection and the availability of market-based information. The challenge in China, as elsewhere, is to identify the data set that is most likely to provide the authorities with some early warning of systemic risks and thus provide an opportunity to respond preemptively.

The central bank and the regulatory agencies share responsibility for the *mitigation* of risk within the financial system. Much of the central bank's contribution to these efforts will come from fulfillment of its other core policy objectives, which are to maintain a sound monetary policy to promote a low-inflation environment and to develop a robust payments infrastructure, including a reliable real-time gross settlement system. The central bank's support for system liquidity through financial market operations is also vital to financial stability. For the regulatory agencies, risk mitigation requires that they pursue the types of best prudential practices identified in the various international standards and codes, tailored where appropriate to national circumstances. History also tells us that progress around issues such as corporate governance, insolvency, creditor protection, and implementation of suitable accounting and auditing standards plays a vital role in promoting financial stability.

However, the global financial crisis has also highlighted the importance of adopting a comprehensive macroprudential framework to help mitigate risks. Success in achieving financial stability will depend critically on complementing microprudential regulations, which aim to enhance the resilience of individual institutions, with effective macroprudential regulation to strengthen the resilience of the financial system as a whole.

The need for *crisis management* arrangements is an acknowledgement that the risk of failure within the financial system is never eliminated, notwithstanding the best efforts in terms of surveillance and mitigation. The authorities need to have contingency plans to respond promptly to a crisis that may involve one or more financial institutions. In most countries, the toolkit for crisis management provides for both "open resolution" outcomes, in which distressed financial institutions are restored to health and remain in business, and "closed resolution" outcomes, in which provision is made for the wind-up and orderly exit of such institutions. Striking the right balance between these open and closed resolution outcomes is critical if financial stability is to be preserved at the least cost to public finances and without an unwelcome and, ultimately, damaging increase in moral hazard. To date in China, the authorities have displayed a strong preference for open resolution outcomes.

Ultimately, the key to an effective financial stability framework is cooperation and coordination between the various agencies, both during the good times when the financial system is in robust health and also in times of crisis. An important question in China is whether coordination arrangements, which appear to be extremely effective in times of crisis, are equally well suited to normal operating conditions.

SURVEILLANCE

Surveillance is a difficult task, not least because the term "systemic risk," while widely used, is actually quite difficult to define and quantify. It's easy to identify once we see it in the form of a broad-based breakdown in the functioning of the financial system, which is normally realized ex post as a large number of financial failures. However, policymakers cannot afford to wait until systemic risk crystallizes into disaster, and so surveillance needs to function, to the extent that it can, in an ex ante mode. That is, it should help the authorities identify sources of systemic risk and the various channels through which these risks are propagated. Accordingly, an effective surveillance framework is one that is predicated on a good understanding of systemic linkages—those interactions that transmit and sometimes amplify risks between the real economy and the financial system and also within the financial system itself. Many of these linkages are intensifying in China as integration into the world economy proceeds apace, and as the financial sector grows in size and complexity.

Cross-sector linkages—those that exist between the financial and nonfinancial sectors—are being gradually reshaped by the evolution of the domestic capital markets and also by the drive to provide better access to finance by the household, small business, and rural sectors in support of domestic consumption.

Cross-border linkages—those between the financial system and the world economy—reflect the need to fund a vibrant manufacturing export sector. But direct linkages are also increasing as financial institutions expand their overseas presence in line with a surge in foreign investment more generally.

Financial linkages—those that transmit risk within the financial system— exist at three levels: (1) cross-market linkages between the domestic money, bond, foreign exchange, and equity markets; (2) cross-institution linkages between bank and nonbank financial institutions; and (3) external linkages between global and local financial institutions and markets.

In China, the transmission of systemic risk through financial linkages is largely contained through the use of administrative controls both on cross-border flows of capital and the deployment of capital domestically. There are, for example, strict controls on cross-investments between bank and nonbank financial institutions, although the government has sanctioned a number of (significant) exemptions as part of a pilot study. In addition, bond markets are divided—with retail trading restricted to the exchanges and wholesale trading channeled through the interbank market—and there are a range of restrictions on equity trading, particularly for foreigners. Nonetheless, there is evidence that financial linkages are intensifying as the traded markets in China expand, providing participants with more liquidity and greater hedging opportunities. External linkages are also deepening as some capital movements are liberalized.

There are two dimensions to systemic risk arising from these various interlinkages. The first relates to the way in which aggregate risk evolves over time. In particular, there is a procyclical bias to risk, with financial institutions tending to take on excessive amounts in the upswing of an economic cycle only to become overly risk-averse in a downswing. This characteristic amplifies the boom-and-bust cycle in the supply of credit and liquidity—and by extension in asset prices—that is so damaging to the real economy. The second dimension is cross-sectional or network risk due to the common exposures and interconnectedness that exist within the financial system—relationships that work to amplify and rapidly transmit shocks between financial institutions. As a result, the failure of one institution, particularly one of significant size or market share, can threaten the system as a whole.

The challenge in China, as in other countries, is to develop a surveillance system that will provide the authorities with some guidance about the amount of risk occurring within the financial system and some early warning of potential problems. In taking the lead on this work, the PBC needs to set itself three key objectives.

The first is to build a comprehensive statistical database, including a broad-based set of financial soundness indicators, so that the authorities can monitor the condition of the financial system on a timely basis.[1] In China, financial soundness indicators are readily available for the largest commercial banks, but coverage is very limited for other key depository and nonbank financial institutions, which together account for around 40 percent of total financial assets. This seems to reflect a number of factors, including the incomplete transition of many smaller financial institutions and nonbank activities to internationally accepted accounting and disclosure standards; methodological and interagency coordination difficulties; and the failure of existing data collection services to keep pace with financial sector growth and innovation. To achieve this first objective,

---

[1]The financial soundness indicators were developed by the IMF, together with the international community, in order to support macroprudential analysis and assess the strengths and vulnerabilities of financial systems.

the PBC will need to collaborate closely with the other prudential regulators, which also have a vested interest in enhanced statistical collection.

The second objective is to identify the economic and financial indicators that can act as an early warning system of potential threats to the financial system. Inevitably, a crisis will reflect the collision of several vulnerabilities of an economic or financial nature. There are often common factors at work: excessive credit growth, particularly associated with a rapid run-up in asset prices; volatile cross-border capital flows; and increased corporate and/or household sector balance sheet leverage. In China, there are also important structural considerations to be taken into account, such as whether the current model of investment-driven growth is sustainable without an accompanying increase in systemic risk.

There is no precise set of economic or financial indicators that will form the basis of an early warning system. A parsimonious but useful set is commonly derived from the behavior of credit and asset prices (Borio and Drehmann, 2009). In particular, there is evidence that sustained rapid credit growth combined with large increases in property prices increases the probability of an episode of financial instability. The challenge in emerging markets like China is to differentiate between an expansion in credit that is the corollary of a successful financial deepening program spurred on by government and an expansion of credit that is suggestive of imprudent borrowing. A good understanding of credit—who is borrowing, how much, and why—is a basic building block of macroprudential surveillance. Similarly, an understanding of the conditionality of credit—both in aggregate and by industry—can provide some valuable insights into the evolving risk environment.

Even more useful, but more data intensive, are leading indicators obtained from the analysis of sectoral balance sheets of the household, corporate, and public sectors. By tracking debt and debt-servicing requirements over time, balance sheet analysis aims to anticipate the potential for higher levels of default should economic growth falter. Similarly, the analysis of state and local government balance sheets may be rewarding if any doubts exist regarding their debt servicing capabilities and whether the central government stands behind them.

Finally, there is always demand for a "snapshot" of systemic risk that provides a sense of whether risks in the financial system are rising or falling. This usually takes the form of an index—a single quantitative measure of financial conditions derived from a weighted sum of variables drawn from foreign exchange, debt, equity markets, and the banking sector (Illing and Liu, 2003; IMF, 2007). A different approach is to separate out the various dimensions of risk and present them in a "map" or "cobweb" form. In each case, the value of these methodologies is heavily dependent on the liquidity and transparency of the financial markets from which the various measures of risks are drawn (IMF, 2007). This means that as financial markets in China deepen and mature, the information content of financial pricing will improve and so will the value that can be derived from the quantitative modeling of systemic risk in China.

The PBC already devotes considerable resources to financial stability and publishes its efforts annually in a comprehensive annual *Financial Stability*

Report.[2] Continuing to enhance its systemic risk monitoring and measuring capabilities will be an important priority for the central bank as it seeks to keep pace with the expanding size and complexity of China's financial system.

MITIGATION

Once an increase in systemic risk has been identified, the challenge is to agree on the policy response that will best address it. What the global financial crisis has taught policymakers is that prudential regulation that ensures the safety and soundness of individual institutions, though vitally important, is not sufficient for this task. What is required is a strengthened set of microprudential regulations targeted at individual institutions but complemented by macroprudential policies that focus on the system as a whole.

In terms of microprudential regulations, it is now clear that leading into the global financial crisis too many financial institutions in too many countries lacked the capital and liquidity needed to absorb sizable economic and financial shocks. Hence, the Basel Committee on Banking Supervision (BCBS), of which China is a member, has undertaken actions to:

- Improve the quantity and quality of capital within the global financial system so that it can more easily absorb losses;

- Adjust capital requirements so that they are more closely aligned with the risks they are meant to protect against and, in particular, more fully capture market risk, counterparty credit risk, risk in securitized portfolios, and the state of the business cycle;

- Apply a gross leverage ratio as a backstop against excessive leverage; and

- Introduce measures to protect against liquidity shortages by requiring larger liquidity buffers and lowering the dependency on less secure forms of funding.

What is also better recognized today is the importance of singling out the largest and most complex financial institutions, that is, those institutions with the potential to do the most damage to the financial system should they fail. There is now global consensus that these systemically important financial institutions (SIFIs), particularly those with a significant cross-border presence, should be subject to more intense supervisory oversight and should hold a capital surcharge. Many countries are considering the addition of a similar surcharge to those SIFIs that have a more limited domestic presence. While these initiatives will help reduce the probability of failures among SIFIs, they will certainly not eliminate them altogether. And as the experience of a number of G20 countries has demonstrated only too well, when SIFIs get into difficulties, the default response is usually to bail them out—an outcome that has been very expensive for the

---

[2]The 2011 edition of the report is available at www.pbc.gov.cn/image_public/UserFiles/english /upload/File/China%20Financial%20Stability%20Report%202011.pdf.

taxpayer and that has perpetuated the underlying problem of moral hazard within the global financial system.

Another reform initiative is the "bail-in" to protect taxpayers from exposure to SIFIs' losses. Bail-in is a statutory power of a resolution authority to restructure the liabilities of a distressed financial institution by writing down its unsecured debt and/or converting it to equity. The statutory bail-in power is intended to achieve prompt recapitalization and restructuring of the distressed institution (Zhou and others, 2012). Of course, bail-in is not a panacea—it is simply one element of a comprehensive solution to the SIFI problem.

The debate about how best to deal with SIFIs is very relevant to China. Reflecting a high degree of concentration in the financial system, the major Chinese banks have a substantial market share and are systemic in size and interconnectedness. While the largest Chinese banks today have relatively simple operations, at least in comparison with the largest U.S. and European banks, this is changing. As noted earlier, cross-investments between banks and nonbank financial institutions have been approved as part of a pilot study. However, nonfinancial companies and industrial houses are able to take up significant stakes in financial institutions and there are no legal impediments to them setting up complex holding company structures that can be very challenging to supervise on a consolidated basis. Ultimately, this all makes for an increasing risk over time of the major banks becoming too large to effectively manage, supervise, or resolve in an orderly fashion. This, in turn, reinforces the importance of identifying a combination of approaches, including bail-ins, to address the systemic risks associated with SIFIs.

However, effective supervision is not just about intensity; it is also about scope. The global financial crisis was propagated in part by institutions outside the regulated sector, that is, in the so-called "shadow" banking system. These institutions—including investment banks, structured investment vehicles, and money market mutual funds—were typically subject to less regulation than the core of the financial system. Events revealed that a number of these institutions were not holding sufficient capital or liquid assets for the risks they were taking, and their weakness soon spread more widely through the financial system. Other shadow institutions, including firms whose activities may not be well defined (such as hedge funds, private equity funds, and commodity trading accounts), were not especially implicated in the crisis. Nonetheless, they can be highly leveraged and closely interconnected with the rest of the financial system, and therefore have the potential to amplify and propagate stresses.

In a regulated banking sector such as China's, strong incentives exist for both borrowers and lenders to shift their activities to markets that are subject to "light-touch" regulation or in some cases to those parts of the financial system that are unregulated altogether. One area of concern over the past few years, for example, has been the rapid increase in the off-balance-sheet activities of Chinese banks as they promoted wealth management products in cooperation with trust companies.

A far broader challenge relates to the "informal" financial markets in China. Efforts to regulate the supply of credit through the banking system have been associated with the growth of a flourishing informal financial sector—part of which provides credit to small and medium-sized enterprises (SMEs), with another part linked to cross-border capital flows into China. The exact size of this market is unknown, but it is clearly sizable, prompting periodic government crackdowns. The existence of a large informal banking system is not without systemic consequences. From a monetary perspective, it will dilute the efficacy of policy actions and thus frustrate efforts to contain the buildup of systemic risks through tighter monetary conditions. Also, where this unregulated market is large, there is always the potential for contagion to the "official" market if the failure of informal institutions—particularly illegal ones—undermines confidence in the financial system more generally. It is likely that there are also significant financial linkages between the two sectors that will transmit risk in times of stress. There would appear to be no quick fix to this problem, which will only be addressed by further deregulating the banking sector and developing financial markets so that they are better able to meet the needs of the retail and SME sectors. Moreover, further efforts to promote banking services to the underserved SMEs would be helpful to prevent risks arising from the informal financial markets.

In terms of macroprudential oversight, the main challenge in China as in other countries is to design a policy framework that will help mitigate the procyclical bias of the financial system and also allow the authorities to respond preemptively to the emergence of systemic risks. Monetary policy will have an important role to play in this regard, but there will be limits to this support as long as the primary objective of monetary policy is price stability. There are also some attractions to identifying policy measures that have an element of "automaticity" about them, so that the burden of deciding exactly when to act, and how much to act, is partly lifted from policymakers. The search for policy measures that might complement the role of monetary policy has so far concentrated on the following:

- *Countercyclical capital requirements,* which would add a buffer to capital requirements based on the current cyclical position of the economy;
- *Variable risk weights* to capital requirements for specific types of lending, such as real estate;
- *Forward-looking provisioning* to link loss provisions to the credit cycle, so banks are forced to put money aside for their potential losses when credit is growing strongly;
- *Collateral requirements* that impose higher collateral restrictions on some activities (examples include loan-to-value limits on secured lending and minimum haircuts or margins on securities financing transactions); and
- *Quantitative credit controls and reserve requirements* that either limit lending directly or indirectly by increasing short-term liquidity requirements.

The choice of instrument depends on the circumstances of individual countries, from the stage of economic development to the structure of the economy. Countries with fixed exchange rate regimes, for example, tend to make greater use of such instruments, given that such an exchange rate arrangement limits the room for interest rate policy.

Although a macroprudential approach is still evolving in tandem with international efforts, China has already made good use of a number of policy measures in its efforts to contain systemic risks. For example, China experienced an unprecedented surge in credit in 2010 as a by-product of the government's successful policy response to the global financial crisis. To help contain this, the authorities tightened monetary policy but also modified a range of prudential regulations directly targeted at reducing exuberance in the economy. These measures included the imposition of a capital surcharge on systemically important banks, the use of dynamic provisioning, the modification of capital requirements, higher reserve requirements, higher loan-to-value ratios, and guidance on loan growth.

The risks posed by overheated real estate markets also prompted the State Council to deploy a range of policies specifically aimed at dampening real estate speculation. These extended to increasing the minimum down payment requirements and loan rates for second homes, temporarily banning loans for third homes, and strengthening property tax collection. These measures were supplemented by actions to increase the supply of housing, particularly low-cost dwellings. Collectively, these measures represent an admirable deployment of macroprudential tools in response to an identified rise in the procyclical dimension of systemic risk. However, there is no indication yet of how these various buffers and requirements will be adjusted as conditions change, suggesting that the macroprudential framework is still a work in progress.

CRISIS MANAGEMENT

Notwithstanding the best efforts to identify and mitigate threats to a financial system, there will still be episodes of financial crisis. These may be idiosyncratic episodes where a single financial institution is in difficulty through mismanagement, but they can also be systemic crises involving multiple institutions. How the authorities respond to these events has an important bearing on the overall stability of the financial system, since failure to quickly contain and resolve problems can rapidly undermine confidence in the financial sector more generally.

Crisis management arrangements vary from country to country, but they tend to share the following key characteristics:

- A clear understanding of the limits to emergency liquidity support from the central bank;

- The existence of adequate powers to ensure that the authorities are able to resolve and restructure a distressed institution to keep it operating—an "open resolution" outcome; and

- The existence of sufficient powers and resources to close a distressed institution in an orderly way—a "closed resolution" outcome.

An effective crisis management framework will be one that combines these options so that problems in the financial system are resolved at minimum cost in terms of both moral hazard and fiscal support.

By their very nature, effective crisis management arrangements require a very high degree of interagency cooperation involving government, the central bank, and financial regulators. Each will have a specific role and each will need to have well-documented contingency arrangements so that it knows how to respond promptly to emerging problems. A crisis itself is no time for developing the protocol and procedures for a speedy and effective resolution of problems.

China's crisis management arrangements fall under the purview of the State Council. Traditionally, the State Council has displayed a strong preference for responding to episodes of financial distress with "open resolution" outcomes in order to avoid any loss of savings that could lead to runs on other institutions and to social discontent. As a result, only a few banks have been closed in the last 10 years and only a small number of rural credit cooperatives have had their licenses revoked in the last five years. These open resolutions have resulted in significant injections of equity to undercapitalized banks and the de-risking of balance sheets through the transfer of poorly performing assets to asset management companies. The restructuring program has also gone hand in hand with an overhaul of governance, which has been somewhat strengthened in the case of the largest banks by their conversion to joint stock companies and listing on the exchanges. This open resolution approach may have helped alleviate social discontent, but it has been expensive for government and has come at the expense of an increase in moral hazard in the financial system.

Like other countries following the recent crisis, China needs to make sure that closed resolution outcomes are also a viable option for dealing with distressed financial institutions, including SIFIs. The toolkit for facilitating both open and closed resolutions includes the legal authority to intervene promptly in a nonviable financial institution; the resources to close, recapitalize, or sell such an institution; and the capacity to manage the intervened institution, including its assets.[3]

However, closed resolutions will only be feasible if there is a financial safety net to protect depositors from loss (a deposit insurance system) and if resources are available to continue to fund the operations of systemically important but nonviable institutions while a resolution strategy is developed. The authorities have given considerable thought to how such a deposit insurance system might operate in China and recognize the importance of this work.[4] Early progress toward implementation of such a system would be a major step toward equipping China with all of the tools needed to manage a modern and dynamic financial system—one in which periodic failures are inevitable.

A related issue is how to organize the resolution function. Again, there is no best practice. In some countries, the deposit insurance, resolution, and asset management functions are combined in a single entity, such as the Federal Deposit Insurance Corporation in the United States. In other countries, the resolution authority is carried out by the supervisors, while deposit insurance is either a

---

[3]Financial Stability Board (2011) outlines the broad principles that have been developed by the G20 countries following the global financial crisis.

[4]IADI and BCBS (2009) outlines the broad principles to be incorporated in such a scheme.

stand-alone entity, such as in Canada, or a pay-box function, as in some European countries. Typically, the asset management function and the interim operation of the intervened financial institution are part of the resolution function, once the supervisor has decided it is necessary to intervene in the bank.

INSTITUTIONAL SET-UP

Strengthening the financial stability framework so that surveillance, mitigation, and crisis management arrangements are effective is obviously a major undertaking that requires the regulatory authorities and the government to collaborate closely. In most countries this cooperation is underpinned by a series of memoranda of understanding that set out the respective responsibilities of financial regulators, particularly with regard to information sharing. Most countries also have protocols and procedures in place to ensure that they coordinate their actions in a financial crisis, usually involving the establishment of a dedicated crisis management committee.

In China, the overarching responsibility for financial stability resides with the State Council, which exercised that responsibility during the global financial crisis by establishing and chairing a high-level committee of key financial agencies that met regularly to assess conditions and consult on policy actions. Each of the agencies also has contingency plans in place for responding to a crisis, including memoranda of understanding to promote cooperation. However, one of the vital lessons of the crisis is that interagency cooperation must be equally effective outside crisis periods so that any buildup of risks can be identified and addressed well before it crystallizes as a systemic event. In other words, an effective macroprudential framework is one in which financial agencies not only share their concerns on emerging risks but also work closely together to resolve them. The general question about China's institutional approach is whether it also needs to be reoriented to give more weight to systemic risks.

There is no single or right set of institutional arrangements for promoting a macroprudential perspective of the financial system. Institutional arrangements need to address country-specific circumstances, including the legal and political environment. One way to do this in China would be to establish a permanent Financial Stability Committee chaired by a very senior official with a clear mandate to monitor systemic risks and make recommendations on the actions needed to address them. Membership of the committee would need to include the PBC, the three supervisory agencies, the Ministry of Finance, and any other relevant macroeconomic agencies. Consistent with its financial stability mandate, there would also be a strong case for the PBC to serve as secretariat of the committee. Having such a permanent committee in place would be broadly consistent with the initiatives undertaken by many other G20 countries to find ways to improve the resilience of their own financial systems and, by doing so, the resilience of the global financial system.

REFERENCES

Borio, C., and M. Drehmann, 2009, "Assessing the Risk of Banking Crises–Revisited," *BIS Quarterly Review,* March: 29–46.

Financial Stability Board, 2011, "Key Attributes of Effective Resolution Regimes for Financial Institutions," October (Basel: Bank for International Settlements). www.financialstability board.org/publications/r_111104cc.pdf.

Illing M., and Y. Liu, 2003, "An Index of Financial Stress for Canada," Bank of Canada Working Paper No. 2003–14 (Ottawa: Bank of Canada).

International Association of Deposit Insurers (IADI) and Basel Committee on Banking Supervision (BCBS), 2009, "Core Principles for Effective Deposit Insurance Systems," June (Basel: Bank for International Settlements). www.iadi.org/NewsRelease/JWGDI%20CBRG %20core%20principles_18_June.pdf.

International Monetary Fund (IMF), 2008, "Financial Stress and Economic Downturns," *World Economic Outlook,* October (Washington: International Monetary Fund).

Zhou, Jianping, Virginia Rutledge, Wouter Bossu, Marc Dobler, Nadege Jassoud, and Michael Moore, 2012, "From Bail-out to Bail-in: Mandatory Debt Restructuring of Systemic Financial Institutions," IMF Staff Discussion Note 12/03 (Washington: International Monetary Fund).

PART II

Macroeconomic Factors Affecting Financial Stability

CHAPTER 4

China's Sovereign Balance Sheet Risks and Implications for Financial Stability

YANG LI AND XIAOJING ZHANG

To examine China's sovereign balance sheet and its potential risk factors relevant to financial stability, this chapter presents a stylized balance sheet for the period from 2000–10 to show that sovereign equity has gradually grown, implying a low probability of a sovereign debt crisis in China. The chapter then discusses China's overall debt-to-GDP ratio (leverage ratio), which is higher than those in other G20 emerging market economies and therefore warrants policy attention, and also analyzes the related structural and institutional aspects relevant for management of the sovereign balance sheet.

The chapter finds that short-term sovereign balance sheet risks in China have emanated mainly from housing credit and local government debts, while medium-to-long-run risk can be attributed to the external sector, corporate debt, and underfunded social security liabilities. These risks are mostly contingent in nature and rooted in China's development model. Finally, the chapter simulates the debt dynamics and shows the importance of maintaining relatively higher GDP growth and thus a positive gap between the GDP growth rate and the interest rate. Transforming the development model, thus, will be the fundamental way to mitigate the risks on the sovereign balance sheet and their potential spillovers onto the financial system.

OVERVIEW

History shows that an economic crisis is often coupled with a debt crisis. With the deepening globalization and growing importance of the financial sector, the dimensions of a debt crisis have gone beyond its traditional fiscal components to include financial stability aspects as well. A proper analysis of sovereign-held financial assets and liabilities is thus vital to better understand the causes and development of the crises and the needed set of policy responses. Indeed, sovereign balance sheet issues are being given greater weight in recent economic literature, as crisis periods since 1980 could be regarded as balance sheet shocks.

In China, the recent development of local government financing vehicles (LGFV or *di fang rong zi ping tai*) have triggered concerns about the country's sovereign debt risk. Some international and Chinese observers have even predicted LGFVs could potentially be a cause for the collapse of the Chinese economy. A sovereign-balance-sheet-based analysis helps examine the assets, liabilities, and net worth of China's public sector, and to clarify the relationships among various economic activities. Since the associated accounting is mainly based on stock rather than flow variables, balance sheet analysis can provide an alternative perspective on the cumulative effects of economic growth over the past decade. In particular, with the help of sectoral balance sheets, the stock-based study is of great interest for investigating the diverse features associated with the ongoing structural trans-formation and institutional changes in China.

Compiling a sovereign balance sheet is not a recent trend. In 1936, two American researchers, Dickinson and Eakin (1936) first applied a corporation's balance sheet framework to undertake macroeconomic analysis. However, this novel perspective became popular in the 1960s mainly due to the work of Gold-smith and Lipsey (1963) and Goldsmith (1982). They constructed and analyzed the overall as well as the sectoral balance sheets of the United States over the period from 1900–80. Later, in the case of the United Kingdom, Revell (1966) presented a sovereign balance sheet for the period from 1957–61, and since 1975 such a financial statement has been published by the British government (Holder, 1998). In Canada, the official compilation of the sovereign balance sheet (in book value and market value) began in 1990. By now, most member countries of the Organization for Economic Cooperation and Development (OECD) have released at least a financial balance sheet.

China started a similar practice relatively late. Although in 1997 and 2007 the National Bureau of Statistics (NBS) published two reports presenting the methodology for compiling China's balance sheet (NBS, 1997, 2007), no official report has yet been released. However, the balance sheet approach has long been used as a statistical tool within the national accounting system. Since the out-break of crises in Latin America and Asia during the 1990s, the balance sheet approach has gained in popularity and use for macroeconomic analysis. Follow-ing the 2007 global financial turmoil, the balance sheet approach became a main analytical tool for scholars, governments, and international organizations. Some Chinese researchers such as Yi (2008) and Li (2009) have started to discuss China's macroeconomic issues using the balance-sheet-approach perspective.

COMPILING CHINA'S SOVEREIGN BALANCE SHEET: A TENTATIVE APPROACH (2000–10)

This section discusses the approach to compiling sovereign balance sheets. Unlike the national balance sheet that covers both the private and public sectors, a sovereign balance sheet focuses only on the government and other state-backed institutions.[1] In the case of China, it encompasses the government (central and

---

[1] In some cases, the state-backed institutions are defined by the government.

local), state-owned financial institutions (including the central bank), and state-owned nonfinancial corporations. In other words, it directly reflects the government's widely defined financial position and risk profile.

A clear structure of a balance sheet statement—assets, liabilities, and net worth—would be vital for the analysis. The *assets* refer to resources that are either in the government's possession or under its control. Specifically, they include six items: business assets, nonbusiness assets, natural resource assets, foreign assets, the social security fund, and government deposits at the central bank. The sovereign *liabilities* include government debts and contingent liabilities due to implicit guarantees. They also include six items: central government debts (domestic and external), government-backed bonds, local government debts, debts of state-owned enterprises, contingent liabilities arising from nonperforming loans (NPLs), and implicit pension debts. Finally, the *net worth* of the government is defined as the difference between assets and liabilities.

Sovereign Assets

China has seen a significant buildup of sovereign assets, specifically the following:

- *State-owned business assets.* The central and local governments hold state-owned business assets for commercial purposes. This includes state-owned assets of nonfinancial corporations and financial institutions. In 2010, the two subcategories of assets were RMB 59.1 trillion and RMB 8.2 trillion, respectively.

- *State-owned nonbusiness assets.* These assets refer to financial and nonfinancial resources, which are generally held by administrative or public institutions. In China, such assets, amounting to RMB 7.8 trillion in 2010, constitute a major component of sovereign assets. Nonbusiness assets have some special characteristics. First, a large proportion of them are fixed assets (more than 40 percent in 2010). Second, they are mainly nonprofit-oriented and devoted to public services. These two characteristics imply low liquidity, indicating the inability of governments to use these assets to pay off debts in the normal course of operations. This is an important aspect to keep in mind when considering the analysis of the sovereign balance sheet presented later in this chapter.

- *State-owned natural resource assets.* These include rural land, forest, subsoil, river, and sea assets. Due to data limitations, we only consider land resources. Drawing on a similar framework used by the World Bank (2006), this type of asset is valued at the net present value of the income derived from using rural land.[2] Employing this method, China's total value of land was estimated to be around RMB 44.3 trillion in 2010. That said, not all

---

[2] The main difference between the current study and the World Bank (2006) study is that we use gross agricultural output value, while the World Bank separately also measures timber resources, nontimber resources, cropland, pastureland, and protected areas. For 2000, however, the results based on these two methods are similar.

these assets are owned by governments (states). In fact, according to China's Constitution (Article 10), land in the rural and suburban areas, which includes housing sites, private plots of cropland, and hilly land, is owned by collectives. Nevertheless, as stipulated in the Constitution, "the state may in the public interest take over the collective land for its use in accordance with the law." Given that, the amount of RMB 44.3 trillion can be viewed as the maximum value of China's land resources that the government is able to mobilize.

- *Foreign assets.* These refer to reserve assets held by the government. China's international investment position increased from US$618.6 billion in 2004 to US$2.9 trillion in 2010.

- *Social security fund.* This fund is financed by the central budget or by transferring state-owned shares in the corporate sector with the second channel being double counted. Specifically, a part of these assets might have been considered as part of the state-owned business assets discussed above (especially during the transfer process).

- *Government deposits at the central bank.* These assets refer to the deposits of central and local governments at the central bank. They include general budget deposits and government fund budget deposits. The deposits at the commercial banks are excluded here, but included in the item of "nonbusiness assets."

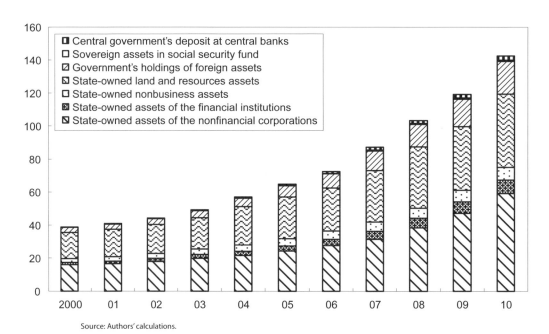

Source: Authors' calculations.

Figure 4.1 Size and Composition of China's Sovereign Assets
(In trillions of renminbi)

A combination of the above items could illustrate the trend and composition of sovereign assets from 2000–10. Figure 4.1 shows that nonfinancial corporations' state-owned assets and reserve assets have increased more rapidly than other items.

Sovereign Liabilities

With heavy state involvement in different forms, the government has accumulated a significant amount of liabilities, as described below:

- *Domestic and external debts of the central government.* These refer to debts the central government owes to domestic and foreign creditors. The external debts of the private sector (Chinese-funded and foreign-funded enterprises and financial institutions), for which the government might be responsible in the case of default, are also included in this subcategory. As shown in Table 4.1, in 2010 the domestic and external debts of China's central government were RMB 6.7 trillion and 2.3 trillion, respectively.

- *Government-guaranteed bonds (quasi-government bonds).* These refer to the bonds issued by various governmental departments and public institutions, including bonds issued by policy banks, which amounted to RMB 5.2 trillion in 2010. It should be emphasized that although the policy (noncommercial) banks do have some market-oriented securities, all their bonds are ultimately guaranteed by the government and thus considered sovereign debts.

TABLE 4.1

Sovereign Balance Sheet of China, 2010
(In trillions of renminbi)

Assets		Liabilities and Net Worth of the Government	
Deposits of government at central bank	2.4	Domestic debts of central government	6.7
Reserve assets	19.7	Sovereign external debts	2.3
Land assets	44.3	Local government debts (excluding LGFV)	5.8
State-owned assets in administrative institutions	7.8	Debts from LGFVs	9.0
State-owned assets in nonfinancial sector	59.1	Nonfinancial state-owned enterprises' debts (excluding LGFVs)	35.6
State-owned assets in financial sector	8.2	Policy banks' debts	5.2
State-owned assets in social security fund	0.8	Nonperforming loans	0.4
		Contingent liabilities due to NPLs	4.2
		Implicit pension debts	3.5
Total assets	**142.3**	**Total liabilities**	**72.7**[1]
		Net worth of the government	**69.6**

Source: Authors' calculations.
Note: LGFV = local government financing vehicles; NPLs = nonperforming loans.
[1]In this context, the sovereign-liabilities-to-GDP ratio reaches the level of 181 percent. But it should be noted that the liabilities are considered from a relatively broader perspective. If the state-owned enterprises' debts (including debts from LGFVs) and implicit pension debts are deducted, the ratio lowers remarkably to 61.3 percent. If following the international norm and not considering the local governments' debts, the ratio will be even lower.

- *Local government debts.* These debts consist of two major parts. One is the debt from the LGFVs, including debt with explicit and implicit guarantee of the government. According to the China Banking Regulatory Commission, this type of debt was approximately RMB 9 trillion by the end of 2010. The other debt is from non-LGFV sources, whose debtors might be local governments and other local public institutions. The National Audit Office reports that these types of debts amounted to approximately RMB 5.7 trillion in 2010.

- *Debts of state-owned enterprises.* Although they are independent corporate entities, state-owned enterprises (SOEs) should assume sole responsibility for their financial condition, although the government is the major investor (or shareholder) and may provide bailouts of last resort in the case of a crisis. Moreover, in this chapter necessary adjustments have been made to avoid double counting of local SOEs' debts and debts due to LGFVs. As of the end of 2010, the debts held by the central and local SOEs were RMB 20.8 trillion and RMB 19.8 trillion, respectively.

- *Contingent liabilities due to NPLs.* These liabilities refer to NPLs held by banks and other financial institutions (such as securities and insurance companies), which amounted to RMB 400 billion in 2010. Contingent liabilities may arise from indisposed NPLs. It is noteworthy that there are many ways to deal with NPLs, such as central government capital injection, issuance of special bonds, and central bank loans. Therefore, the NPLs were just transformed into different forms, but by no means did they disappear from the economic system. Such government-backed troubled assets, which

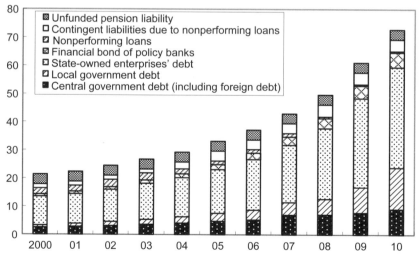

Source: Authors' calculations.

Figure 4.2 Size and Composition of China's Sovereign Liabilities
(In trillions of renminbi)

were estimated to be RMB 4.2 trillion in 2010, are regarded as contingent liabilities in the sovereign balance sheet.

• *Underfunded pension liability.* Because of commitments over time, a huge amount of implicit pension obligations (underfunded pensions) have accumulated. Given the absence of official data, this study uses the average value of various estimates offered by Chinese and international institutions, which was approximately RMB 3.5 trillion in 2010.

A combination of the above items illustrates the trend and composition of sovereign liabilities from 2000–10 (Figure 4.2). Governmental debts (both central and local), SOEs' debts, and contingent liabilities due to NPLs have increased more rapidly than other items.

Results for China's Sovereign Balance Sheet

After putting together the asset and liability profile, China's sovereign balance sheet is shown in Figure 4.3. Over the past 11 years, both sovereign assets and liabilities have expanded considerably, but by different magnitudes. Sovereign assets expanded faster than liabilities and consequently net worth has been increasing.

The risk of an imminent debt crisis in China thus appears to be negligible. Table 4.1 shows detailed data for 2010. Total net worth amounts to RMB 69.6 trillion (175 percent of GDP). Nevertheless, the poor liquidity of some types of assets makes it necessary to adjust the size of the estimated sovereign assets.

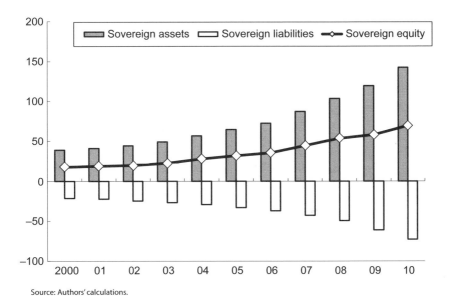

Source: Authors' calculations.

Figure 4.3 China's Sovereign Assets, Liabilities, and Net Worth
(In trillions of renminbi)

Specifically, two changes are involved. First, state-owned nonbusiness assets are excluded because of their nonprofit administrative functions. Second, since the natural resource assets (e.g., land) are not entirely convertible to cash, we use annual land sale revenue in 2010 (known as *tu di chu rang jin*) to replace the RMB 44.3 trillion shown in Table 4.1. After these adjustments the amount decreases from RMB 142.3 trillion to RMB 93 trillion. As a consequence, net worth shrinks to around RMB 20 trillion. Despite the enormous difference between the two methods, net worth remains positive and thus China's sovereign balance sheet seems to be resilient to a full-blown debt crisis. It indicates that Chinese authorities have sufficient financial resources to pay back all of the country's debts, including contingent liabilities.

However, the above estimations should be interpreted with caution. First, several factors may underestimate the size. For instance, the change of land use (farmland to urban land) may not fully reflect market value, and some categories of assets remain denominated in book value rather than market value.[3] Second, some assets, such as nonbusiness assets, cannot be easily liquidated. The calculations may also overestimate the value of the total assets.

On the liability side, the inclusion of contingent liabilities due to NPLs remains disputable. In reality, it depends on the loss-given-default probability of the NPLs. However, this analysis does not have sufficient information to estimate the exact size of losses, and so the entire NPL stock is taken as losses that could devolve on the government. Therefore, the sovereign liabilities may also be overestimated.

OVERALL DEBT LEVEL AND LEVERAGE RATIO IN CHINA

This section takes into account the debt level and leverage ratio of all main economic sectors, including households, nonfinancial corporations, financial institutions, and government (McKinsey Global Institute, 2010, 2012). The purpose is to better understand China's overall financial risks by examining other interrelated contagion channels.[4]

Debts and liabilities differ from each other in several ways. Total debt consists of "all liabilities that are debt instruments" (IMF, 2011, p. 3). These include IMF Special Drawing Rights; currency and deposits; debt securities; loans; insurance, pension, and standardized guarantee schemes; and other accounts payable. Other liability items that "do not require the payment of principal and interest" (p. 3)—namely, equity, investment fund shares, financial derivatives, and employee stock options—are not considered debt.

---

[3]Shen and Fan (2012) show that for the listed companies, the state-owned assets are underestimated if the book value is used in lieu of market value.

[4]The transformation from NPLs to government's contingent liabilities serves as an example of financial risk contagion from the private to the public sector.

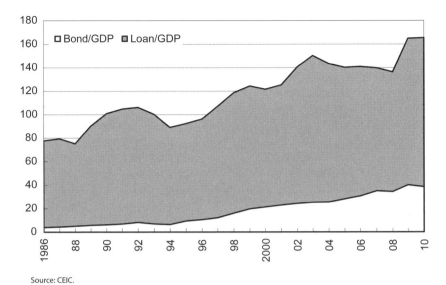

Source: CEIC.

Figure 4.4 China: Bonds and Loans
(Percent share of GDP)

Constrained by data, this section takes a narrow definition of debt by investigating two categories of liabilities: loans and bonds.[5] The former constitute the major part of total debt in China, although the debt share of the latter has increased rapidly in recent years (Figure 4.4).

The debt structure varies in different sectors: for households, loans are the sole item on the liability side; nonfinancial corporations' debts include both loans and corporate bonds; financial institutions' debts are composed of policy-related financial bonds and other bonds; and government debts refer to the domestic and external debts held by the central government. For the purpose of international comparisons, local government debt is excluded from the analysis.[6]

Figure 4.5 shows the trends of overall and sectoral debt-to-GDP ratios for 1996–2010. As can be seen from the figure, the leverage ratio increased significantly during and immediately after the three macroeconomic shocks over this period: the Asian financial crisis of 1997–98, the bursting of the dot-com bubble in 2000, and the global financial tsunami in 2008. In this sense, the ratio can be a useful tool to analyze financial crises.

International comparisons show that China's debt-to-GDP ratio has been relatively low (Table 4.2). The total debt of all sectors accounts for 169 percent of GDP but remains low compared with other major developed economies. For

---

[5]In fact, we do not take into account other debt securities such as promissory notes, commercial paper, and transferable loans. See IMF (2011) for a detailed discussion of debt securities.
[6]According to IMF (2011), local debts are not considered government debts, partly because in many countries the central government is not responsible for the budgets of local governments.

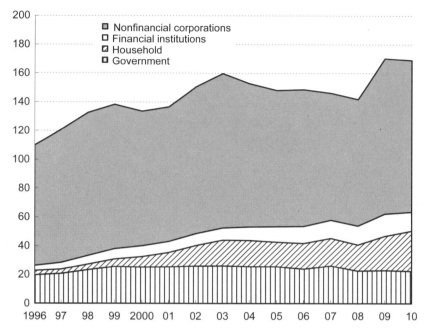

Sources: CEIC; and authors' calculations.

Figure 4.5   China: Debt Level by Sector
(Percent share of GDP)

TABLE 4.2

International Comparison of China's Debt Structure and Overall Leverage Ratio
(Percent of GDP)

	Household Debt	Nonfinancial Corporation Debt	Financial Institution Debt	Government Debt	Total Debt
Japan	67	99	120	226	512
United Kingdom	98	109	219	81	507
Spain	82	134	76	71	363
France	48	111	97	90	346
Italy	45	82	76	111	314
Korea	81	107	93	33	314
United States	87	72	40	80	279
Germany	60	49	87	83	279
Australia	105	59	91	21	276
Canada	91	53	63	69	276
China	**28**	**105.4**	**13**	**22.4**	**168.9**

Sources: China's data come from authors' calculation and refer to 2010. Data for other countries are from McKinsey Global Institute (2012) and refer to the second quarter of 2011 (except for Italy, which refer to the first quarter of 2011).

example, the debt ratios of both Japan and the United Kingdom exceed 500 percent, and those for other countries are higher than 200 percent. There are, however, a few warning signs for China. First, China's debt load appears heavier than those of major emerging countries. As reported in McKinsey Global Institute

(2012), the debt-to-GDP ratios in 2010 for Brazil, India, and Russia were 148 percent, 122 percent, and 72 percent, respectively. Second, owing to the global financial crisis, China's debt level has increased significantly in recent years. Third, as mentioned above, our analysis does not take into account local government debt, which represented around 20 percent of Chinese GDP in 2010 (a level similar to the debt level of the central government). These concerns suggest an accumulation of implicit financial risks and deserve attention.

Debt also varies in different sectors (Table 4.2). The debt burden of China's nonfinancial corporation sector is heavy, but the burden of the household and financial institution sectors is relatively low. To a large degree, this phenomenon reflects the characteristics of China's current development pattern and financial structure. In fact, despite some positive changes over the past year (as direct capital-market-based financing has gained importance), the enterprise sector still relies heavily on indirect financing. As a consequence, loans remain the major liabilities of enterprises. If economic growth is robust, such a financing pattern benefits from relatively lower cost and risk. Nevertheless, in the event of declining growth, the troubles of nonfinancial corporations can easily spread to the financial sector through defaulted loans.

There are two caveats to this analysis. First, by no means do we suggest that the optimal debt-to-GDP ratio is zero. Under certain circumstances, a low debt burden might lead to inefficient allocation of financial resources. In theory, there should be a certain critical point at which the benefit-risk balance can be achieved. Such an intuition is supported by a recent study by Cecchetti, Mohanty, and Zampolli (2011). Using data from flow of funds accounts for 18 OECD countries, the authors find that the threshold debt level (still as a share of GDP) is 85 percent for the government and households and 90 percent for nonfinancial corporations. As shown in the table, this differs sharply from China.

The second caveat is the fact that various sectors are closely interrelated complicates the analysis. It is misleading to draw conclusions by focusing on a single sector. McKinsey Global Institute (2010) presents a good example: in 1995, the debt-to-GDP ratio was 148 percent for the Japanese nonfinancial corporation sector. However, it steadily declined, and by 2005 the ratio had decreased to 91 percent. Despite this deleveraging process, concerns remained regarding Japan's macrofinancial stability because during 1995–2005 the country's public-debt-to-GDP ratio soared from 84 to 180 percent, mainly due to the transmission of debt loads between sectors. Therefore, both overall and sectoral analyses are needed to understand the macrofinancial and financial stability interconnections.

EXPANSION OF CHINA'S NATIONAL BALANCE SHEET

From 2000–10, China's national balance sheet expanded substantially. On the asset side, three categories of assets saw a significant increase: foreign assets, infrastructure assets, and housing assets. The expansion reflects the fact that China has experienced accelerated industrialization and urbanization over the past decade. By following the export-oriented industrialization strategy, China has become the manufacturing center of the world, and accordingly runs large trade surpluses. As a consequence, vast amounts of foreign assets have been accumulated (mainly denominated in U.S. dollars). By the end of 2011, China's foreign exchange reserves amounted to US$3.3 trillion, about 20 times as large as in 2000. However, as the urbanization process accelerates, investment in urban infrastructure needs to expand rapidly—and in fact it has, growing by an average rate of 18.4 percent per year (3.57 times over in real terms) during the period from 2000–10. Such investment has exceeded 10 percent of GDP in several years and has been as high as 15 percent in 2009 and 2010. Meanwhile, this process has created a boom in the urban housing market. According to our estimates, the total value of residential assets in urban areas was RMB 71.9 trillion in 2010, approximately seven times as large as in 1998.

Similarly, the liabilities of government and SOEs expanded more significantly than those in the private sector. To a certain degree, this trend reflects the characteristic of an "investment-driven" government, as the government still plays a crucial role in making large-scale investment decisions and tends to intervene in microlevel activities (sometimes even getting involved in the production process). This is especially the case at the local level. To boost local growth, and to finance various large-scale projects, the local governments commonly rely on off-budget mechanisms, such as the LGFVs. The latter are mainly dedicated to municipal construction, transportation facilities, and land purchase and reserve. Moreover, in parallel with heavy direct interventions in the market, China has had to provide explicit or implicit guarantees for the contingent liabilities owed by other sectors, including NPLs and pension debts.

ASSESSING FINANCIAL RISKS

Conventional wisdom suggests that the sovereign balance sheet is exposed to insolvency and structural risks. The first kind of risk relates to the long-term fiscal capacity and economic growth prospects. This section focuses on risks of a structural nature. These consist of the following three categories of mismatches found on China's sovereign balance sheet, all of which can lead to liquidity risk:

(1) *Currency mismatch risk.* China is holding a huge amount of official reserve assets that are exposed to the volatility of exchange rates. It is clear that China will suffer losses, at least in book value terms, due to the depreciation of foreign currency, especially the U.S. dollar.

(2) *Maturity mismatch risk.* China's urbanization is mainly supported by long-term investment. Commercial banks often encounter the problem of mismatches between long-term loans and short-term debts (i.e., sources of funds, which are mainly in the form of deposits). Local governments are also commonly confronted with the mismatch between debt maturity and cash flows.

(3) *Capital structure mismatch risk.* This refers to a situation in which financing is overly dependent on liabilities, and consequently the equity share is relatively small. An international comparison shows that the total debt of China's nonfinancial corporations accounts for 62.4 percent of the nation's overall debt, which is 30 to 40 percent higher than the share of nonfinancial corporation debt in the sample of countries. Such a high debt burden and leverage ratio reflects the inherent vulnerability of China's financial system, which is characterized by the dominance of the banking sector and indirect financing.

Based on various indicators, the direct risk exposure of the banking sector to *housing finance* is manageable. However, given factors such as the high mortgage-loan ratio in the banking sector, the close downward and upward linkage of the housing industry to other industries, and the overdependence of LGFVs on land sale revenue, banks' indirect risk exposure to the housing sector could be large if the housing market were to undergo a severe negative shock. It should also be noted that although China's overall housing-value-to-GDP ratio remains quite low—compared to household disposable income—urban housing prices appear to be higher in China than in some developed countries. China, thus, must guard against a possible scenario of a housing price boom.

Economic transition and population aging may add to the rapid accumulation of *underfunded pensions*. The current deficit in the private accounts of pension funds is around RMB 1.4 trillion. This debt load will be further aggregated in view of the broadening coverage of the pension system (especially covering urban and rural residents who are not formally employed) and deficits in health care insurance and unemployment insurance. As a last resort for funding shortfalls, the Chinese authorities are increasingly concerned about contingent debts and the ever-increasing liabilities associated with longevity risk as people live longer.

The sovereign-dependent sectors may also suffer from potential contagion risk through the balance sheet channel. Because of the relationship between claims and liabilities, the sectoral balance sheets are interconnected. Despite the fact that the government can mobilize financial resources among sectors to deal with debt payment problems, the debt burden of the sovereign does not decline. For example, although the NPLs in the banking sector decreased from RMB 2.17 trillion in 2000 to RMB 430 billion in 2010, on the sovereign balance sheet the contingent liabilities arising from the NPL clean-up soared from RMB 1.4 trillion to RMB 4.2 trillion. It is believed that to a large extent, the bad assets of the banking sector have been transferred from that sector to the sovereign.

Regarding the sustainability of the government debt burden, our scenario analysis shows that the development path of the government debt-to-GDP ratio is ultimately determined by the gap between the economic growth rate and the interest rate. From a macroeconomic perspective, if this gap remains sufficiently large, the government debt burden will stay at a low and sustainable level and thus the related risks seem small at present.

CONCLUSIONS AND POLICY RECOMMENDATIONS

Examining China's national balance sheet in general and sovereign balance sheet in particular leads to drawing several preliminary conclusions. First, during 2000–10, China's sovereign balance sheet expanded substantially. This trend can be explained by the accelerated industrialization and urbanization on the asset side and the government-dominated development model on the liability side.

Second, the narrowly defined net sovereign assets (assets minus liabilities) remain positive. This indicates that the Chinese government has sufficient financial resources to cover its debts. Therefore, the general risk exposure of China's sovereign balance sheet is manageable, and the possibility of a near-term sovereign debt crisis in China seems negligible.

Third, the immediate risks in China's sovereign balance sheet lie in housing finance and local government debts. In the medium to long term, the risks may mainly come from the external sector, corporate debts, and underfunded pensions. It should be noted that most of these risks can be viewed as contingent debts and are closely related to China's growth model.

Fourth, the analysis of both the overall debt level and the debt-to-GDP ratio shows that while China's debt load appears higher than those of other emerging countries, its general debt burden is still mild and manageable. However, there are several noteworthy and cautionary trends:

- In 2010, total corporate debt in China exceeded GDP, and the corporate-debt-to-GDP ratio was higher than the generally observed threshold of 90 percent for OECD countries.

- The household debt load is relatively low and thus has a large amount of room to increase in the future.

- As demonstrated by international experience, as China's economy enters into a more advanced development stage, the government will likely change its functions, and consequently its net wealth will tend to shrink or even become negative.

- Scenario analysis shows that the gap between the economic growth rate and the interest rate determines the sustainability and risks of the debt burden.

Based on the above risk assessment, a change in China's growth model appears essential in order to cope with the sovereign balance sheet risks. Policy recommendations toward that end include the following:

- Currency mismatch risk needs to be lowered. China should slow its accumulation of foreign exchange reserves by boosting domestic demand and weakening its dependence on external demand. Meanwhile, China should promote international use of renminbi and encourage private agents to keep foreign assets and invest overseas. More importantly, given that the creditor currency mismatch cannot be resolved in the short term, China should actively employ the sovereign wealth fund mechanism to reduce the currency mismatch risk.

- Financial stability risks of local governments need to be controlled, especially as they relate to maturity mismatch problems. Government interventions in microlevel economic activities should be limited. To promote market-oriented reform and the transformation of government's role, the debtor entity's responsibilities should be better defined and diversified. Meanwhile, the central and local government fiscal relationship needs to be redefined, and alternative financing channels through the private sector should be used more to support urban and infrastructure development.

- To improve the structure of capital, China needs to further financial reforms to encourage the corporate sector to rely on equity financing rather than debt financing. This will help reduce China's overall debt leverage.

- To deal with the funding gap in the pension system, China should adjust its income distribution policies and deepen the reform of SOEs. In particular, mobilizing more profits from these enterprises and pushing ahead the process of reducing state-owned shares could be some of the alternative solutions.

REFERENCES

Cecchetti, Stephen G., M. S. Mohanty, and Fabrizio Zampolli, 2011, "The Real Effects of Debt," BIS Working Paper No. 352 (Basel: Bank for International Settlements).

Dickinson, Frank Greene, and Franzy Eakin, 1936, *A Balance Sheet of the Nation's Economy* (Urbana: University of Illinois).

Goldsmith, Raymond W., 1982, *The National Balance Sheet of the United States, 1953–1980* (Chicago: University of Chicago Press).

Goldsmith, Raymond W., and R. E. Lipsey, 1963, *Studies in the National Balance Sheet of the United States* (Princeton, New Jersey: Princeton University Press).

Holder, Andrew, 1998, "Developing the Public-Sector Balance Sheet," *Economic Trends*, No. 540 (November), pp. 31–40.

International Monetary Fund (IMF), 2011, *Public Sector Debt Statistics: Guide for Compilers and Users* (Washington: International Monetary Fund).

Li, Yang, 2009, "Yao Cong Zi Chan Fu Zhai Biao Lai Kong Zhi Zi Chan Pao Mo," manuscript presented at Summer Davos World Economic Forum (in Chinese). http://money.163.com/09/0910/15/5IS2VHQJ00253NDC.html.

McKinsey Global Institute, 2010, "Debt and Deleveraging: The Global Credit Bubble and Its Economic Consequences." www.mckinsey.com/insights/mgi/research/financial_markets/debt_and_deleveraging_the_global_credit_bubble_update.

———, 2012, "Debt and Deleveraging: Uneven Progress on the Path to Growth." www.mckinsey.com/insights/mgi/research/financial_markets/uneven_progress_on_the_path_to_growth.

National Bureau of Statistics of China (NBS), 1997, 2007, *Methodology for Compilation of China's Balance Sheet* (in Chinese). China Statistics Press.

Revell, Jack, 1966, "The National Balance Sheet of the United Kingdom," *Review of Income and Wealth*, Vol. 12, No. 4, pp. 281–310.

Shen, Pei Long, and Huan Fan, 2012, "Liquidity Assets Balance Sheet Based Government Debt Risk Research in China," *Economic Research Journal (Jing Ji Yan Jiu)* 47, no. 2. (in Chinese).

World Bank, 2006, *Where is the Wealth of Nations? Measuring Capital for the 21ˢᵗ Century* (Washington: World Bank).

Yi, Gang, 2008, "Zhong Guo Neng Gou Jing Shou Zhu Jin Rong Wei Ji De Kao Yan," *Qiushi* 22 (in Chinese).

CHAPTER 5

Systemic Liquidity, Monetary Operations, and Financial Stability in China

Nuno Cassola and Nathan Porter

This chapter considers the various ways in which domestic liquidity, monetary policy operations, and financial stability intersect in China. It highlights how the operations and facilities of the People's Bank of China (PBC) influence liquidity and eventually financial prices, as well as the role they could play in mitigating a crisis. The chapter also discusses other stability and efficiency aspects of liquidity management in China, as well as some of the main implications for liquidity management of advancing financial liberalization.

OVERVIEW

Historically, China's financial system has been highly liquid, reflecting the impact of persistent foreign exchange inflows. With ample liquidity, banks following a relatively conservative business model, and with access to high-quality collateral, the prospect of a near-term liquidity crisis has been limited. China has not faced any systemic banking crisis since the restructuring in the early 2000s, including during the period of heightened global stress following the collapse of Lehman Brothers in 2008. However, one lesson of the global financial crisis is that even abundant central bank liquidity can be insufficient to prevent a systemic liquidity crisis (IMF, 2010). Indeed, such crises can result directly from friction in the functioning of markets (market liquidity) or an inability of institutions to meet their short-term funding needs (funding liquidity), possibly due to counterparty risk. Moreover, in the case of China, liquidity has always been unevenly distributed throughout the system and liquidity conditions have recently tightened, making the ongoing management of liquidity increasingly important.

This chapter focuses on the interaction of liquidity management and systemic liquidity risk in China (Box 5.1). While aggregate central bank liquidity cannot prevent a liquidity crisis, the central bank's operating framework, interacting with well-functioning financial markets, will limit this systemic risk. Beyond documenting the current institutional set-up and functioning of money and fixed-income markets, the chapter also describes some changes that will strengthen both aggregate and institutional-level liquidity management in all environments,

Box 5.1 What Is Liquidity?

Three concepts of liquidity are relevant to systemic liquidity management.[1] The first, *aggregate liquidity*, is the extent of liquid funds the central bank supplies to the financial system. The second is *market liquidity*, which relates to the depth, breadth, and resilience of markets, so that parties may trade an asset on short notice, at low cost, and without affecting its price. The final concept is *funding liquidity*, which refers to the ability of a solvent institution to raise funding on short notice and make agreed-upon payments in a timely manner. In developed financial markets, under normal market conditions, market and funding liquidity risk are low, provided the central bank ensures aggregate liquidity to the banking system that is consistent with economic and financial stability, since funds cycle through the banking system and move to where the greatest shortage is. However, systemic liquidity risk can arise due to information asymmetries across market participants and incomplete markets (e.g., poorly functioning hedging markets), irrespective of the amount of aggregate (central bank) liquidity.

This chapter measures the aggregate liquidity position of the banking system using the concept of its structural liquidity position, which reflects the impact of exogenous factors beyond the People's Bank of China's (PBC) control on funds available to the system. Specifically, based on the stylized balance sheet depicted in Table 5.1.1 (bold elements in the table), structural liquidity is defined as $S = NFA - BN - GOV - K$. When this is positive, the banking system has a structural liquidity surplus with respect to the central bank, meaning that it has no need to obtain (net) funding from the central bank.

TABLE 5.1.1

Stylized People's Bank of China Balance Sheet

Assets	Liabilities
Net foreign assets (NFA)	**Bank notes in circulation (BN)**
Net domestic assets (NDA)	**Government deposits (GOV)**
	Minimum reserve requirements (MRR)
	Excess reserves (XR)
	PBC paper (B)
	PBC capital (K)

Note: PBC = the People's Bank of China.

A structural liquidity surplus does not, per se, eliminate the risk of a systemic crisis. Indeed, during periods of market or funding liquidity stress, a vicious link between market and funding liquidity can occur as limited funding prompts "fire sales" of assets, which in turn limits the ability of institutions to raise funds as collateral values fall. As a result, liquidity channels can propagate a financial crisis as the deterioration of either market liquidity or funding liquidity leads to a systemic liquidity crisis irrespective of the extent of aggregate liquidity if counterparty risk becomes important. Indeed, empirically, funding and market risk are often correlated, with market liquidity conditions highly correlated across markets and funding liquidity conditions correlated across institutions. Given the financial instability generated in such a crisis, there is a role for the central bank to provide liquidity in a way that breaks this vicious cycle.

---

[1]Nikolaou (2009) provides an excellent summary of the literature on the meaning of liquidity and the interaction between these three types of liquidity.

irrespective of the amount of aggregate liquidity. These changes can ensure the management framework is not only aimed at withdrawing liquidity during periods of significant liquidity surplus but also flexible enough to provide timely and targeted liquidity in the event of a local or general liquidity shortage resulting, say, from an unexpected reversal of capital inflows or a rise in counterparty risk.

The nature of the potential liquidity strains faced by Chinese banks highlights the critical role of the PBC operations and framework in mitigating liquidity stresses, and suggests some necessary reforms. Unlike large Western banks pre-Lehman, many Chinese banks have lower exposure to funding and especially market risk. They have large—and historically stable—deposit funding, a negative loan-deposit gap, limited leverage and exposure to derivatives, and predominantly hold high-quality securities that can easily be collateralized to maturity. However, these features alone do not eliminate liquidity risk. Funds are unequally distributed through the system, with some banks highly reliant on interbank funding. Banks' large required reserves cannot be used as a buffer, and only a limited share of banks' liquid securities are held on their trading book. Together these characteristics mean that banks may have only a relatively limited share of truly liquid assets on the balance sheet at any time. To limit the resulting risk, a number of refinements to the PBC's framework would ease the task of liquidity management for many banks, as well as ensure that the PBC is in a position to quickly provide liquidity through its standing facilities and operations. Such reforms would include the introduction of reserve averaging, automation of existing PBC standing facilities, and strengthening the ability to undertake high-frequency liquidity operations.

These reforms will also help mitigate the risk of liquidity crises going forward as new financial products spread and China's financial system becomes increasingly open and less bank dominated. In such an environment, market and funding liquidity risks are likely to be higher, allowing a localized liquidity shortage to transmit to other institutions through a traditional run or tighter wholesale funding conditions, the impact on financial prices due to the need to liquidate assets quickly, or failed money market transactions as both funding and market liquidity stresses rise in tandem. As mentioned in Box 5.1, such events can occur even with ample aggregate liquidity in the system. The refinements to the operating framework mentioned above should limit the contagion by allowing the PBC to target its liquidity support to institutions in ways that break contagion across institutions.

In general, the conclusions of this chapter are to move operations in the direction of greater reliance on indirect, rather than direct and administrative, instruments, and to make standing facilities operate in a more transparent and automatic way. Not only should these changes enhance system stability in the case of extreme events but they should also improve the efficiency of (and thereby information conveyed by) financial prices and the allocation of funds by reducing the distortions related to the use of administrative tools. This will become increasingly important as domestic (and eventually external) liberalization proceeds and quantitative-based liquidity management becomes less reliable.

LIQUIDITY MANAGEMENT: FRAMEWORK, INSTRUMENTS, AND FACILITIES

The focus on aggregate liquidity management has largely reflected the need to sterilize large foreign exchange inflows. To do this, the PBC sets an annual broad money target, although it has increasingly paid attention to the information provided by interest rates. While the exchange rate regime is a de jure "managed float," and despite increased flexibility and gradual application, the bilateral rate with the U.S. dollar has remained tightly managed. The PBC has been able to pursue both domestic quantitative targets and an exchange rate target due to China's relatively effective capital controls. Although the PBC's current intermediate monetary policy targets are monetary aggregates, the money multiplier is already relatively unstable. This instability will continue to increase over time given the increasing extent of intermediation outside the banking system, suggesting limits on the effectiveness of managing aggregate liquidity through quantity targeting, and the possibility that liquidity operations may add to aggregate volatility.

To achieve its aggregate monetary and liquidity objectives, the PBC has a rich set of policy instruments that can be broken into three categories:

- *Market-based instruments.* The PBC regularly undertakes open-market operations (OMOs) through both repo transactions and the issuance of PBC bills to manage liquidity. OMOs are typically conducted twice weekly, on Tuesday and Thursday,[1] with the PBC determining the maturity varieties of OMOs based on banks' liquidity management needs. For example, while the majority of OMOs have occurred at one- and three-month maturities, during the peak initial public offering (IPO) activity in 2006 and 2007 the PBC moved to shorter (seven-day) interventions.

- *Standing facilities.* The PBC has several standing facilities that are able to provide emergency funding during times of stress and absorb liquidity on a regular basis. It has intraday and other lending facilities, and a rediscount facility. These facilities were augmented during the recent crisis through the creation of term auction and currency swap windows.

- *Administrative tools.* The PBC uses a number of direct administrative tools, including mandatory reserve requirements, the setting of retail benchmark lending and deposit interest rates (Figures 5.1 and 5.2), and direct window guidance, where the PBC communicates the intentions of monetary policy and guides credit decisions in order to ensure sound economic developments and financial stability. Benchmark interest rates set the ceiling on retail deposit interest rates and the floor on retail lending rates, with the

---

[1]Eligible participants are chosen by the PBC. Currently there are around 50 eligible participants, including both banks and nonbanks (securities firms, insurance companies, and fund managers). The list is adjusted over time depending on past operations and credit ratings.

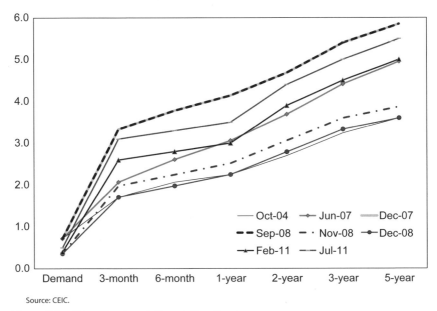

Source: CEIC.

Figure 5.1   China: Benchmark Deposit Rate Structure
(In percent)

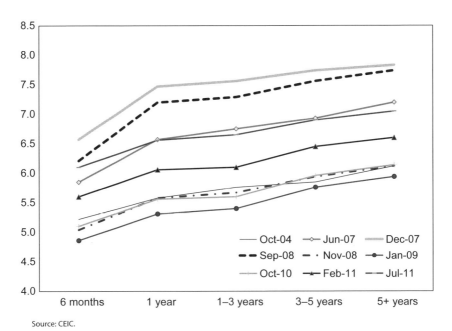

Source: CEIC.

Figure 5.2   China: Benchmark Lending Rate Structure
(In percent)

regulation affecting the entire term structure.[2] Reserve requirements must be met daily, and since early 2011 they are dynamically differentiated over time depending on each bank's credit and other behavior. Adjustments are announced in advance, with some adjustment period provided for banks. Both required and excess reserves are remunerated.

The PBC's standing facilities operate in a fundamentally different way from those in other countries. In particular, the use of the facilities is not automatically triggered at the discretion of eligible financial institutions. The PBC maintains considerable discretion over the use of the facilities. In other places, standing facilities (for solvent institutions) are designed to be large, immediate (on demand), and automatic and predictable. It is these three characteristics that allow them to effectively limit the impact and spread of a liquidity crisis. Moral hazard concerns are dealt with through the (high) penalty rates that the use of the facility incurs and through strengthened supervisory inquiry and appropriate (but ex ante transparent) haircuts on collateral. While the PBC already has an impressive array of facilities, the discretionary and capped nature of its facilities, together with limited information on acceptable collateral, means that the facilities cannot play their full financial stability role as smoothly and quickly as possible.[3] There also seems to be a stigma associated with the use of these facilities, meaning that financial institutions are reluctant to consider using them. Moving the facilities toward being automatic, immediate, stigma-free, and large should substantially limit stability risks in the event of an extreme event. The limited nature of the standing facilities is evident from the fact that short-term market interest rates have exceeded standing facility charges at times of stress, a development discussed later in the chapter.

In China, required reserves are high and do not provide a buffer against shocks. Reserve requirements have to be met strictly each day rather than on average over some maintenance period (as is common elsewhere). The absence of reserve averaging increases liquidity risks, since reserves cannot provide a buffer. Averaging reserve requirements would, therefore, improve stability, reduce distortions, and improve the market position of smaller banks. In addition, these requirements are exceptionally high and are currently, on average, just under 20 percent of deposits. Since these reserves do not act as a buffer, banks have typically held even higher reserve levels for operational purposes and liquidity insurance; although, as described later in this chapter, tightening liquidity conditions in recent times have led banks to reduce this buffer.[4]

---

[2]The deposit rates are generally considered binding, while the lowest lending rate—90 percent of the administered benchmark rate—has traditionally been binding on a quarter to a third of new loans. The share of new loans at this floor, however, fell dramatically in 2011, reaching a minimum of around 5 percent in early 2012. The share ticked up later in 2012 and was around 11 percent in September 2012.

[3]The PBC does not impose any haircut for Treasury bonds and central bank paper, but there seems to be less clarity over the margins applicable on other paper, such as commercial bills.

[4]The absence of reserve averaging also increases the volatility of money market interest rates (Bartolini and Prati, 2003).

By enhancing the buffer role of reserves, as well as reducing the implicit tax they make on financial activity, the introduction of reserve averaging would seem to be a critical reform that could be easily implemented. The successful introduction of reserve averaging should, for instance, help stabilize liquidity conditions at the bank level, even if it were to require additional liquidity draining by the PBC in the short term, which could be achieved through additional OMOs.

The stability concerns resulting from the structure of reserve requirements are accentuated given the dynamic differentiated nature of these requirements—individual institutions may face a sudden change in their reserve requirement. Dynamic differentiation could increase financial instability given its potential differential impact on sets of smaller institutions, and therefore provide incentives to move intermediation outside the regulated financial system. Given this, it may be better to limit the extent of this feature, leaving macroprudential concerns to be addressed by other prudential policies (e.g., capital adequacy and credit quality, that is, through lending standards), since reserve requirements are not primarily a macroprudential tool.

DEVELOPMENTS IN DOMESTIC LIQUIDITY

China's financial system has traditionally been flush with liquidity, although more active monetary management has reduced those levels. This largely reflects autonomous monetary injections. In fact, China's significant structural liquidity surplus increased by almost five times between end-2005 and end-2009, but the rate of increase has slowed—only increasing another 30 percent by end-2011 (Figure 5.3). The growth largely resulted from the accumulation of foreign exchange reserves, and is principally the counterpart of China's persistently large balance of payments surpluses. Ultimately this liquidity surplus has shown up in commercial banks, which as a group hold many more deposits than they require for lending or to meet the regulatory requirements of the PBC and the China Banking Regulatory Commission.[5] More recently, the pace of the increase in the structural liquidity surplus has slowed to below that of foreign reserve accumulation, which most likely reflects deliberate changes in PBC liquidity operations. However, even with this liquidity surplus, there remains a potential for systemic liquidity events, given that the surplus is unevenly distributed across banks; there are informational asymmetries between banks; and there are imperfections in the PBC's toolkit, as described later in the chapter.

PBC management of aggregate or central bank liquidity through its instruments seems to have become more aggressive. The impact of policy actions to offset the effect of "autonomous" monetary injections (e.g., from foreign reserve accumulation) is often measured through the central bank policy of sterilization.[6] Before

---

[5]Commercial banks are not allowed to lend more than 75 percent of deposits.
[6]Policy sterilization—the sum of changes in required reserves and OMOs—reflects the monetary actions undertaken by the central bank to offset autonomous changes in structural liquidity.

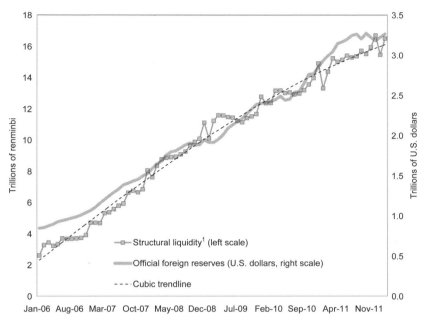

Sources: CEIC; and authors' estimates.
[1]The People's Bank of China (PBC) net foreign assets (excluding other net assets) + net credit to government – currency in circulation – PBC capital.

Figure 5.3 China: Structural Liquidity and Foreign Reserves
(In trillions of renminbi and U.S. dollars)

2010, PBC policy actions (as measured by sterilization) had only partly offset the rise in structural liquidity. However, since end-2009, sterilization has responded more than proportionally to changes in structural liquidity (Figure 5.4), resulting in a steeper response of sterilization and structural liquidity. The PBC has relied mostly on reserve requirements in this more aggressive policy, probably reflecting their relative cost and comparative advantage in absorbing liquidity both quickly and for a long time. Given the size of the banking system, a small change in the required reserve rate can quickly absorb (or release) considerable liquidity, as seen by the impact of the reduction in the requirement in December 2008. However, the use of OMOs has increased considerably, and since 2010 has been important in injecting liquidity, given the extent of liquidity withdrawn through reserve requirements. This is an important change in the behavior of the PBC (Figure 5.5). Reserve requirements have, all else being equal, moved the system toward a deficit, with OMOs providing the additional liquidity needed by financial institutions. This can be seen in the behavior of money market rates during this period.

The more aggressive monetary response may have made aggregate management easier. When, as in China, a banking system has a positive structural liquidity position, the central bank must manage aggregate liquidity through the liability

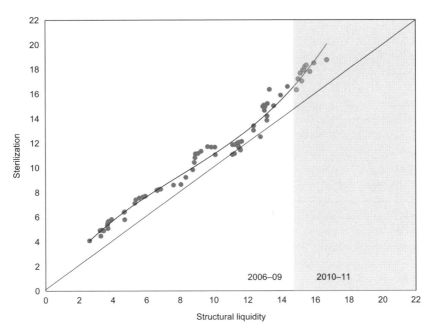

Sources: CEIC; and authors' estimates.

Figure 5.4 Structural Liquidity and the People's Bank of China Sterilization Policy
(In trillions of renminbi)

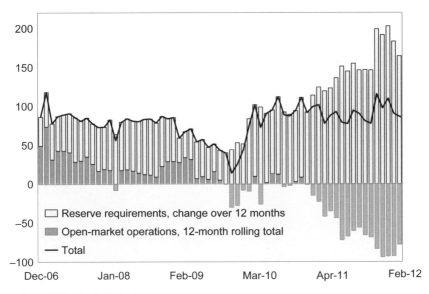

Sources: CEIC; and authors' estimates.

Figure 5.5 Composition of Policy Sterilization
(In trillions of renminbi)

side of its balance sheet. Typically this is more challenging and costly due to the distortions created by sterilization, since financial institutions are not required to deal with the central bank for funding, at least in the aggregate, making it more difficult for the central bank to influence liquidity conditions (Gray, 2006; Gray and Talbot, 2006). In the case of a liquidity surplus, the default liability expansion—excess reserves—may directly lead to monetary expansion, as banks generally do not, for their operational needs, have to participate in central bank liquidity draining operations. Consequently, the tightening of liquidity is likely to have improved the traction of the PBC's policy for its macroeconomic objectives because banks are more likely to rely on the PBC for refinancing.

However, the rise in funding liquidity stresses is evident in the recent behavior of money market rates. The PBC's standing facilities should, in principle, define an interest rate corridor, with the emergency lending or discount rate at the top and the excess reserve rate at the bottom. This corridor is wide, with a median width of over 200 basis points between 2002 and 2011, compared with the current typical corridor of 50 basis points in countries with interest rate monetary policy targets. Moreover, the access limits imposed on these facilities, and the discretion maintained by the PBC, means the corridor is "soft" in the sense that it is not always binding on money market interest rates. This is clearly illustrated when repo rates significantly breach the top of the corridor, as was seen in late 2007, and as has been more endemic since late 2010 (Figure 5.6). To

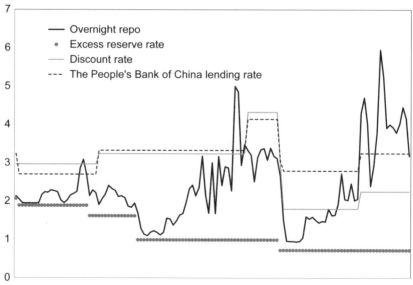

Source: CEIC.

Figure 5.6   China: Interest Rate Structure
(In percent per annum)

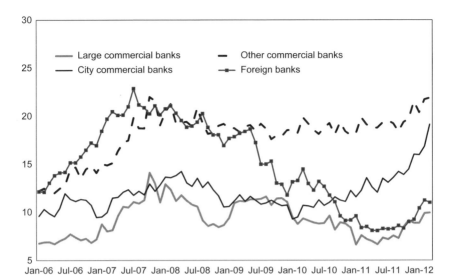

Sources: CEIC; and authors' estimates.
Note: Prior to January 2010, "large commercial banks" were referred to as "state-controlled banks." Since January 2010, the data on other commercial banks and city commercial banks reflect data for medium-sized and small banks, respectively.

Figure 5.7   China: Interbank Funding
(In percent of liabilities)

the extent that spikes in money market rates are attributable to clear transitory factors that do not affect the stance of monetary policy—such as temporary tightness due to a large IPO—the PBC is not inclined to intervene aggressively to smooth short-lived volatility and keep the interest rate within the corridor. However, more systematic violations of the corridor through the ceiling suggest persistent tight liquidity conditions that could have stability implications.

This heightened stress, together with the uneven distribution of funds in the banking system, raises the importance of well-functioning money markets and nimble PBC liquidity management for stability. This uneven distribution leaves many institutions dependent on the money markets and on holding higher excess reserves (Figures 5.7 and 5.8). Specifically, China's "big five" commercial banks, and many of the midsized joint stock banks, have surplus funds, while smaller commercial banks, policy banks, credit cooperatives, and nonbanks are typical net borrowers in this market.[7] Consequently, despite a system that has been flush with liquidity, particular sets of institutions can be vulnerable to liquidity shocks and are forced to maintain higher excess reserves.[8] Indeed, the switch from OMOs to reserve requirements for liquidity draining (sterilization)

---

[7]Porter and Xu (2009) provide a more detailed discussion of the parallel historical development of the interbank and exchange traded bond markets.
[8]For foreign banks, the higher average reflects both higher buffer stocks and, in the case of some banks, a business model with limited reliance on retail deposit taking.

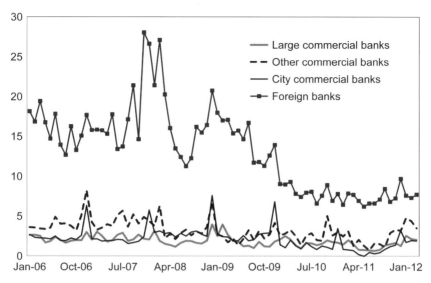

Source: IMF staff estimates based on aggregated balance sheet data.
Note: Prior to January 2010, "large commercial banks" were referred to as "state-controlled banks." Since January 2010, the data on other commercial banks and city commercial banks reflect data for medium-sized and small banks, respectively.

Figure 5.8   China: Estimated Excess Reserve Ratios
(In percent of deposits)

TABLE 5.1

China: Aggregated Bank Balance Sheet *(In percent of assets net of interbank claims, as of December 31, 2011)*			
Assets		**Liabilities**	
Cash	0.5	Retail deposits	81.4
Deposits at the People's Bank of China (including excess reserves)	17.5	Net interbank	−8.9
Loans	66.2	Securities	7.9
Securities	7.5	Other	16.6
Other	8.2	**Equity**	3.0

Source: The People's Bank of China.

operations, ceteris paribus, effectively tightened conditions at a bank level given the nonexistent buffer role reserves play in the absence of reserve averaging. As a result, some banks are left with relatively limited liquid assets (Table 5.1), especially after a period of rapid loan growth, increasing their volatility. The imbalance is also reflected in the patterns of interbank funding, in which the larger state-controlled banks are predominantly the borrowers in the unsecured market, while in the collateralized repo market they are the dominant lenders to the other financial institutions. The recent spikes in money market rates suggest that funding conditions have been tight for some institutions.

Since Chinese banks cannot average their required reserves, excess reserves have been required to play an essential buffer role. In recent times, these buffers

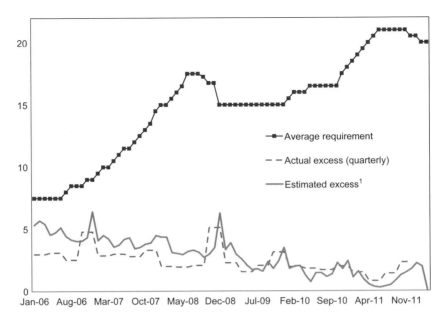

Sources: CEIC; and authors' estimates.
[1]IMF staff estimates based on aggregated balance sheet data.

Figure 5.9   China: Bank Reserves
(In percent of deposits)

have been relatively low. The daily nature of the requirement means that it is principally an aggregate liquidity management tool for the PBC rather than a liquid asset for banks. Across the banking system these excess reserve buffers have averaged around 2–3 percent of deposits, but the actual holdings vary substantially by type of bank, although they were at historically low levels in 2011 (Figure 5.9). Supporting their buffer stock role, excess reserves are also relatively insensitive to their opportunity cost. On the other hand, interest rates react to changes in excess reserves, seemingly consistent with the PBC using quantitative liquidity changes (brought about by repo and bill transactions) to influence short-term money market interest rates. Specifically, as illustrated by the impulse responses (Figures 5.10 and 5.11) from a simple two-variable vector autoregression (VAR)—including the excess reserves ratio over total deposits and the spread between the overnight rate (SHIBOR) and the rate of the remuneration of excess reserves—a positive shock (around the trend) to the excess reserve ratio leads to a temporary reduction in the spread (around the trend), but a shock to the spread does not have any impact on the excess ratio.[9] So, with buffers lower than that traditionally required for the smooth functioning of the system, liquidity shocks could have larger stability implications.

---

[9]Besides the constant term, a time trend was added to the VAR because in the sample period both the excess reserves ratio and the interest rate spread have declining (linear) trends.

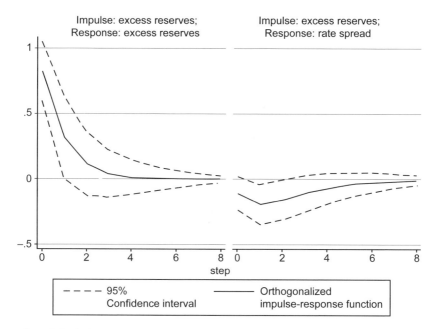

Source: Authors' estimates.

Note: Vector autoregression (1 lag); excess reserves ratio; spread overnight SHIBOR over rate of excess reserves; constant.

Figure 5.10 China: Responses to an Increase in the Total Excess Reserves Ratio

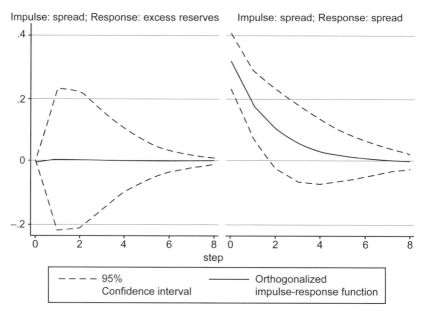

Source: Authors' estimates.

Figure 5.11 China: Responses to an Increase in the Spread

As such, the interbank money markets, and the efficiency of their operation, are central to intermediation. Recent international experience has shown that a liquidity crisis can occur even when aggregate liquidity is ample if the distribution of funds in the system is uneven and institutions are sufficiently interconnected. Although such events have not in the past spread across institutions in China to become a systemic event, this remains a risk for the future. In the case of China, a deterioration in the liquidity of the markets for repo collateral is less likely to be disruptive than was seen in the recent crisis in developed markets, given the high-quality (near-sovereign) securities mostly used as collateral. However, this could change as new forms of collateral become increasingly important (Chu, Wen, and He, 2010), and frictions in the system could exacerbate a localized crisis.

In addition, ongoing structural changes have contributed to tighter liquidity conditions. Indeed, the ongoing process of disintermediation from the banking sector, as well as the development of the offshore renminbi market, has tightened conditions (Chu, Wen, and He, 2011). The rise in wealth management products has been associated with increased depositor mobility (given that these products offer higher returns than the ceiling on deposit rates), and the payouts associated with these products often also raise liquidity stress, as they are products generally not matched with the payment profile of the underlying product, which can cause banks to use their own funds or tap the money markets. More generally, the disintermediation leads to a general drain in liquidity and often returns to the banks "in the form of loan repayments rather than new deposits" (Chu, Wen, and He, 2011, p. 4). The development of the offshore market can also lead to destabilizing cross-border flows, and while much of the renminbi funds raised offshore (in Hong Kong SAR) remain there, corporates can use onshore renminbi to repay offshore obligations, resulting in funds leaving the system.

Risks arising from sudden changes in market and funding liquidity make it important that the PBC be able to respond quickly and relatively automatically. Therefore, developing the ability to undertake daily liquidity management would improve liquidity risk surveillance and crisis management. Although during normal times the ability to undertake such frequent liquidity operations may bring little marginal benefit, and indeed may not even be necessary under a reserve averaging regime, during times of stress the financial stability benefits could be significant. This will require additional effort in forecasting liquidity accurately at very high (daily) frequencies to ensure that high-frequency operations reduce rather than exacerbate market volatility. In particular, if a crisis involves heightened counterparty risk, then central bank operations become an important contributing element to the ongoing smooth functioning of the financial system (Cassola and Huetl, 2010). This is even more important when, as in China, required reserves cannot play a buffer role for financial institutions.

MONEY MARKETS, FIXED-INCOME MARKETS, AND THE INTEREST RATE REGIME IN CHINA

The PBC is at the center of fixed-income pricing in China. Not only do its OMOs influence money market interest rates as described above, it also sets benchmark lending and deposit rate structures, which influence the interest rates in the money and bond markets. This section lays out the behavior of China's interest rates and suggests some areas for operational reform that may improve the efficiency of these price signals. We find some anomalies in the operation of the money markets, and bond markets display some inefficiency at shorter maturities, likely reflecting regulation, segmentation, and illiquidity. Despite these inefficiencies, prices seem to reflect economic expectations and transmit shocks across yield curves.

Efficiency of fixed-income prices in the money and bond markets is critical for their functioning and, hence, market liquidity. Indeed, there are several reasons to suspect that these prices are far from efficient. Despite no formal segmentation, the secured and unsecured fixed-income and money markets appear segmented.[10] China's bond markets have traditionally been segmented between those for retail investors and those for institutional investors. Although the impact of this segmentation has been reduced, with some large banks now able to operate in both markets on a pilot basis, the distortions are likely to exacerbate market illiquidity in normal times, and especially during times of stress. Removing the final divisions in the bond market, strengthening existing standing facilities (including by making them automatic), and liberalizing financial prices would likely address these remaining anomalies and improve the functioning of these markets.

Money Market Interest Rates

China's money markets include a collateralized (repo) market and an uncollateralized (call-loan) market. Collateralized lending activity clearly dominates, averaging 10 times the size of the unsecured market. Large banks dominate the lending in the repo market, with smaller banks and other financial institutions generally short of liquidity (Figure 5.12). In the unsecured money market the roles are reversed, with smaller banks predominantly lending to the larger banks (Figure 5.13). Financial—policy and commercial bank—bonds are the most popular instrument for repo purposes, but PBC paper and, increasingly, the newer middle-term notes are also used (Figure 5.14).[11] Although most of the collateral is very high (near sovereign) quality, Chu, Wen, and He (2010) report the

---

[10]The segmentation of the bond market dates from 1997 and prevents banks from trading in the exchange market. Since 2004, bonds trading in one market have been able to be moved to the other platform, but since this requires moving bonds across depositories, it can take substantial time (up to a day). In early 2010, the authorities announced a pilot scheme to allow some commercial banks to operate in both interbank and exchange markets.

[11]Middle-term notes are medium-term paper (up to five-year maturity) issued by (listed or unlisted) companies.

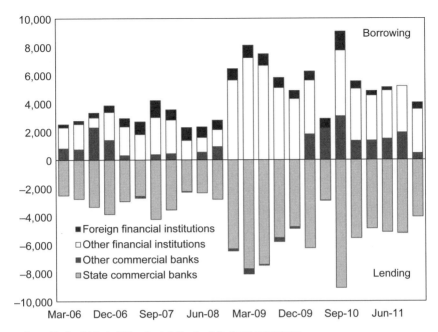

Source: The People's Bank of China, *Quarterly Monetary Policy Report,* various issues.

Figure 5.12 China: Flow of Funds in the Interbank Market—Repos
(In billions of renminbi)

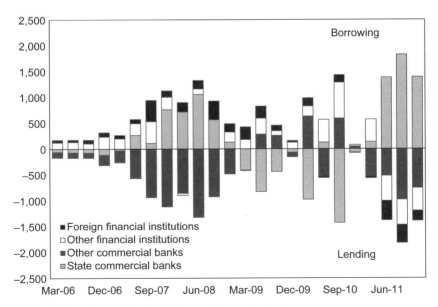

Source: The People's Bank of China, *Quarterly Monetary Policy Report,* various issues.

Figure 5.13 China: Flow of Funds in the Interbank Market: Call Loans
(In billions of renminbi)

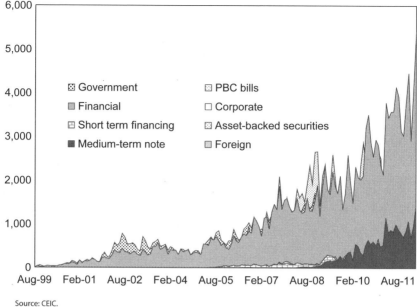

Source: CEIC.
Note: PBC = the People's Bank of China.

Figure 5.14 China: Interbank Repo Turnover
(In billions of renminbi)

increasing use of discounted short-term bills as collateral, as well as corporate medium-term notes, deteriorating the quality of the collateral pool.[12] Such a change in the nature of collateral increases the likelihood of systemic risks if it becomes sufficiently widespread, and haircuts on these bills may be smaller than suggested by their risk characteristics (Chu, Wen, and He, 2010).

While the money markets are highly active, and key to intermediation in China, two pricing anomalies can be identified:

- *Secured interest rates are typically above unsecured rates.* The weighted average of the repo rate persistently exceeds the unsecured rate, particularly since January 2006 (Figure 5.15). Given the quality of the securities pledged for repos (and the haircuts applied), this suggests problems in the pricing of short-term credit. Market participants generally attribute this to a reflection of counterparty risk, as only large banks are typically able to borrow in the unsecured market. However, the security provided for the repo transaction, and the higher liquidity in the repo market, should imply even lower interest

---

[12]The China Government Depository Trust and Clearing Co. Ltd. (CDC) is the only institution entrusted by the Ministry of Finance to be the depository for government securities. In addition to the interbank and over-the-counter bond markets, government securities may also be traded in the stock exchanges. For this purpose, the China Securities and Clearing Corporation Ltd. holds an omnibus account at the CDC.

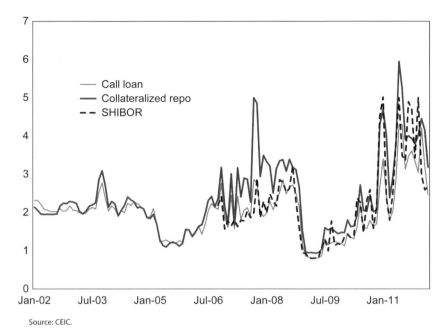

Source: CEIC.

Figure 5.15   China: Interbank Overnight Funding Rates
(In percent)

rates. As such, an average premium of over 50 basis points—between the overnight repo and uncollateralized call-loan rates—seems high.[13] Reportedly, tiering is common in interbank pricing, and although conditional on a particular bank borrowing in both secured and unsecured markets, the rate of interest charged in the unsecured market is higher. This gap should then likely reflect factors other than pure counterparty risk. In particular, given the dominance of a few very large banks, it seems likely that relative market power plays an important role, particularly around times when money market conditions are especially tight due to IPOs or seasonal factors.[14]

- *The short-term money market yield curve is always positively sloped,* irrespective of whether the interest rate cycle is on an upward, flat, or downward phase. This suggests that interest rates do not accurately reflect the expected path of short-term interest rates. This feature is illustrated in Figure 5.16

---

[13]Although only overnight rates are shown in the figure, there is a substantial gap between repo and SHIBOR rates out to one year.
[14]Feyzioglu (2009) also suggests market concentration as a possible explanation for the independence between profitability and efficiency observed across Chinese banks. The extensive use of pledged, rather than outright, repos may also play a role, as these are in principle relatively more expensive.

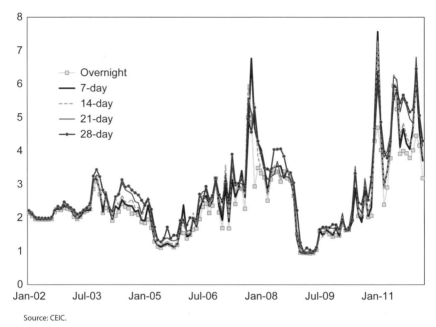

Source: CEIC.

Figure 5.16 China: Interbank Collateralized Repo Rates
(In percent)

with five very short-term repo rates (1-day, 7-day, 14-day, 21-day, and 28-day maturities). Given their very short-term maturity, the term premia should normally be very small and constant. However, spreads are relatively wide (between 25 and 60 basis points) and are positive irrespective of the stage of the interest rate cycle: end-2008 and end-2009 share the same patterns, while in the former period policy rates were being cut and in the latter policy rates were kept constant. This not only suggests some mispricing but could lead to problems on the rare occasions the curve inverts, since market participants are unfamiliar with such behavior.

Bond Turnover and Pricing

This section looks at the behavior and efficiency of bond market prices. Bond yields should (bidirectionally) reflect shocks that affect other yields as well as convey expectations about future macroeconomic developments. However, given the segmentation and other distortions in the Chinese financial market, this may not turn out to be the case.

Since segmentation, market turnover has been higher in the interbank (institutional) bond market, with inconsistencies in the pricing of securities across the retail and institutional Treasury markets. Despite this, and somewhat surprisingly, median bid-ask spreads tend to be lower for Treasury bonds across most maturities, although the market for one-year bonds seems equally liquid (Figure 5.17).

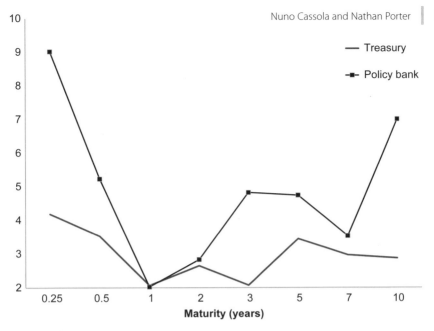

Source: CEIC.

Figure 5.17 China: Bond Market Bid-Ask Spreads, April 2010 to June 2011
(In basis points)

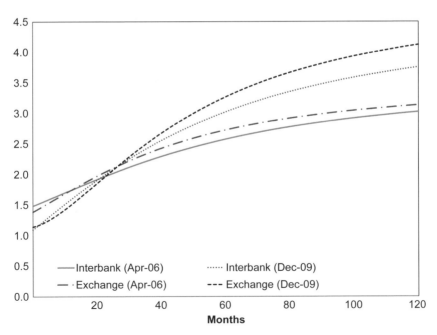

Source: Authors' estimates.

Figure 5.18 China: Treasury Bond Yield Curves
(In percent)

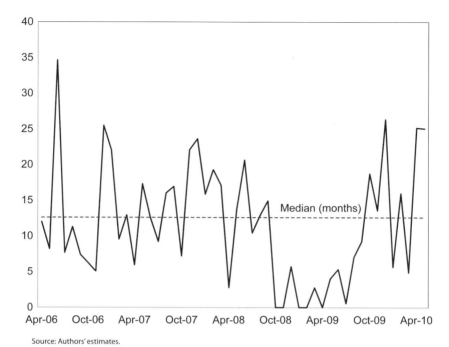

Source: Authors' estimates.

Figure 5.19 China: Interbank and Exchange Market Yield Curve Crossing
(In months)

The segmentation of the Treasury bond market—between retail and institutional (interbank) markets—has allowed different pricing for these bonds. This is apparent from the fact that the yield curves of the bonds trading on the separate markets tend to cross. The maturity of crossing has varied over time around a median of 12 months (Figures 5.18 and 5.19). As such, segmentation has clearly led to distorted price signals.

Offshore Market Development

The development of the offshore bond market poses some risks to liquidity management in China. The reform process has led to the creation of a rapidly expanding set of renminbi financial products and prices outside of mainland China. Given China's binding capital controls, these prices tend to differ from those on the mainland, creating the incentive for capital flows to arbitrage these differences. This has particularly been the case since July 2010, when the PBC and Hong Kong Monetary Authority signed a Memorandum of Cooperation allowing nonbank financial institutions as well as non-trade-related nonfinancial corporations to open renminbi accounts in Hong Kong SAR. A key part of the functioning of this scheme is the convertibility constraint, by which banks acting as counterparties to non-trade-related renminbi conversion cannot automatically net their position with the clearing bank (Bank of China, Hong Kong). These convertibility restrictions are designed largely to preserve the mainland's capital account restrictions.

Long-term development of the offshore renminbi market is likely to bring many benefits. Possibly an early tangible benefit will result from the introduction of new (and different) types of investors in the domestic bond market. Nonetheless, it is likely to complicate liquidity management and may raise some financial stability concerns.[15] Having said that, the development of an offshore market does not require complete capital account liberalization, and there are ways to manage the emerging risks as the market develops. While the complete "going out" of the renminbi may be impossible without an open capital account, the substantial restriction that remained on the use of the U.S. dollar during the 1960s and 1970s did not seem to have impeded the international use of the dollar at the time.

The expansion of offshore renminbi activity may pose risks to the PBC's ability to control domestic monetary conditions. Nonetheless, moving toward liquidity management targeting domestic interest rates is likely to ease the overall management task as the offshore market grows. Specifically, changes in offshore activity—as well as the endogenous money creation resulting from offshore lending—complicate controlling credit, domestic interest rates, and the exchange rate. However, provided capital controls remain effective, the PBC is likely to maintain control over monetary conditions. The reforms outlined above aimed at developing the offshore renminbi market clearly limit the extent of capital account opening but may possibly make evasion easier by making trade misinvoicing easier. If so, then additional measures to restore the strength of capital controls may be needed to maintain monetary control.

Beyond issues related to liquidity and monetary management, the development of a deep offshore market could eventually also have implications for the PBC's financial stability role. The large expansion of renminbi lending by foreign banks made possible by offshore market development means that the PBC may be required to provide renminbi liquidity support to non-Chinese banks in the case of tight liquidity in the offshore renminbi market. Indeed, as offshore use of the renminbi expands, this could be even more relevant for the PBC than it was for the U.S. Federal Reserve during the 2007–09 financial crisis, as few foreign central banks are likely to have significant renminbi assets in their reserve portfolios. However, during the financial crisis the PBC gained some experience in providing renminbi swap arrangements with other central banks (although none have actually been used), demonstrating that it has already developed the necessary infrastructure.

---

[15]He and McCauley (2010) provide an excellent survey of the lessons for emerging economies that may wish to internationalize their currency.

CONCLUSIONS AND CONSIDERATIONS FOR FURTHER LIBERALIZATION

This chapter has surveyed liquidity management operations by the PBC and the operation of key fixed-income markets in China. The PBC has effectively managed domestic liquidity conditions in recent times, particularly given the remarkably large increase in structural liquidity since 2006. However, the chapter argues that future financial stability would benefit from reforming (and reducing the stigma associated with) the PBC's standing facilities, developing an ability over time to undertake OMOs at a daily frequency, and introducing reserve averaging. Clarifying the PBC's liquidity management objectives and moving toward indirect liquidity management instruments should also ease the PBC's management task as the money multiplier becomes less stable, also aiding macroeconomic and financial stability. Finally, the efficiency of financial prices should improve as the financial sector is further liberalized and market liquidity grows.

Further financial and interest rate liberalization should bring a number of benefits, and the need is becoming increasingly urgent. Market-determined interest rates should become a more informative guide to domestic monetary conditions and provide more efficient price signals to guide investment allocation. Moreover, liberalization is also likely to result in access to bond issuance for an expanded set of corporates, particularly for short- and medium-term notes, and expand available saving and investment products for individuals. The disintermediation already under way, as well as the tightening of liquidity conditions, makes the need more urgent. Indeed, market liquidity should improve with the removal of a number of distortions.

As discussed above, improperly sequenced liberalization is likely to increase risks in ways that dominate the benefits from reform. While a complete sequencing of financial sector reforms is discussed in Chapter 2 of this book, this chapter concludes with two sequencing considerations relevant to liquidity management.

- *Domestic liberalization.* Domestic liberalization will likely increase both the level and volatility of interest rates and, as discussed, should be accompanied by tight monetary policy to limit the risks posed by a competition-driven expansion of lending. With interest rate volatility likely to rise, and the depth of hedging markets currently limited, a concurrent move to interest rate targeting should also smooth the transition during the liberalization process. At the same time, moving the exchange rate closer to its equilibrium level should add a further dimension to the tightening of monetary conditions, as well as slow the autonomous rise in structural liquidity. Ultimately, greater flexibility in both exchange and interest rates will deepen the hedging markets, allowing for greater market-based hedging opportunities.

- *External liberalization.* Complete external liberalization ahead of domestic liberalization could lead to substantial and destabilizing capital flows, particularly if the exchange rate is considered to be near equilibrium at the time and domestic interest rates remain low. Moreover, a vibrant offshore market would likely make these pressures stronger and significantly complicate monetary management if attempted too early and, especially, if attempted before the PBC moves to the use of indirect policy instruments. Consequently, domestic financial and interest rate market reform should precede external liberalization, with the exchange rate close to equilibrium.

REFERENCES

Bartolini, Leonardo, and Alessandro Prati, 2003, "Cross-Country Differences in Monetary Policy Execution and Money Market Rates' Volatility," FRB Staff Report No. 175 (New York: Federal Reserve Bank of New York).

Cassola, Nuno, and Michael Huetl, 2010, "The Euro Overnight Interbank Market and ECB's Liquidity Management Policy During Tranquil and Turbulent Times," ECB Working Paper No. 1247 (Frankfurt: European Central Bank).

Chu, Charlene, Chunling Wen, and Hiddy He, 2010, "Chinese Banks: No Pause in Credit Growth: Still on Pace with 2009," *China: Special Report,* Fitch Ratings, Hong Kong SAR, December.

———, 2011, "Chinese Banks: Cash Cushions Thinning as Liquidity Erodes and Forbearance Burdens Rise," China: Special Report, Fitch Ratings, Hong Kong SAR, December 2.

Feyzioglu, Tarhan, 2009, "Does Good Financial Performance Mean Good Financial Intermediation in China?" IMF Working Paper No. 09/170 (Washington: International Monetary Fund).

Gray, Simon T., ed., 2006, "Central Bank Management of Surplus Liquidity," Handbooks in Central Banking Lecture Series No. 6 (London: Centre for Central Banking Studies, Bank of England).

Gray, Simon T., and Nick Talbot, 2006, "Monetary Operations," Handbooks in Central Banking No. 24 (London: Centre for Central Banking Studies, Bank of England).

He, Dong, and Robert McCauley, 2010, "Offshore Markets for the Domestic Currency: Monetary and Financial Stability Issues," HKMA Working Paper No. 02/2010 (Hong Kong SAR: Hong Kong Monetary Authority).

International Monetary Fund (IMF), 2010, "People's Republic of China—Staff Report for the 2010 Article IV Consultation," IMF Country Report No. 10/238 (Washington: International Monetary Fund). www.imf.org/external/pubs/ft/scr/2010/cr10238.pdf.

Nikolaou, Kleopatra, 2009, "Liquidity (Risk) Concepts: Definitions and Interactions," ECB Working Paper No. 1008 (Frankfurt: European Central Bank).

Porter, Nathan, and TengTeng Xu, 2009, "What Drives China's Interbank Market?" IMF Working Paper No. 09/189 (Washington: International Monetary Fund).

CHAPTER 6

Capital Flows, International Use of the Renminbi, and Implications for Financial Stability

SHAUN K. ROACHE AND SAMAR MAZIAD

China's Twelfth Five-Year Plan identifies greater integration with the global financial system as a strategic priority. The focus and attention given to financial integration is entirely appropriate, as China will need to combine its large role in global trade with a comparatively important position in the global financial system if strong and balanced growth is to be achieved and sustained over the medium term.

Much progress has already been made. Some restrictions on the capital account have been lifted, with a particular focus on allowing increased opportunities for professional investors. International use of the renminbi has also been increasing. Both developments are closely linked, as they increase China's integration into the global financial system and also rely on important complementarities, including the careful sequencing of reforms. Increasing openness of the financial sector is taking place against the backdrop of steady domestic financial reform and transition. For now, China's capital control regime remains fairly comprehensive and effective, and this has limited the risks to domestic stability sometimes presented by capital flows. But flows are increasing and in net terms are becoming comparable in size relative to the economy or the financial system to those of other large, more open emerging markets. With the liberalization of flows and internationalization of the renminbi likely to continue, this will present policymakers with some financial stability challenges.

This chapter will review recent progress in the liberalization of capital flows and the internationalization of the renminbi and assess how this process may evolve in the future. In particular, it discusses what this process means for domestic financial stability. The experiences of other countries indicate that the appropriate sequencing of reforms is critical to safe navigation toward full international financial integration. China has made an excellent start on this path, and by following some important principles, prospects for successful global integration are bright.

RECENT TRENDS IN CAPITAL FLOWS AND INTERNATIONALIZATION OF THE RENMINBI

Capital Flows Now

One pressing challenge facing China is that the immediate pressures of global capital flows could run ahead of efforts to gradually open the capital account. Notwithstanding China's tightly controlled capital account—which has proven to be very effective over a long period of time—net capital inflows to China unrelated to foreign direct investment (FDI) have been increasing and now appear to be large (as estimates later in this chapter will show). China faces the same challenges posed by increasing capital flows as do many emerging market economies. A number of structural developments are driving these capital flows, including wider economic growth and interest rate differentials, and a structural reallocation in the portfolios of institutional investors (IMF, 2004, Chapter 4; IMF, 2011, Chapter 2). While these factors suggest that China and other emerging economies will have to manage higher net inflows over a sustained period, historical experience also suggests that these flows can reverse rapidly. However, from a medium-term perspective, a sustained flow of capital to large emerging markets is likely to remain a feature of global finance in the post–global crisis world. This would necessitate a shift in emerging market policies and financial sector frameworks to effectively manage this trend.

Capital flows unrelated to direct investments are not all speculative and potentially destabilizing, although a large proportion typically is. Speculative capital flows are often defined by the motivation of the investor to earn a return over a short horizon and the ease with which such investments can be liquidated and transferred. In China, such flows are sometimes measured indirectly due to the possibly large volume of unrecorded capital flows evading capital controls.

One common approach to estimating the total flow of non-FDI capital is to subtract the trade balance, FDI, and estimated currency valuation effects from the monthly change in foreign exchange reserves. Although an approximation, this provides some guide as to the scale and high frequency pattern of speculative flows. In recent years, there is evidence that the size of these flows has picked up, with annual net flows of between US$60 billion and US$80 billion (or 1 to 1.5 percent of GDP) per year from 2008–11 (Figure 6.1). Importantly, the volatility of these flows has also increased, with very large net reversals that often coincide with changes in global financial conditions, including in 2008 and late 2011. This provides strong evidence that net flows to China are strengthening linkages with global financial markets.

Progress in Internationalizing the Renminbi

China also faces the unique challenge that comes with the internationalization of its currency. Internationalization refers to a currency's use outside the issuer's borders, including for purchases of goods, services, and financial assets in transactions by nonresidents (Kenan, 2009). By its very nature, currency internationalization

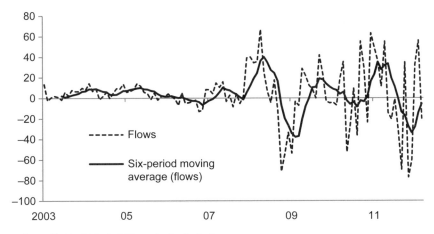

Sources: The People's Bank of China; and authors' estimates.

Figure 6.1   China: Estimated Unrecorded Capital Flows
(In billions of U.S. dollars, net)

will involve an increase in the flow of capital into and out of China. It is essentially an organic, evolutionary, and market-driven process in which there emerges progressively wider use of a currency as a unit of denominating cross-border trade and as a global store of value. While currencies from a number of advanced and emerging market countries have achieved a significant degree of international use, it is widely recognized that China's currency has the potential to evolve into a "global" currency (Maziad and others, 2011). Broadly speaking, the renminbi already meets the prerequisites for cross-border use in terms of potential demand for the currency. International demand for the renminbi exists due to China's large economic size and strong growth prospects, its central role within the Asian supply chain, and its role as a very large global exporter of a diverse range of goods.

The Chinese authorities have begun to advance the renminbi's role as an international currency. Renminbi cross-border trade settlement expanded fourfold during the first nine months of 2011 to reach almost RMB 200 billion, supporting a rapid rise in renminbi deposits in Hong Kong SAR. In addition, the People's Bank of China (PBC) is facilitating access to the renminbi through currency swap lines with other central banks within and outside Asia, while several countries have announced plans to add the renminbi to their foreign exchange reserves.[1]

---

[1]Between December 2008 and July 2010, the PBC established currency swap lines of about RMB 800 billion with eight central banks, including those of Argentina, Belarus, Hong Kong, Iceland, Indonesia, Malaysia, Singapore, and South Korea. In November 2011, Premier Wen Jiabao proposed expanding the use of swap lines with countries that belong to the Shanghai Cooperation Organization, including Russia, Kazakhstan, Kyrgyzstan, Tajikistan, Uzbekistan, and China. India, Iran, Mongolia, and Pakistan take part as observers. In January 2012, China signed the first currency swap agreement with an Arab nation, the United Arab Emirates, worth RMB 35 billion.

Since the start of renminbi internationalization efforts, foreigners have been able to develop and trade a wide range of renminbi-denominated financial instruments in Hong Kong, making it the first financial center for renminbi investments offshore. The following are some of the other recent highlights in renminbi internationalization:

- *Renminbi deposits and financial instruments.* Once offshore, renminbi liquidity is reclassified as "CNH" without restrictions on its end use as long as it remains offshore.[2] Renminbi deposits offshore have increased rapidly and by end-2011 accounted for 10.4 percent of total deposits in Hong Kong. The first offshore renminbi mutual fund was created in 2010, and the list of offshore renminbi products has already become substantial. Beyond active spot and forward foreign exchange markets, renminbi cross-currency swaps, certificates of deposit, interbank lending, and some structured products are available in Hong Kong. In 2010, the PBC expanded the channels through which offshore renminbi could flow back to the mainland. In particular, central banks and qualified financial institutions were allowed to invest renminbi directly in the onshore interbank bond market, subject to individual quotas.

- *Renminbi bonds.* The supply of the renminbi-denominated assets offshore has lagged demand and the rapid growth of the pool of renminbi deposits in Hong Kong. Issuers of renminbi bonds or "Dim-Sum" bonds benefit from this excess demand and are able to raise funds offshore at much lower yields in comparison with onshore issuers, as shown in Figure 6.2 for government bond yields. This is an important channel for renminbi funds to be transferred back onshore, creating a feedback loop between onshore and offshore renminbi markets. This market has grown rapidly with the stock of outstanding renminbi bonds, reaching about RMB 167 billion by end-2011, while market structure shifted from sovereigns to banks and corporates. Issuance is mostly by businesses with a natural renminbi hedge that take advantage of lower yields offshore compared with renminbi or dollar funding on the mainland (Maziad and Kang, 2012). The dominant role of domestic issuers in the offshore renminbi market is very unusual compared with other offshore markets. The absence of alternatives for offshore renminbi investments and appreciation expectations has caused offshore renminbi bondholders to maintain their position, limiting secondary market volume. Plans are in place to expand the issuance of Treasury bonds in Hong Kong, in part to support market development and establish a benchmark risk-free interest rate.

- *Renminbi FDI.* In October 2011, the authorities formalized the use of offshore renminbi for FDI on the mainland. This development would make

---

[2]The acronym CNH is used to represent the exchange rate of the renminbi that trades offshore in Hong Kong.

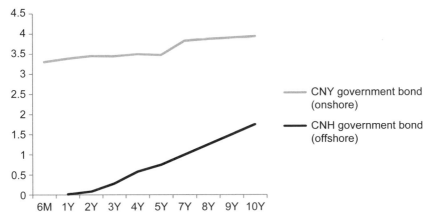

Sources: Bloomberg; and IMF staff.
Note: The acronym CNY is used to represent onshore renminbi within China. CNH is used to represent the exchange rate of the renminbi that trades offshore in Hong Kong.

Figure 6.2   Government Bond Yield
(In percent)

renminbi-denominated FDI more transparent under a standardized framework, giving foreign enterprises greater incentive to use the renminbi in their cross-border transactions and potentially speed up two-way circulation of renminbi funds both in and out of the mainland. In the longer run, this should further spur the development of offshore renminbi products in Hong Kong and increase the confidence of enterprises to raise funds there for investments on the mainland. Under the rules, FDI flows have to be backed by actual settlement or business needs to be settled within three months of the transaction, and applications for renminbi FDI totaling more than RMB 300 million will be subject to approval by the Ministry of Commerce, while those of lesser amounts will be subject to approval by branches of the ministry at the provincial level.

- *Portfolio flows.* Prior to August 2011, a narrow set of qualifying institutions, including renminbi–trade settlement banks, qualifying central banks, and the Bank of China in Hong Kong and Macau (the offshore clearing bank for trade settlement), were able to invest in the interbank bond market onshore. In the package of measures announced in August 2011, the long-awaited "mini QFII" (Qualified Foreign Institutional Investor) scheme was finally given the official green light with an initial quota of RMB 20 billion (and the relevant administrative rules were announced by the Chinese authorities in December 2011). This is effectively a renminbi-settled version of the current U.S. dollar–settled QFII. Although the size of the quota is small, reflecting concerns over capital inflows, it is nevertheless an important step toward greater RMB internationalization.

TABLE 6.1

Top Five Contributors to Global Financial Depth			
(In percentage share of global financial depth weighted by GDP)			
1989			**2009**
Advanced countries	**92.8**	**Advanced countries**	**82.4**
United States	32.5	United States	29.4
Japan	28.3	Japan	13.2
United Kingdom	5.7	United Kingdom	7.8
Germany	5.3	Germany	6.1
France	4.5	France	5.4
Emerging markets	**7.2**	**Emerging markets**	**17.6**
Brazil	1.9	China	7.2
China	0.9	Brazil	1.6
Hong Kong SAR	0.7	Hong Kong SAR	1.6
Korea	0.7	Korea	1.2
India	0.5	India	1.1

Source: Goyal and others (2011).

Domestic Financial Sector Absorption

The absorptive capacity of China's financial system will need to be upgraded to ensure that structural demand by global investors for Chinese assets does not become a destabilizing force. In turn, this will require sustained effort over the medium term to develop and deepen the financial sector to ensure stability and economic resilience.

Despite progress in financial development and allowing some access (within specified quotas) under the QFII and capital outflows under the Qualified Domestic Institutional Investor (QDII) program, China's financial markets remain comparatively less developed and largely closed according to traditional measures of financial depth. However, China fares better using a new proxy for financial depth, measured as an index of total financial claims (both domestic and external) over GDP for individual countries and for the world as a whole (Table 6.1). The index shows that advanced economies (United States, euro area, Japan, and United Kingdom) contribute most to "global financial depth," followed closely by China (Goyal and others, 2011). However, this measure only captures total financial stocks as one proxy for depth and needs to be augmented with additional information on capital account openness and international tradability. On this front, China's capital account remains largely closed.

IMPACT ON FINANCIAL STABILITY

How might capital flows, increasing capital mobility, and renminbi internationalization affect the prospects for financial stability in China? Some lessons can be learned from the experiences of other emerging economies over the last 30 years. In many cases, large net capital flows have had broad effects, affecting bank lending, corporate leverage through bond market issuance, asset prices, and real estate markets. There are some key sources of financial instability that could be identified, and each of these can interact with capital flows. These include disturbances arising from the linkages between the financial sector and macro economy and structural weaknesses in the financial sector.

Broad Risks

The direct macroeconomic impact of capital flows does not yet appear to be a major financial stability risk for China. International experience has shown that large capital inflows can fuel domestic demand, real exchange rate appreciation, current account deficits, and a sharp expansion in bank credit (e.g., Mexico in 1994 and Thailand in 1997). When the perceived risk-return profile of exposure to these countries then unexpectedly worsens, inflows can reverse sharply, swamping offsetting changes in private and government savings. In turn, this can lead to large adverse changes in financial conditions—including vanishing liquidity, collapsing asset prices, and shrinking credit—that inflict significant real economic damage.

These direct linkages between capital flows and the macro economy in China are much weaker than they were in other notable cases, including Southeast Asia in the late 1990s. In particular, consumption (and consumer credit) has not taken off and reached excessively high levels and the current account remains in surplus. The impact of capital inflows on monetary aggregates has been relatively modest compared to the effect of very large current account surpluses. In fact, China faces the challenge of reorienting the economy toward domestic consumption to rebalance the drivers of economic growth away from relying on external demand for its exports.

Perhaps the more critical channel of risk in China lies in the remaining structural weaknesses of the broader macroeconomic framework and the institutional and regulatory framework of financial sector oversight. China has made significant progress in developing and strengthening its financial sector, but remaining structural weaknesses mean that capital flows could contribute to the buildup of excessive risks. One weakness is the broader monetary framework and reliance on administered interest rates (notably ceilings on deposit rates) to manage liquidity, along with the limited investment opportunities available to market participants.

These features of the macro framework, interacting with increased capital flows, may lead to capital seeking higher returns in specific and possibly unproductive sectors of the economy, leading to large price distortions and volatility in these areas (e.g., the real estate market). Shortcomings in some of China's asset markets may also impede price discovery and risk management, and lead to excessive price volatility. For example, the equity market lacks liquidity and is extremely volatile, due in part to the lack of transparency in terms of regulation and corporate governance. Capital flows can amplify this volatility and increase the impact of mispriced risks.

Capital Flows and Risks for China's Banks

Notwithstanding these shortcomings, Chinese banks, which dominate the financial system, appear fairly well insulated against the effects of capital flows. This reflects a number of factors. First, strict capital controls have helped keep capital flow volumes modest relative to the size of the banking sector. Net flows are rising but remain dwarfed by the size of banking system assets and deposits. Other factors have been more important than capital flows in contributing to the growth in bank deposits and liquidity, notably large current account surpluses and precautionary saving by households with few investment alternatives.

Second, foreign exchange risks are concentrated at the central bank, rather than at commercial banks. China is exposed to a large currency mismatch on its balance sheet as a result of its current account surplus, its monetary policy and exchange rate regime, and the renminbi's fledgling status as an international currency. However, strict quantitative controls on offshore foreign currency borrowing by commercial banks ensure that this mismatch is concentrated on the balance sheet of the PBC.

Linkages across Exchange Rate Markets

What risks could stem from the flourishing offshore market for renminbi? Given heavy management of the onshore spot market and capital controls, linkages between onshore and offshore exchange rates should be limited. However, both rates have tracked each other quite closely, with the exception of some divergence in late 2010 and again in late 2011, suggesting some de facto links. For example, market participants offshore might extract policy signals from onshore markets, though onshore market participants might believe that price developments offshore better reflect global market conditions due to closer global financial integration.

Empirical results using a bivariate generalized autoregressive conditional heteroskedasticity (GARCH) model to capture mean and volatility spillovers across onshore and offshore markets suggest that cross-market spillovers exist (Maziad and Kang, 2012). In particular, the analysis shows that (1) developments in the offshore spot market could influence the onshore spot market in terms of both level and volatility during a period of offshore market dislocation, and (2) the onshore market drives price movement offshore under normal market conditions, while developments in the offshore market could still affect the volatility of price movement in the onshore market. In contrast to the pattern of influence in the spot markets, the offshore forward market moves ahead of the onshore forward market. In particular, as shown in more detail in Maziad and Kang (2012), today's offshore forward rates have a predictive impact on tomorrow's onshore forward rates, but not vice versa, and the offshore forward market also has an influence on the onshore forward market through the channel of volatility spillover.

There is also evidence that the offshore market could influence onshore markets through volatility channels. Given that volatility in the offshore market has been higher than that in the onshore market,[3] these findings imply that offshore market developments should be monitored carefully, as they could affect exchange rate volatility on the mainland. In addition, during a period of offshore market dislocation, developments in the offshore market could influence the onshore exchange rate in terms of level and volatility. This is perhaps because market participants believe that price developments offshore more adequately reflect global market conditions.

Linkages with Asset Markets

Perhaps the most active transmission channel from capital flows to financial conditions is through domestic asset markets. For many investors, the potential for large returns provided by domestic Chinese real estate and equity markets may provide a sufficiently large incentive to evade capital controls. In recent years, domestic equity markets in China have been highly volatile and have experienced sustained periods of rising prices. Real estate prices have been less volatile, but prices have risen significantly since 2005. In both cases, the returns to investors during price upswings have been significant, providing strong incentives for those investors that extrapolate investment returns from the past and are considering evading capital controls to gain exposure to China.

Real estate exposures of Chinese banks have expanded rapidly at the same time that net speculative inflows have increased. The real estate market accounted for just under one-fifth of total domestic loans at the end of the first quarter of 2010. There are a number of channels through which real estate can affect commercial banks in China. For example, increases in the price of real estate may increase both the value of bank capital (to the extent that banks own real estate) and the value of real estate collateral, leading to a decline in the perceived risks of property-related lending. Higher prices can also lead to higher volumes of activity, both in the resale market and in new developments, which in China are largely bank financed. Both effects would increase the exposure of bank balance sheets to the real estate sector, all else being equal. The real estate market could also affect China's banks more indirectly. For example, a real estate price correction could trigger a negative spillover to local government financing vehicles, as banks adjust down land collateral valuations, recall loans, or halt debt rollovers.

Capital flows can contribute to overshooting real estate prices and, in the event of a sharp reversal in flows, expose financial sector vulnerabilities that had built up during the upswing. There are two features of capital flows that could contribute to excessive price moves in domestic real estate markets. First, capital flows are driven in part by external factors, including global interest rates, exchange rates, and risk appetite. This can cause flows to be volatile and less sensitive to local real estate market conditions, such as affordability, and often more volatile than domestic sources of real estate demand. It can also lead to periods

---

[3]In 2011, Standard Chartered Bank reported that volatility of offshore spot exchange rates was higher than that of the onshore spot rate by 40 to 50 percent (based on daily data).

of sharp reversals in the direction of speculative flows. Second, capital flows are often associated with financial cycles triggered by waves of optimism underpinned by favorable developments in the real side of the economy. This optimism contributes to the underestimation of risk and the overextension of credit. The real estate market plays a central role in such cycles because increases in real estate prices tend to boost banks' willingness and capacity to lend. This was a notable feature of the Asian financial crisis in the 1990s.

Capital flows could also influence domestic equity market prices. Capital flows, in part, are driven by global financial conditions. Global liquidity conditions could affect equity market returns in those emerging economies that receive capital inflows, including China. The effects of global liquidity on equity returns and reserve accumulation are particularly strong for economies with fixed exchange rate regimes, and the volatility of liquidity is also transmitted to flow-receiving economies.

The equity market is a relatively accessible investment for cross-border investors, including speculators with large volumes to invest. Competition among brokerages has kept commissions very low and provided retail investors with easy access to the equity market. There is evidence that retail equity brokerage accounts are used by nonretail participants to gain easy access to the market and avoid the strict oversight of institutional investors, a route to the market that can also facilitate the investment of capital inflows. Gray market money managers, corporates, and rich individuals, along with average individual retail investors, may all play some role in diverting net inflows into equities.

The direct linkages between the equity market and the rest of the financial sector are weaker than for the real estate market. This has insulated banks and other financial institutions from the effects of equity market volatility. In particular, banks have been prohibited from participating in the equity market, either as investors, asset managers, or brokers. Weak equity-bond return correlations have also insulated the valuation of bonds on bank balance sheets from the effects of equity price declines. Finally, equity markets also play a minor role in the intermediation of capital. This limits the feedback from the equity market through the real economy and back to the financial sector (e.g., through the impact of the cost of equity on capital expenditures and economic growth).

The most likely linkage between capital flows, equity markets, and the rest of the financial sector is through wealth effects, which could influence the supply-demand balance for real estate or encourage increased demand for credit. Equity markets can provide a signaling function, given the timely way they respond to macroeconomic news and their forward-looking perspective, which can also increase linkages across the financial sector. However, Chinese markets have a very low signal-to-noise ratio, which may be partly explained by the markets' structural weaknesses. Looking ahead, the linkages between equity markets and banks may strengthen in the future if banks are permitted to diversify away from lending and to participate in equity markets, either directly or indirectly.

The effects of capital flows on China's equity and real estate markets may involve quite complicated dynamics, in part due to the interrelations between these markets. Very little is known about the relationships between capital flows and domestic asset markets, in part because these linkages have been evolving as China's macroeconomic policy regime and financial system develops, new policies are introduced, and the private sector broadens the exposures of its wealth portfolio. Capital control evasion also means that many of these capital flows are not recorded in official data and are therefore difficult to track and follow through the financial system. Any empirical analysis should be sufficiently flexible to allow for complicated dynamics and linkages.

Empirical analysis based on vector autoregressions (VARs) indicates that capital flows can help predict equity and real estate prices.[4] Granger causality tests based on VAR models provide strong evidence that current and past net capital flows affect future equity and real estate prices. There is also evidence that Granger causality runs in the opposite direction; in particular, past changes in equity and real estate prices can help to predict future capital flows, which suggests that capital can be "pulled" by domestic market developments as well as "pushed" by global financial conditions.

How large an effect can capital flows have on asset markets? For equities, the effects are modest and dissipate quickly, but a larger impact is felt by the real estate market. The effects of capital flows were quantified by tracing out the estimated dynamic response to a standard deviation shock to net capital flows, which accounted for about US$15 billion. The effects of a change in exchange rate expectations were computed in a similar way, with a standard deviation shock representing a change of about 1 percentage point. The results described below, as shown in Figure 6.3, are based on a VAR model including real estate prices estimated over the 2005–10 period.[5] The results show that:

- *The impact of a shock to net capital flows is either modest or short-lived (real estate prices) or insignificant (equity prices).* Shocks to flows also tend to dissipate quickly, with the cumulative change in flows close to the initial shock.

- *Exchange rate expectations have large and statistically significant effects on both capital flows and asset markets.* For example, a 1 percentage point increase in anticipated renminbi appreciation leads to an additional capital inflow of over US$20 billion, an increase in equity prices that peaks at 7 percent (but dissipates thereafter), and a near 1 percent sustained increase in real estate prices. This effect can work in reverse, with expectations for a weaker renminbi leading to lower net inflows and declining asset prices.

---

[4]A natural way to investigate the possibly complicated dynamics between capital flows and assets markets is by using VARs. In this framework, capital flows, asset market returns, and the expected appreciation of the renminbi implied by nondeliverable forwards—found to be associated with flows—are taken to be endogenous variables. In other words, each of these variables is assumed to be affected by changes in the other variables.

[5]The results for a model excluding real estate prices and estimated over a longer sample period (1997–2010) are qualitatively similar.

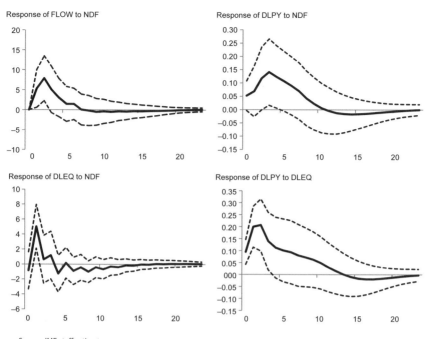

Source: IMF staff estimates.
Note: Variables included are the log level of capital flows (FLOW), the change in the 12-month log nondeliverable forward-spot exchange rate spread (NDF), the change in the log equity price (DLEQ), and the change in the log property price (DLPY). Dotted lines represent 95 percent confidence intervals.

Figure 6.3 Impulse Responses from Vector Autoregressions, 2005–10
(In percent)

- *Linkages between markets could amplify the effects of capital flows.* A standard deviation 8 percent shock to equity prices leads to an increase in real estate prices that is sustained and significant, with a cumulative impact of 1.25 percent.

Overall, the results indicate that capital flows to and from China affect domestic asset prices, but the dynamics are complex and work through a number of channels. In particular, the impact of capital flows is higher and significant when driven by exchange rate expectations. A change in market perceptions regarding the path of the renminbi has large and significant effects on capital flows, and this in turn feeds through to asset prices. In contrast, direct shocks to capital flows have more modest and generally insignificant effects on asset prices. This suggests that anticipated currency gains, underpinned by past perceptions of a "one-way bet," have provided important incentives even though asset price volatility may be significantly higher than exchange rate volatility (i.e., equity market losses could easily wipe out currency gains).

In addition, linkages between asset markets, particularly from domestic equities to real estate, may be key transmission channels for capital flows. Although the impact of capital flows on equities is modest and dissipates quickly, rising equity prices lead to relatively persistent increases in real estate prices. This may reflect wealth effects, with higher equity prices bolstering balance sheets and encouraging or allowing potential real estate investors to increase real estate–related borrowing. It may also be due to switching between markets. If capital flows initially go into equity markets, due in part to their higher liquidity, then this may have knock-on and long-lasting effects on real estate prices. Until now, effects on financial stability appear to be limited, but they are likely to grow with financial openness.

THE ROAD AHEAD

Sequencing the Reform Process

As international experience suggests, there is no "one-size-fits-all" approach to sequencing financial sector liberalization (Johnston and Sundararajan, 1999). This consideration is particularly important given the unique characteristics of China's financial system. Reforms should be tailored to each country's unique circumstances and the prevailing macroeconomic and financial conditions. However, some broad principles of international best practice can be identified. A key overarching precondition throughout the process of change is the presence of adequate legal, regulatory, and supervisory frameworks to monitor financial institutions and manage risks.

In China, the appropriate pace and ordering of reforms will involve balancing trade-offs. For example, greater exchange rate flexibility would allow for more effective handling of monetary policy and lessen the steady injection of liquidity into the system from the balance of payments surplus. However, such reform could also weaken corporate profitability, worsen the quality of bank credit, and increase foreign exchange risk on financial and corporate sector balance sheets. Similarly, the regime of capital controls allows liquidity to be absorbed and interest rate reform to be phased in, while allowing for the management of the pace of inflows that may be attracted by rising nominal interest rates. However, a phased opening up of the capital account should not proceed ahead of developing domestic capital markets and strengthening their regulatory foundations.

In this context, a broad sequencing for reforms can be surmised by adapting international experience to China's specific circumstances. This suggests the need to absorb liquidity from the financial system, adjust relative prices, and increase reliance on indirect monetary tools before interest rates are liberalized and quantitative restrictions are lifted. Initially the banking system is likely to continue to play a dominant role, but over time the conditions should fall into place for the rest of the financial sector to take a larger share of the intermediation function. Advancing the reform agenda, particularly financial deepening and the development of robust macroeconomic and regulatory frameworks, would provide the necessary preconditions for full capital account liberalization.

Indeed, capital account opening should be sequenced after the bulk of financial sector reform has been achieved. Although some countries have successfully opened the capital account before financial sector reform, the current scale of global capital flows and the increasing sophistication and interconnectedness of global financial markets imply much larger risks for this strategy now than in past decades. Capital account reform should proceed in stages, based on the relative stability and maturity of flows. The early stages of capital account liberalization should focus on stable long-term sources of financing such as direct investment inflows. The intermediate stage should liberalize longer-term portfolio flows, with full liberalization—including short-term flows—achieved when the bulk of financial sector reform has been implemented.

Unique Risks from Further Liberalization of the Renminbi[6]

An international currency requires a robust financial system and an open capital account. As international experience suggests, failing to supply internationally traded stores of value to the rest of the world limits the scope for currency internationalization. Rapid developments in the offshore market reflect the prospects for the Chinese currency as a global currency and the strong cross-border linkages that would accompany the process, particularly the potential for increased capital inflows. Promoting cross-border use of the renminbi poses additional risks to financial stability, especially at a time of transformation in China's financial system. Potential risks could be broadly divided into two types: market development risks and financial stability risks.

- *Market development risks:* Part of investors' interest in an offshore renminbi has been driven by expectation of renminbi appreciation. Thus, in the absence of a sufficient supply of renminbi-denominated assets, there is a risk that market development may lose momentum or stagnate as appreciation expectations are met or become less one-sided. In late 2011, market expectations of currency appreciations moderated in light of lower growth projections and generalized risk aversion due to the debt crisis in Europe, resulting in lower demand and deleveraging of CNH-denominated investments, while the accumulation of renminbi deposits in Hong Kong decelerated and the stock actually shrank for the first time in October 2011. To keep the momentum for market development beyond appreciation expectations, the channels to invest renminbi funds productively onshore would have to be expanded. Similarly, two-way currency movements would foster the development of a well-functioning offshore renminbi bond market and facilitate balanced demand for the currency, both for funding and investing. A major deterrent for non-Chinese firms to issue CNH-denominated bonds despite low yields is the risk of currency appreciation. If issuers perceived a two-way currency movement, it would encourage non-Chinese firms to take on renminbi-denominated liabilities, and thus contribute to expanding the stock of renminbi-denominated assets offshore. Recent measures to allow renminbi-

---

[6]This section is based on Maziad and Kang (2012).

denominated inward FDI and the launch of the mini-QFII are steps in this direction.

• *Stability risk:* Generally speaking, financial stability risks due to offshore market development would be limited, given the size of the offshore market of about 10 percent of onshore base money, and the effectiveness of controls on the flow of capital onshore. However, going forward the process of renminbi internationalization and the strong demand for renminbi assets would expand the channels of feedback and arbitrage across onshore and offshore markets. Particularly, as mainland businesses gain greater access to credit through offshore subsidiaries of mainland banks or issue renminbi bonds offshore, some of the effectiveness of the credit rationing onshore could be undermined. In the long run, this could lead to disintermediation of large Chinese firms from the banking system onshore as they forge ties with banks offshore or borrow directly in the offshore bond market. Eventually, as the offshore market grows, larger cross-border flows could undermine the effectiveness of credit controls and administered interest rates onshore as offshore banks extend credit directly to firms onshore. This could potentially lead to some loss of monetary control due to access to credit offshore at unregulated interest rates, and to exchange rate pressure on the renminbi offshore that would lead to currency appreciation. Bearing these potential risks in mind, greater strides toward currency internationalization should be phased in as part of the process of financial sector reform and gradual capital account liberalization.

CONCLUSIONS

The paths toward greater capital account openness and internationalization of the renminbi share many similarities. At the broadest level, both involve increasing integration into the global financial system, which can bring rewards but also import risks, particularly from increased international use of the currency and associated volatile capital flows. From a financial stability perspective, both require careful sequencing to ensure that China's domestic financial stability is not compromised. China has already shown that a dual strategy of increasing international use of its currency, while at the same time gradually opening up the financial system to greater capital flows, can succeed. One component of increased openness need not come before the other; indeed, in many cases they must proceed simultaneously. In part, success so far reflects the steady application of the important principle that domestic financial sector reforms—including deepening and liberalizing domestic financial markets, enhancing regulation and supervision, and bolstering legal frameworks—are prerequisites for large-scale international liberalization. This principle should continue to guide the reform process in China, particularly as the largest challenges, including adapting the monetary and exchange rate policy framework to increased global integration, remain to be fully addressed.

REFERENCES

Goyal, R., C. Marsh, N. Raman, S. Wang, and S. Ahmed, 2011, "Financial Deepening and International Monetary Stability," IMF Staff Discussion Note No. 11/16 (Washington: International Monetary Fund).

International Monetary Fund (IMF), 2004, "Institutional Investors in Emerging Markets," *Global Financial Stability Report*, April (Washington: International Monetary Fund).

———, 2011, "Long-Term Investors and Their Asset Allocation: Where Are They Now?" *Global Financial Stability Report*, September (Washington: International Monetary Fund).

Johnston, R. Barry, and Vasudevan Sundararajan, 1999, "Managing Financial Sector Liberalization: An Overview," in *Sequencing Financial Sector Reforms: Country Experiences and Issues,* ed. by B. Johnston and V. Sundararajan (Washington: International Monetary Fund).

Kenan, Peter B., 2009, *Currency Internationalization—An Overview* (Princeton, New Jersey: Princeton University).

Maziad, Samar, and Joong Shik Kang, 2012, "RMB Internationalization: Onshore/Offshore Links," IMF Working Paper 12/133 (Washington: International Monetary Fund).

Maziad, Samar, Pascal Farahmand, Shengzu Wang, Stephanie Segal, and Faisal Ahmed, 2011, "Internationalization of Emerging Market Currencies: A Balance Between Risks and Rewards," IMF Staff Discussion Note No. 11/17 (Washington: International Monetary Fund).

PART III

Strengthening Financial System Oversight

CHAPTER 7

Structure of the Banking Sector and Implications for Financial Stability

SILVIA IORGOVA AND YINQIU LU

The turnaround of the Chinese banking system has been impressive. Supported by capital injections and key policy reforms—including improved prudential standards and gradual financial liberalization—the banking system is moving toward better disclosure, gradually improved corporate governance, and increased reliance on market mechanisms.

To analyze China's potential financial stability risks, it is pivotal to distill the key structural factors and distortions that define the Chinese banking system. Structurally, there are several features that, taken together, set China apart from financial systems in other countries: (1) the preeminence of large domestic commercial banks in domestic financial intermediation; (2) sizable structural liquidity in view of high domestic savings due to limited investment alternatives; (3) low remuneration of deposits associated with remaining interest rate controls; (4) the dominant role of the state both in terms of bank ownership and its influence on the credit allocation process, reflected in the importance of quantitative lending targets for monetary policy; (5) regulatory emphasis on maintaining low nonperforming loan (NPL) ratios; and (6) the nontrivial role of the shadow banking sector.

This chapter outlines these structural traits and discusses their relevance for China's financial stability. In particular, the chapter argues that it is vital to curb the adverse structural incentives in the system to avert the potentially undesirable accumulation of credit risks and to address internal macroeconomic imbalances. In particular, China needs to address capital allocation distortions to provide for more balanced economic growth. More broadly, policies should seek to reduce moral hazard and improve the credit risk management and corporate governance of banks. For example, emphasis on lending to state-owned enterprises (SOEs) and meeting explicit NPL targets lowers the incentives of banks to adopt better risk management practices and curbs the extension of credit to intrinsically riskier borrowers, such as small and medium-sized enterprises (SMEs). Moreover, to curb the incentive of excessively using the banking system for fiscal policy purposes—such as for funding local infrastructure projects—future reforms at the local level should seek to reduce fiscal revenue-expenditure mismatches faced by local governments. The chapter elaborates on the link between such structural factors and the need for local governments to indirectly secure funding via the domestic banking system, and also establishes a link between structural traits and China's financial stability. It makes the point that such reforms are a complex undertaking that go beyond the financial sector.

KEY STRUCTURAL CHARACTERISTICS OF THE CHINESE BANKING SYSTEM

Dominance of Large Banks in Domestic Funding

Banks plays a dominant role in the Chinese financial system. Credit in China is primarily channeled through banks, with domestic equity and bond markets playing a relatively small role in the intermediation of financial capital. The role of bank finance in economic growth is considerably more preeminent than in other G20 countries, with bank loans accounting for 67 percent of domestic funding at end-2011 (Figure 7.1). Banking system assets grew to RMB 114 trillion at end-2011, equivalent to 240 percent of GDP.

Banking sector activity is still dominated by large commercial banks (LCBs) and joint-stock commercial banks (JSCBs); however, the degree of concentration has been declining. Collectively, the five LCBs and the 12 JSCBs accounted for 65 percent of the broader banking system assets at end-2011

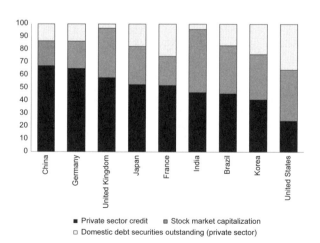

Sources: Bank for International Settlements; Bloomberg; IMF, International Financial Statistics; and IMF staff calculations.

Figure 7.1   Size of Selected Countries' Financial Systems, end-2011
(In percent of total)

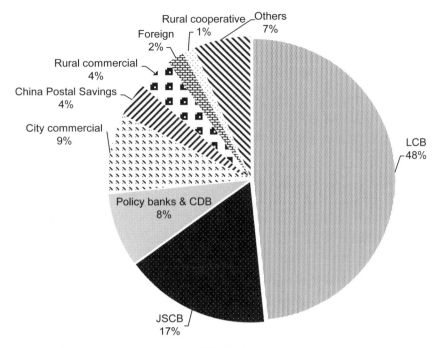

Figure 7.2 Banking System Assets by Type of Bank, end-2011
(In percent of total)

Sources: China Banking Regulatory Commission; and IMF staff calculations.
Note: CDB = China Development Bank; JSCB = joint-stock commercial banks; LCB = large commercial banks.

(Figure 7.2).[1] Unlike other types of banks (with the exception of certain city commercial banks), LCBs and JSCBs are permitted to operate on a broader (national) scale, with deposit-taking and lending operations spanning urban and rural areas. Their market power remains considerable, despite a marginal decline in recent years. A measure of market concentration—the Herfindahl-Hirschman index (HHI)[2]—reveals that banking sector concentration, both on the lending and deposit sides, has declined over time, from 0.15 at end-2005 to 0.11 at end-2011 for lending and from 0.12 to 0.09 for deposits.

---

[1]The five LCBs are the Industrial and Commercial Bank of China (ICBC), Bank of China (BOC), Agricultural Bank of China (ABC), China Construction Bank (CCB), and Bank of Communications (BComm). The 12 joint-stock commercial banks are China CITIC Bank, China Everbright Bank, Hua Xia Bank, Guangdong Development Bank, Shenzhen Development Bank, China Merchants Bank, Shanghai Pudong Bank, Industrial Bank, China Minsheng Bank, Evergrowing Bank, Zhe Shang Bank, and Bo Hai Bank.
[2]The HHI ranges between 0 and 1, and is estimated as the sum of the squares of banks' market shares in the banking system's total assets.

High Structural Liquidity and Interest Rate Controls

Bank funding in China relies heavily on deposits due to high domestic saving rates and limited investment alternatives. Deposits account for over 80 percent of system-wide liabilities, and 172 percent of GDP, among the highest levels compared to selected G20 countries (Figure 7.3). The absence of well-developed domestic capital markets results in a high retention of savings in the banking sector. Total deposits in the banking system have been growing rapidly, increasing by an average of 17 percent annually since end-1999. As of end-2011, total deposits stood at RMB 80.9 trillion, of which 49 percent was in the form of household deposits.

The low remuneration of domestic deposits has been a key by-product of financial repression in the Chinese banking system. Remaining interest rate controls account for periodic swings of real deposit rates in China to negative levels during some periods (Figure 7.4). Structurally, over the long term, real deposit rates have, on average, been lower than in many other countries. The very low and at times negative real rates have deprived savers of a reasonable rate of return on deposits. In conjunction with the very high savings rates in the domestic banking system, the low interest rates paid on domestic deposits have provided an implicit subsidization of domestic corporate funding.

The low real interest rates have also accounted for periodic fluctuations in the composition of bank deposits in recent years. The evolution of bank deposits has followed closely the upswings and downswings in the domestic equity markets, reflecting domestic depositors' search for higher yields. From the viewpoint of households' portfolio allocation, the high opportunity cost of holding savings

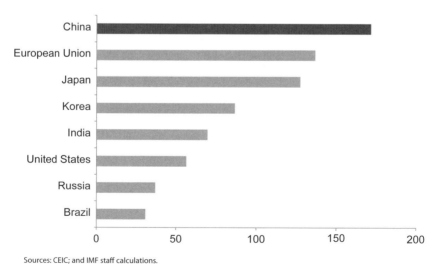

Sources: CEIC; and IMF staff calculations.

Figure 7.3   Select Banking Systems' Aggregate Deposits, end-2011
(In percent)

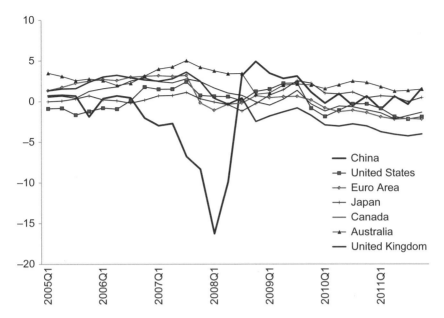

Sources: Bloomberg; IMF, International Financial Statistics; and IMF staff calculations.

Figure 7.4 Real Deposit Rates in Select G20 Countries
(In percent of GDP)

and time deposits in a low real interest rate environment induces depositors to shift away from longer-term deposits to more liquid demand deposits, and subsequently invest these into the equity market. For example, the upswing in the equity markets in January 2010 was associated with a sharp acceleration in the reallocation of household savings deposits into demand deposits, with the latter increasing at 45 percent on an annual basis at their peak (Figure 7.5).[3] The inverse relationship between the size of savings deposits and equity market returns—shown to be statistically significant in earlier studies—has been linked, at least in part, to the structurally low—and even negative—real savings deposit rates (Figure 7.6).[4]

Low deposit remuneration and limited investment opportunities have also accounted for a high share of household savings allocated to the real estate market. Such transfers draw down household deposits and have a strong distributional effect on the domestic economy, as they amount to a wealth transfer from

---

[3]Savings deposits are open-term deposits that do not incur early withdrawal penalties. Generally, there is no cost for depositors to shift away from savings deposits because, unlike time certificates of deposit (CDs), they do not have predetermined maturities and do not incur penalties for premature withdrawals.

[4]See Burdekin and Redfern (2009) for the relationship between savings deposits and equity market returns in China.

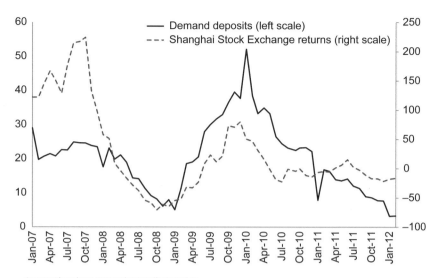

Sources: Bloomberg; CEIC; and IMF staff calculations.

Figure 7.5   Demand Deposits and Returns on the Shanghai Stock Exchange
(In percent, year-on-year growth)

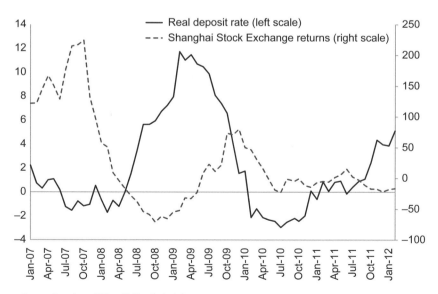

Sources: Bloomberg; CEIC; and IMF staff calculations.

Figure 7.6   Household Real Deposit Rate and Returns on the Shanghai Stock Exchange
(In percent, year-on-year growth)

households to large SOEs and the government. The transfer is effectuated by household savings withdrawals to make down payments on house purchases, a process that ultimately benefits the government and enterprises as the principal players in the real estate market.[5] The limited investment opportunities for domestic households—other than deposits and, to an extent, the equity market—increase the attractiveness of real estate investments and augment the scale of such transfers.

Banks' real estate exposures expanded particularly rapidly during the 2009 government-led stimulus.[6] The real estate market turned into an important recipient of domestic credit, accounting for about 19.5 percent of total domestic loans by end-2011. Direct bank exposures to the sector took two principal forms: mortgage loans and loans to real estate developers, with the former accounting for RMB 7.1 trillion, or 13 percent of total domestic loans as of end-2011, and the latter for RMB 3.5 trillion, or slightly more than 6 percent of the total.

In addition, the remaining interest rate controls and limited risk pricing make bank profitability dependent not only on the margin but on lending volumes. The government effectively ensures a minimum interest margin by administratively setting a deposit rate cap and a lending rate floor. Such a guarantee on the margin is meant to ensure the long-term stability of banks' profit margins. In an environment in which Chinese banks do not rely fully on risk-pricing mechanisms, banks' margins closely mimic the guaranteed margins. Thus, if either margins or lending volumes contract, the two need to move in opposite directions to avert a negative impact on banks' profitability. However, given that lending volumes are determined by credit quotas, the government effectively has an impact both on the margin and on loan quantities (Box 7.1). For example, Chinese banks' sizable stimulus-led credit growth in effect partially offset the compression in the net interest margins. Moreover, the potential negative effect on the profitability of Chinese banks is exacerbated by their strong dependence on interest income and limited earnings diversification.

---

[5]Higher household savings withdrawals translate into higher government and corporate savings via land and housing sales. In China, all land is owned by the state, with a significant portion of local government revenues derived from the sale of land usage rights. Corporates, particularly many large, centrally owned SOEs, include real estate developers with significant power in bidding up the price of land.

[6]The housing sector reform has been a catalyst for the sizable expansion of mortgage lending in recent years. The reform has had a tangible impact on banks' housing-related lending in two ways. The first impact is through the rapid evolution of the housing market following the monetization of housing allocation set forth by the Notification of the State Council on Further Deepening of the Urban Housing System and Accelerating Housing Construction, introduced in 1998. By explicitly prohibiting employers from direct provision of housing to employees, the Chinese authorities effectively opened up the housing market to private developers and indirectly to bank-based financing. The second impact has been through introduction of a series of rules and regulations on mortgage lending, such as management measures on individual housing loans (1998), which set base lending standards such as loan-to-value ratios and mandatory income verification.

The Predominant Role of the Government

The government has a strong influence on banks' credit allocation and lending patterns. The government—primarily via the Central Huijin and the Ministry of Finance—continues to be the largest direct shareholder of the five LCBs and the three policy banks, and has sizable indirect shares in JSCBs via its SOEs (Table 7.1). Although since 2005 the LCBs and a number of JSCBs and smaller banks have had successful initial public offerings (IPOs), as of end-2011 the central government continued to hold a majority stake in the top four LCBs, with private sector and strategic investor ownership still relatively limited.

The government also has a bearing on banks' management decisions. As the principal shareholder of domestic banks, the government has the right to appoint bank directors and senior management.[7] While LCB and JSCB listings on exchanges have improved corporate governance and led to an increasing share of independent directors on banks' boards, there is still a prevalent practice for the government to nominate directors and senior managers and set up remuneration schedules.

The use of window guidance and quantitative lending targets continues to influence the commercial nature of banks' credit policies. While the 1993 Law on Commercial Banks established LCBs as commercial entities with full responsibility for their own profits and losses, their credit allocation decisions are still influenced by policy intervention (Brehm, 2008). Window guidance—a form of voluntary moral suasion to exert pressure on banks to adhere to official guidelines—is a key component of credit transmission in China and has been used as a tool to limit or expand loans to parts of the system. While the PBC defines and carries out monetary policies, the China Banking Regulatory Commission (CBRC) has been intermittently involved in window guidance policies. For example, the CBRC's 2009 annual report provides explicit guidance for domestic banks on priority sectors that they are expected to target, and on their broader role in domestic economic development.[8] Banks have also been required to set up units specializing in small enterprise lending (CBRC, 2010).

The use of quantitative lending targets—including mandated rapid domestic credit growth to counteract macroeconomic shocks—poses a risk of credit quality deterioration. Rapid credit expansion, ceteris paribus, is linked to a decline

---

[7]Key personnel appointments are normally carried out by the Organization Department of the Communist Party of China Central Committee.

[8]The annual report states that "[i]n the meantime, the CBRC required banking institutions to actively optimize their credit portfolio and allocation, so as to give bank credit a full play in the transformation and restructuring of the national economy. Specifically, banking institutions were urged to increase agricultural and SME loans, develop green credit, support energy-saving enterprises and projects, provide consumer credit for purchasing first homes, household appliances, automobiles and agricultural equipment, and facilitate key projects in line with national industrial policies. Overall, the banking industry played a pivotal role in underpinning economic recovery and restructuring in 2009" (CBRC, 2010, p. 8).

Box 7.1. The Credit Channel in China

Banks are the key source of credit transmission in the Chinese economy. Their predominant role is defined by their considerable size compared to recently established nonbank institutions.

Quantitative credit targeting in China is closely related to domestic monetary policy. To manage credit transmission, the People's Bank of China (PBC) relies on quantitative tools, including (1) administrative aggregate credit growth targets (both aggregate and for individual banks); (2) preferential credit to underdeveloped geographical areas or industries; and (3) restrictions on excess credit flows to specific industries (Figure 7.1.1). The PBC also makes use of indirect instruments, such as required reserves, which transmit changes in the monetary base via required reserves to bank deposits, and subsequently to the domestic loan supply. However, the PBC does rely heavily on quantitative mechanisms when it wants to reinforce short-term policy outcomes. The response to the global financial crisis is a good example: while both deposit and interest rates were cut significantly and required reserve ratios declined as well, the PBC relied on the cancellation of the credit quotas to support a considerable expansionary policy.

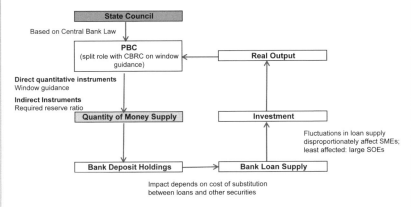

Source: IMF staff.
Note: Open-market operations are mainly used to withdraw liquidity from the financial system and maintain the stability of the renminbi. Open-market operations affect the credit channel via banks' purchases of central bank bills. The PBC issues these bills when foreign exchange pressures force it to excessively sterilize. Some banks are subjected to directional issuance. CBRC = China Banking Regulatory Commission; SMEs = small and medium-sized enterprises; SOEs = state-owned enterprises.

Figure 7.1.1   Credit Channel in China

Effective transmission of these monetary policy signals hinges on the inability of banks to easily substitute between loans and other types of securities. Such substitution, if possible, would thwart targeting of domestic loan levels and would reduce the overall effectiveness of the credit transmission mechanism. In this sense, a potential expansion of Chinese banks' domestic capital market activities may reduce the effectiveness of the current credit transmission framework. Lastly, fluctuations in the bank loan supply affect the level of domestic investment, with smaller borrowers such as small and medium-sized enterprises being affected most significantly.

While the importance of the interest rate channel in China is slowly increasing, interest rates remain a limited tool for credit policy transmission. They hold limited informational content, given that the lack of sufficient investment options and the relatively high propensity to save make domestic savers relatively insensitive to interest rate changes.

TABLE 7.1

Ownership of Large Commercial Banks, end-2011
(In percent of total)

	Huijin	Ministry of Finance	Total
Industrial & Commercial Bank of China	35.4	35.3	70.7
Bank of China	67.6	0.0	67.6
Agricultural Bank of China	40.0	39.2	79.2
China Construction Bank	57.1	0.0	57.1
Bank of Communications	0.0	26.5	26.5

Sources: Company reports.

in marginal returns. The evolution of NPLs and bank capitalization levels after periods of rapid credit growth points to an inverse relationship between such growth and the quality of banks' assets. Quantitative lending guidance—which is still used in China—limits the incentives of banks to apply prudent risk management practices, given that they are expected to meet high lending targets.

Regulatory Limit on Leverage and Emphasis on Low Nonperforming Loan Ratios

Policy limits on NPL accumulation have induced banks to curb credit risks by lending to borrowers supported by explicit or implicit government guarantees, or to delay NPL recognition altogether.[9] The use of explicit NPL targets distorts banks' incentive structure, leading to limited risk-taking, and unintentionally holding back the adoption of better risk management practices, including sound underwriting practices and prompt loan workouts. Instead, the targets encourage banks to shift NPLs off balance sheet and resort to debt rollovers. In principle, an improvement of banks' risk management practices tends to be incompatible with the short-term goal of minimizing NPL accumulation. The development and implementation of risk management procedures, effective internal monitoring systems, and credit officer training are time-consuming and cost-intensive. Moreover, given that profitability measures are estimated on a post-provisioning basis, a potential enhancement of banks' risk management standards could initially have a negative impact on profits to the extent that weak loans are recategorized as NPLs.

The Role of the Shadow Banking System

The shadow banking system in China has grown considerably in recent years, taking on the role of an alternate funding source for domestic entities. Estimates

---

[9]See CBRC's *Guidance for the Governance and Supervision of State Owned Commercial Banks* (GaS-LCB), issued in April 2006, which defines required performance criteria for domestic banks, including a minimum NPL ratio of 5 percent and returns on investment of at least 0.6 percent (Article 6.1).

of the size of the shadow banking system vary considerably, given its highly non-transparent nature and the varied assumptions on the types of activities that it encompasses. The broadest spectrum of these activities entails both formal funding mechanisms and informal funding channels. The formal mechanisms include bank-based, off-balance-sheet lending (mostly via entrusted loans), credit-related and wealth-management-related trust products, lease financing, credit guarantees, microfinance, company-to-company lending, offshore borrowing, private equity funding, and regulated pawnshops.[10] The informal funding channels include underground banks, private peer-to-peer lending, and unregulated pawnshops. Estimates at different points of time in 2011 and based on varied coverage assumptions put shadow banking lending in the range of RMB 8.5 trillion to RMB 15 trillion.[11] This is equivalent to approximately 16 to 29 percent of bank lending, suggesting that shadow banking is nontrivial for domestic funding. Informal lending—the most nontransparent portion of the shadow banking sector, given its unlicensed nature—is estimated to account for about RMB 3 trillion to RMB 4 trillion.[12]

The expansion of the shadow banking system in China is driven by idiosyncratic factors. Unlike other countries—including the United States, where activity in the shadow banking sector is driven by market mechanisms (such as securitization)—the growth of shadow banking in China is largely lending-driven and is defined by certain peculiarities of the country's financial structure, including (1) the constrained availability of bank funding, particularly for SMEs and higher-risk borrowers, given banks' limited risk pricing capacity; (2) insufficient remuneration on bank deposits and limited financial investment opportunities, which induce private lending amid a search for higher yields; (3) government "moral suasion" directed to banks responsible for the high share of bank credit to domestic SOEs, which in the absence of viable investment opportunities is onlent in the informal market; and (4) regulatory arbitrage, with banks prompted to use alternative channels to circumvent loan target limits. Key features of the system are high interest rates and relatively short tenures of extended loans.

Shadow bank activities can exert negative pressures on financial stability through their amplifying effects on procyclicality and the transmission of risks to

---

[10]Entrusted loans are loans extended by a financial institution to a borrower expressly designated by a specific depositor, and subject to depositor-specified terms about the amount, structure, and purpose of the loans. The financial institution thus acts as an agent for the funds entrusted by the depositor. The considerable increase in entrusted loans in China has been related to the strict ban on direct bilateral borrowing and lending between commercial entities under existing regulations.

[11]The RMB 8.5 trillion estimate is by Nomura Securities as of November 2011, while the estimate of RMB 14 trillion to RMB 15 trillion is by Société Générale as of June 2011. UBS puts shadow bank lending at RMB 10 trillion as of October 2011.

[12]Société Générale estimates underground banking to account for RMB 3 trillion to RMB 4 trillion as of June 2011; UBS puts its size at RMB 3 trillion (October 2011); and Credit Suisse estimates it at RMB 4 trillion (September 2011).

the broader financial system. The shadow banking system affects procyclicality by facilitating higher leverage in the economy at a time when conditions in certain sectors, such as real estate, are buoyant. Countercyclical credit limits meant to constrain the level of lending in the economy effectively propel smaller borrowers—such as SMEs and property developers—that have limited access to bank funding to resort to the informal lending market.[13] In addition, banks have an incentive to revert to informal securitizations to improve their capitalization and open up opportunities for further lending. Indeed, in the aftermath of the global financial crisis, banks shifted some credits off balance-sheet and repackaged them as wealth management products, subsequently sold to investors.[14] Credit risks in the shadow banking sector are also linked to those in the mainstream banking sector, for example via SOEs relending bank loans in the informal market to arbitrage the interest spread between the two markets.[15] Moreover, shadow bank lending has implications for monetary stability, including consumer price index and asset inflation. For example, in the post-crisis environment informal lending supported the uptick in property investments, with funding to the real estate sector accounting for up to 60 percent of total lending by some estimates (Credit Suisse, 2011).

Case Study: The Link between Banks and Local Governments

The exposure of Chinese banks to local governments increased markedly as a result of the economic stimulus initiated after the onset of the global financial crisis. Local government financing platforms (LGFPs)—vehicles set up by local governments to support project financing, particularly in infrastructure—played a key role in the implementation of the stimulus. They provided local governments with a platform for accessing off-budget financing to support local (mostly infrastructure) projects and thus to maintain robust economic growth in their localities. LGFPs grew rapidly after relatively limited activity prior to the crisis. It is estimated that local government debt almost doubled from RMB 5.6 trillion at end-2008 to RMB 10.7 trillion at end-2010, with bank lending via LGFPs accounting for RMB 8.5 trillion, or 80 percent of total local government debt at end-2010 (National Audit Office of the People's Republic of China, 2011).

The rapid expansion of bank credit to LGFPs was related to structural features of the Chinese banking system. The preeminent role of commercial banks

---

[13]The tightening of banks' credit limits leaves commercial banks largely targeting large SOEs, given the priority put on such loans. This creates a potential for a freeze of credit to certain borrowers, such as SMEs.

[14]Such transfer of credit risks prompted a temporary regulatory hold on further securitizations and a requirement for banks to reincorporate trust loans on their balance sheet by August 2012.

[15]Credit Suisse (2011) estimates that roughly 60 percent of informal lending is funded by mainstream banks through various channels (including SOE relending), 20 percent by private entrepreneurs, and about 20 percent by individuals.

in domestic financial intermediation and the sizable structural liquidity in the banking system could ensure an uninterrupted supply of bank credit and sufficient volume to meet the sizable borrowing requirements of local governments. The use of quantitative lending targets and the temporary easing of these targets at the time of the economic stimulus unleashed the potential for a considerable expansion of credit to local governments. Moreover, the guarantee of banks' interest margins through interest rate controls made banks depend on expanding lending volumes to boost profitability. Overall, banks have strong incentives to make use of the sizable stimulus-related expansion of LGFP loans to maximize market share and shareholder value.

The considerable growth of LGFP-related lending was also underpinned by peculiarities in the incentive structure of China's local governments and the government fiscal decentralization process. China's system of top-down appointments and fast rotations of local government officials fosters an environment in which local officials primarily pursue short-term targets rather than long-term outcomes. Moreover, emphasis on relative performance in the promotion of local officials is conducive to herding behavior, as similarities in decision-making protect officials from underperforming relative to peers. Thus, their incentive to achieve a rapid promotion induces local government officials to take on relatively high risks even at the cost of potential debt overhang problems. This translated into strong incentives for local governments to support massive infrastructure investments at the time of the post-crisis stimulus. The burden of such investments fell largely on local governments due to the decentralization of government expenditures and the centralization of fiscal revenues under the 1994 fiscal reform. The sizable local government fiscal imbalances, coupled with legal restrictions on local government funding via bank borrowing or bond issuance, induced a massive expansion of LGFPs in order to secure bank funding.

Implicit support from local governments was a critical driver for the rapid development of the LGFPs, given the emphasis by banks on low NPL ratios. Typically, the establishment of LGFPs was supported by initial capital injections from local governments, mostly in the form of land use rights (Figure 7.7). Moreover, implicit government support permitted funding at more favorable terms, as local governments' fiscal revenues and collateral, such as land, acted as an implicit guarantee for the repayment capacity of LGFPs. All in all, LGFPs could leverage on the reputation, fiscal revenues, or guarantees of local governments, with which their incentives are largely aligned. In addition, in some cases—particularly smaller local banks—it is conceivable that local governments may have exerted pressures on banks to expand LGFP lending, given that a good relationship with their local government could permit banks to accrue business benefits.

The overly rapid growth of LGFP borrowing accounted for the accumulation of potentially sizable credit risks and amplified government contingent liabilities. The various potential risks embedded in LGFP-related exposures include the following:

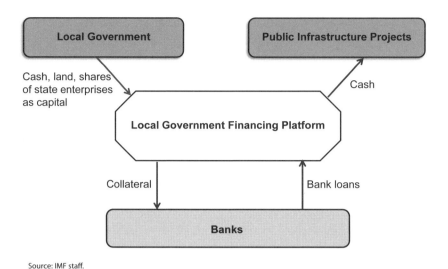

Source: IMF staff.

Figure 7.7 Typical Structure of Local Government Financing Platforms

- Local governments' conflicting incentives as principal agents for national economic growth targets under tight budgetary constraints are conducive to the potential accumulation of credit risks for the banks, which fund them. Local officials are motivated to fund a maximum number of large-scale projects to support sufficient growth in their respective regions. This contributes to a trade-off between the scale of needed funding and the potential for the accumulation of credit risks, given that not all projects could be put to productive use.

- Risks to LGFP-funded projects are linked to a sharper-than-anticipated downward correction in real estate and land prices. A potential correction in the real estate sector and a spillover to LGFPs could test the resilience of the banking system, as banks may face lower land collateral valuations, and may need to recall loans or halt debt rollovers. Given that many LGFP-funded projects are financed via long-term loans disbursed in phases, early-stage long-term projects may face difficulties reaching completion and repaying outstanding debt.

- The incentive structure of Chinese banks may exacerbate such risks in view of (1) previous use of implicit and/or explicit local government guarantees, which may have subdued perceived risks by banks at the time of underwriting; (2) deficiencies in banks' ability to carry out adequate risk pricing and credit underwriting; and (3) limited motivation to recognize potential credit losses in a policy environment that emphasizes maintaining low NPL levels.

KEY POLICY ISSUES

Going forward, it is important to ensure that domestic banks set credit policies based on commercial considerations, independent of government objectives. In this respect, it would be useful to establish clear, nonoverlapping mandates between policy and commercial banks, with development functions fully allocated to policy banks. In addition, decoupling the government's monetary and fiscal objectives from reliance on commercial banks would eliminate undue influence on the decision-making of those banks. In this regard, it would be necessary to increase the use of indirect monetary policy instruments (such as required reserves), curb reliance on quantitative credit targets, and do away with window guidance.

Work toward further liberalization of domestic interest rates should be given a top priority. A shift away from policy-determined interest rates would lead to stronger price competition that would induce banks to price risks more effectively, allowing them to manage funding costs to reflect those risks. Liberalization could lead to the compression of net interest margins on the back of intensified domestic competition. The key to successful liberalization is to ensure that banks are able to absorb higher levels of risks without posing a danger to domestic financial stability. Banks would need to significantly improve their risk management practices to be able to absorb such risks. In fact, the authorities are already moving in this direction, most recently providing banks with some discretion to raise deposit rates above the existing cap.[16]

Further capital market deepening would expand the range of investment opportunities and contain the channeling of savings to the shadow banking sector. The development of capital markets would also (1) increase the allocational efficiency of the domestic financial system by providing households with alternative investment channels to low-yielding bank deposits; (2) heighten banks' attention to risk-return trade-offs, given the likely contraction in the availability of domestic deposits; (3) provide a source of noninterest income for domestic banks; and (4) decrease the degree of complacency in banks' liquidity management that may have developed as a result of the ample liquidity and stability of the domestic deposit base.

While the authorities have already introduced measures to curb LGFP-related risks, policy responses need to be more nuanced and respond to risks in particular market segments and locales. Such responses would require more transparency, and hence better information, about the scale and nature of banks' exposures. For example, apart from their size, LGFP funding mechanisms and the viability of many of the projects undertaken remain unclear. Moreover, the differences in the nature of the exposures of banks across locales and by type of bank—which may account for divergent vulnerabilities across the banking system—are not

---

[16]As of June 7, 2012, the PBC permits banks to set deposit rates at up to 110 percent of the benchmark rate, above the prior requirement to match the policy rate.

reflected in estimates of potential buffers. Also, at the local level, the authorities need to curb structural fiscal revenue-expenditure mismatches and limit incentives for excessive risk-taking to contain potential financial stability risks.

Further reforms should also seek to constrain the structural incentives that induce growth in the unregulated shadow banking sector. Specifically, the lack of sufficient risk-pricing mechanisms in the mainstream banking sector adversely affects the ability of banks to service borrowers with higher risk profiles than large SOEs. The introduction of a broad set of reforms—including a gradual withdrawal of the state from its dominant role in the financial system, further interest rate liberalization, and further enhancement of banks' risk management systems—could support more robust bank lending to higher-risk borrowers that are currently serviced by unregulated institutions. In addition, the government may want to consider legalizing unregulated financial institutions, while expanding the perimeter of regulation and supervision to such entities to curb potential system-wide risks. The policy initiative of formally registering illegal banks as microlenders—first introduced in the Wenzhou and Zhejiang Provinces and the Chongqing municipality in 2008–09—may be a useful pilot for moving further in the direction of integrating these institutions into the formal system. System-wide monitoring of financial sector risks is pivotal both from a monetary policy and financial stability point of view.

The risk management frameworks of banks need to be improved to enhance risk-taking and improve resilience to potentially adverse economic conditions. Perhaps most importantly, banks need to shift to active risk management that reflects the ongoing concerns of their own bank management or board of directors, rather than merely following regulatory guidance. Risk management practices should be both geared to bank-specific issues and be preventive in character, in that they should be conducted to prevent or at least mitigate potential losses. More rigorous analysis of potential loan performance risks, for example, could indicate reductions in exposures to specific sectors that may not be viable from a bank's risk-return viewpoint. Such analysis would also capture sector-specific market supply and demand effects, and lead to a natural slowdown in lending when imbalances appear likely. In addition, commercial banks would need to enhance the evaluation of risks under the varied economic and market conditions at loans' points of origination. Banks should also enhance the quality and scope of the underwriting features of their loan activities; assess and manage collateral associated with loans on an ongoing basis; and improve risk management practices to support their going-concern values. Finally, domestic regulators should consider pooling data on key risk factors and exposures across banks—including geographic and sectoral exposures and corresponding probabilities of default and loss-given-default—in order to support more robust assessments of bank-related risks that account for variability in regional and sectoral economic conditions.

REFERENCES

Brehm, S., 2008, "Risk Management in China's State Banks—International Best Practice and the Political Economy of Regulation," *Business and Politics,* Vol. 10, No. 1, Article 2.

Burdekin, R.C.K., and L. Redfern, 2009, "Stock Market Sentiment and the Draining of China's Savings Deposits," *Economics Letters,* Vol. 102, No. 1: 27–29.

China Banking Regulatory Commission (CBRC), 2010, *Annual Report 2009.* http://zhuanti.cbrc.gov.cn/subject/subject/nianbao2009/english/zwqb.pdf.

Credit Suisse, 2011, "China: Rising Risk in Informal Lending," September 28. https://doc.research-and-analytics.csfb.com/docView?language=ENG&format=PDF&document_id=804496540&source_id=em&serialid=zRcEVDVhNw34S9eMWilTXmTioYyyu5u0Sf9Mol0EFx0%3D.

National Audit Office of the People's Republic of China, 2011, *Report on the Local Government Debt Audit Work,* No. 35.

CHAPTER 8

Practical Experiences in Strengthening Banking Supervision and Regulation

HUAQING WANG[1]

Since the global financial crisis erupted in 2008, strengthening financial supervision and regulation has become the consensus of the international community. As a member of the Financial Stability Board (FSB) and the Basel Committee on Banking Supervision (BCBS), the China Regulatory Banking Commission (CBRC) has been an active participant in the international policy dialogues regarding financial regulatory reform and new standard-setting. At the same time, the CRBC is also a determined implementer of reforms, endeavoring to put in place internationally agreed-upon reforms in line with the Chinese reality. In a bid to promote industry stability and improve supervisory effectiveness, the CBRC has participated in the Financial Sector Assessment Program (FSAP). And in its effort to promote the sustainable development of the banking sector, the CBRC is introducing a set of new capital, liquidity, and leverage rules that signify the integrated implementation of Basel II and Basel III in China. Given the unique situation in China, the CBRC has, in practice, paid particular attention to the seven areas of work described below.

First is to strengthen the supervision and regulation of large, complex banks. The FSB has confirmed the Bank of China as one of the 29 global systemically important financial institutions. Considering that many other Chinese banks have the potential to be listed as global systemically important banks, the CBRC is working to build the domestic supervisory framework, including drafting supervisory guidelines on the assessment and supervision of the systemic importance of commercial banks, strengthening the consolidated supervision and increasing the supervisory frequency and intensity of large banking groups, hosting supervisory colleges for large and internationally active Chinese banks, and formulating recovery and resolution plans for such banks in cooperation with other related government agencies. Starting as early as 2010, large, complex banks in China were subject to an additional 1 percent capital

---

[1] Huaqing Wang was the disciplinary commissioner of the China Banking Regulatory Commission when contributing this chapter. He now serves as the disciplinary commissioner of the People's Bank of China.

surcharge in addition to the conservation and countercyclical capital buffer applied to all banks.

By drawing upon our past lessons, we have also attached great importance to improving the corporate governance, internal controls, and compensation practices of large banks, which we believe is an important backstop to effective supervision. In order to facilitate early warning as well as dynamic monitoring of the overall risk profile of each large banking group, we have improved the supervisory rating system to cover 13 prudential regulatory indicators under seven categories: capital adequacy, asset quality, risk concentration, provisioning coverage, affiliates and subsidiaries, liquidity, and operational risk control.

The CBRC's second area of work is to strengthen the supervision of risk concentration. In China, local government funding platforms (LGFPs) have, for many years, played an important role in funding local infrastructure construction and welfare programs. In particular, these LGFPs were instrumental in stoking local economic recovery in recent years. However, the rapid expansion of bank loans to the LGFPs triggered our concerns as early as 2009. To mitigate the potential risks, we required banks to review and revaluate each and every loan, to classify their LGFP exposures in accordance with underlying project cash flow and collateral, and, where necessary, to promptly reschedule or resolve potential problem loans. In the meantime, we are exploring market means to attract social capital to participate in the LGFPs, and working closely with the relevant government agencies to have local governments set aside a portion of their fiscal budget as an additional buffer. All these measures have been proven effective to underpin the commercial viability of the LGFP loans.

The third area of work is to strengthen the supervision of real estate lenders. As part of joint ministerial efforts to control property prices, the CBRC has leveraged its policymaking to differentiate reasonable demand for home ownership from speculative investment in the real estate market. For instance, we apply dynamic loan-to-value (LTV) ratios as well as different down payment policies for purchasing the first and second home, respectively. We require banks to conduct diligent review of the creditworthiness of borrowers and determine mortgage rates based on stringent risk assessments. We support lending for affordable housing projects, but this must be done with proper controls and under the principle of commercial viability. To stay on top of the risks that come along with real estate lending, we require banks to launch intensive stress testing with multidimensional stress scenarios. Such exercises help both banks and regulators maintain dynamic monitoring and evaluation of banks' resilience and accurately assess the impact of price declines and macroeconomic changes on the quality of banks' real estate loan portfolios. Finally, banks are required to develop their risk management strategies by factoring in the full picture of exposures to key geographical regions and related industries.

The fourth area is to strike a balance between financial innovation and prudential supervision. Financial innovation and related supervision have always been the focus of the CBRC's endeavors to highlight the role of the banking sector in serving the real economy. In our view, the effectiveness and desirability of financial innovation should be measured by banks' performance in meeting the fundamental demand of real economic activities. The CBRC encourages financial innovation as long as it helps banks nurture the diversity and advisability of financial products, lower the cost to customers, and effectively manage inherent risks. For instance, by providing wealth management services, commercial banks offer their customers a diversified range of tailor-made products and services, and help their customers maintain and increase the value of their assets against market volatility. The increasing engagement in financial innovation, however, also exposes banks to greater risks of different types. As a solution, the CBRC has issued *Guidelines on the Financial Innovation of Commercial Banks*, which requires that financial innovation be conducted under the principles of "cost accountable, risk controllable, and information sufficiently disclosed." We have also introduced a host of detailed rules governing banks' wealth management activities, credit card business, derivatives trading, bond underwriting, etc. In addition, we constantly improve our tools and techniques for offsite surveillance and onsite examinations, enhance the synergy of different supervisory functions in the supervision of financial innovation, and strengthen our undertakings in consumer protection and public education.

The CBRC's fifth area of work is to prudently carry forward the pilot programs for cross-sector operations and financial holding company supervision. When China enacted its banking law in 1995, it adopted the Glass-Steagall approach to separate banking from other financial businesses. In recent years, with the approval of the State Council, some banks have been permitted to engage in insurance and securities businesses on a pilot basis. In carrying out such pilot programs, the CBRC has pursued a three-step strategy: (1) prepare a solid regulatory and policy framework; (2) conduct rigorous application review and approval; and (3) limit the pilot scope to a few selected eligible banks. Accordingly, a "primary supervisor" arrangement is adopted in light of the shaping of financial holding companies as a result of the pilot operations. Undoubtedly, the trend toward cross-sector operations is posing new challenges to both banks and bank regulators. In response, the CBRC is careful to ensure that banks engage in cross-sector business with compatible corporate governance, necessary firewalls and controls, and adequate consolidated management capability. We closely monitor the performance of banks' cross-sector operations and take prompt supervisory actions when the returns on assets and equity of banks' nonbanking business fall below the average levels of the corresponding industry, and when the overall performance of banks is negatively affected by the cross-sector operations. Finally, we are promoting collaboration and information sharing with other regulatory authorities in order to avoid gaps and overlaps in institutional oversight.

The sixth area of work is to attend to the supervision of shadow banking activities. In the current international financial arena, the shadow banking sector mostly consists of mutual funds and structured investment vehicles, which are either under-regulated or not regulated at all. The assets of these shadow banks involve virtual off-floor trading, which is typically highly leveraged. Shadow banks as so characterized have yet to be found in China. As banking regulators, we pay close attention to the financial activities and assets that have dealings with banks but are not fully or not at all reflected in banks' financial statements. Such activities are identified in the following areas: business cooperation between commercial banks and trust companies, credit asset transfers between financial institutions, banks' wealth management activities, bond underwriting, private equity participation by commercial banks, etc. The CBRC has been keeping these activities on its radar screen. We require banks to fully account for and build adequate buffers against the underlying risks that may arise from the off-balance-sheet activities of commercial banks. We also set forth the requirements for better information disclosure by banks and trust companies, the setup of effective firewall mechanisms between banks and nonbank financial institutions, and more stringent large exposure limits. Our goal is to extend out regulatory coverage as much as to prevent regulatory arbitrage, deal with hidden risks, and ultimately ensure financial system stability.

The seventh and final area of the CBRC's work is to support and regulate the development of a diversified financial system. In this respect, the CBRC enters into close partnership with local governments with shared goals of fostering an ecosystem favorable to the development of microfinance firms. This ecosystem has in turn enhanced the financial inclusion of farmers, small businesses, and communities neglected by the regular banking sector. To this end, we are also working to promote the development of lending-related services such as credit guarantees so as to enhance the credit capacity for intermediation. As the financial system has grown increasingly diversified over recent years, the CBRC is also working together with the relevant government agencies to regulate the safe and sound development of various financing entities and vehicles. At the same time, the CBRC is engaged in various endeavors involving the financial education of the public, including launching nationwide education campaigns under such themes as "Better Finance for a Better Life," and "Understand Finance Better, Protect Wealth Better" in a bid to enhance public awareness and fend off financial risks.

CHAPTER 9

Seeking the Middle Ground for Supervision

Jonathan Fiechter and Aditya Narain

As China moves to strengthen its supervisory system, it is faced with a choice. Should it follow the supervisory model adopted by many Western countries of allowing a fair degree of independence on the part of bank management to determine the bank's business strategy? Or should China continue with its current approach of a relatively comprehensive and heavy-handed approach to regulation and supervision, which grants less discretion to bank management?

The Western supervisory model, which is being questioned following the global financial crisis, is characterized by a high degree of reliance on financial institutions' own systems, policies, and management incentives to align risks with supervisory expectations. Supervision and regulation are less intrusive and supervisors permit banks viewed as having sophisticated risk management approaches and good corporate governance the freedom to determine their business strategy (e.g., pricing of products, management of the balance sheet, and a range of financial services) within the parameters of the statutory framework. This model assumes that financial market innovation is normally benign, and great reliance is placed on market discipline to give banks the incentive to avoid taking on excessive risk. In some cases, this approach to supervision has been characterized as a "light-touch," with a reliance on the market to act as a governor to limit excessive risk-taking.

While this model appears to have worked very well during the early part of the last decade, the experience from the crisis includes significant failures in the risk management practices of banks along with weak corporate governance. Because of the systemic importance of many of these banks, governments were unwilling to permit the weaker ones to fail (particularly following the failure of Lehman Brothers) because of the risk that such failures might cause system-wide financial instability. As a consequence, since the start of the crisis, there has been a rethinking of the reliance on market discipline and bank management to manage and control the risk assumed by banks—that is, a questioning of the philosophy underlying the regulatory paradigm in the major financial markets in the advanced economies. Consideration is being given to more prescriptive regulation, more intrusive supervision, and less faith in the accuracy and timeliness of market-based indicators of soundness such as ratings produced by credit rating agencies. In an effort to restore the application of market discipline, policies are being discussed to reduce the complexity and interconnectedness of large banks so that potential failures pose less of a threat to financial stability. This is part of an overall supervisory theme of returning to the basics.

In contrast to the model in the West, the supervisory model for emerging markets in Asia such as China has taken a more paternalistic approach, characterized by a rules-based prudential framework that is heavily prescriptive and conservative, backed by intrusive supervision and a focus on compliance with rules that may go beyond prudential standards. Financial institutions are often viewed like public utilities, with an obligation to serve the economic development needs of the domestic economy even when such services do not always meet a market test. Such regimes may include controls on interest rates paid on deposits and lending rates, a focus on ensuring that banks provide infrastructure finance, and an expectation of bank funding of major state-owned entities (SOEs). The result may be that domestic banks act in a way that is more akin to that of a development bank.

While such regimes may work well initially in underdeveloped financial systems, they need evolve as the real sector becomes more developed. As the demand for credit by private companies and consumers grows, financial systems geared to meeting the needs of major corporations and project finance will need to evolve to meet the disparate demands of households and smaller businesses that lack government backing. A rules-based and conservative prudential regime that discourages innovation and change may unintentionally serve as an impediment to the development of a more robust and diversified financial system. Moreover, the primary focus of the major banks on government-oriented lending with an implicit government backstop may prevent a risk culture from emerging within the banks.

While it is recognized by many officials that China needs a more dynamic and innovative banking system that will require a change in the approach to supervision and regulation, the decision for the Chinese leadership is where to position the regime in the spectrum defined by the two extremes. This chapter draws on the findings of the IMF's 2010 Financial Sector Assessment Program (FSAP) of China to take a look at the strengths of the current system and the challenges that are to be navigated. It then recommends priorities for the authorities as they transition to a supervisory regime that may be better suited to overseeing a financial system that can meet the needs of the evolving Chinese economy.

CHINA'S FINANCIAL SYSTEM

The modern Chinese financial system is very young, mirroring the developments in the real economy. The reform of the banking system began in the 1980s, when commercial banking was separated from the People's Bank of China (PBC). At the outset, the commercial banks were expected to operate as direct lending arms of the government. In the following decade, however, initiatives were undertaken to develop a dual system of policy banks and commercial banks, with the intention that government-oriented policy lending would be shifted into specialized policy banks and out of the commercial banks. This goal has not yet been achieved.

The Chinese financial system is dominated by the rapidly growing banking sector, with nonbank financial institutions accounting for only a fraction of the system. The banking system accounts for nearly 80 percent of net new lending every year. In the past two decades, the banking sector has become extraordinarily large, with assets of over 200 percent of GDP. Two Chinese banks are in the top three globally by market capitalization.

By contrast, China's capital markets, which date to the 1990s, remain relatively shallow. Over 60 percent of outstanding bonds were issued by the government, with the majority of the remaining bonds issued by either the large commercial banks or the policy banks (which are state-owned and provide a range of development finance services in support of infrastructure, agricultural development, export insurance, etc.)

Not unexpectedly, given the relatively young age of the financial markets, there has been a lot of change since the 1980s. The banking system has undergone an extraordinary evolution, with the number of banking entities reduced from more than 40,000 to less than 5,000 through a series of restructurings and mergers of credit cooperatives into commercial banks. The Chinese government has on two separate occasions rescued the large state banks by making massive capital injections and transferring the banks' nonperforming loans (NPLs) to state-sponsored asset-management companies. To reduce the likelihood of this happening again, the government has emphasized improving corporate governance in these institutions through the introduction of experienced outside directors, and has become more cautious in using the nonpolicy banks to carry out government policy objectives.

The regulated financial markets in China are subject to strict government controls. Key financial prices remain regulated, which distorts the incentives to save and invest, limits the ability of institutions to price for risk, and constrains the conduct of monetary policy. Despite gradual interest rate liberalization over more than a decade, retail interest rates remain partly regulated, with deposit rates subject to a cap and lending rates to a floor. Banks can price lending above the floor to a degree, and do so in practice.

Expanding access to financial services has been a priority of the government. Efforts are being made to improve access to bank finance by small and medium-sized enterprises and households, and, at the local level, to find alternatives to bank funding of projects sponsored by local governments. These initiatives are in response to a system of bank financing that has been largely limited to large corporate entities (which are typically owned or controlled by the state) and projects supported by the local governments.

In the past five years, as the Chinese economy has experienced the adverse impact of the global slowdown, the government has again encouraged high levels of commercial bank lending as a way to stimulate the economy. The heavy involvement of the state in the financial system has done more to influence the strategic direction of the financial system than market forces.

CURRENT STATUS OF SUPERVISION

Regulation and supervision of China's banking system has made very impressive progress in the past few years, led by a forward-looking regulator (the China Banking Regulatory Commission–CBRC) with a clear safety and soundness mandate. The CBRC was spun off from the PBC in 2003 as a stand-alone prudential authority and is widely credited with having made significant achievements in its short existence. It has played a key role in driving professionalism, risk management, corporate governance, internal control, and disclosure in the major banks, as well as in enhancing international recognition of the Chinese banking system. This task has been helped by the fact that the objectives and responsibilities of authorities involved in banking supervision are clear. The CBRC's mandate has enabled it to focus primarily on the mission of safety and soundness, and that has helped it become a high-quality organization, although it has also been used to enforce the meeting of the government's policy goals by the banks. Under this mandate, the CBRC has been very successful in articulating to banks and the public the need to balance both safety and soundness objectives with the need to achieve economic and social progress.

The legal framework has been very supportive. Laws, rules, and guidance that the CBRC operates under generally establish a benchmark of prudential standards that is of high quality and was drawn extensively from international standards. The CBRC has the authority to take a wide range of corrective and remedial actions, and the large numbers of enforcement actions it has taken and disclosed demonstrates its willingness to use them. CBRC staff is legally protected from the consequences of acts committed in good faith. The CBRC also has the legal authority to share information with other regulators, domestically and internationally, and does so through networks of Memoranda of Understandings.

The CBRC has the necessary building blocks for effective onsite and offsite supervision, but in common with a number of supervisory agencies in other countries, it needs to continue to build its cadre of experienced supervisors. There is a system to capture frequent and periodic information from banks and an acknowledgment that with the evolving risks, even more data need to be collected. Supervisory approaches are increasingly risk-focused, reflecting the need to carefully assign scarce resources to areas of the highest risk. Credit risk is viewed as the most important risk facing Chinese banks and will remain so for some time. It has received the most focus from banks and the CBRC and, with some exceptions, is generally well controlled, particularly in the large banks. Not surprisingly, the risk management policies and credit underwriting standards are weaker in the rural institutions. The rules and practices for problem assets and related provisioning for the listed banks are generally adequate. They are based on the equivalent of the accounting rules and regulatory requirements for classifying loans of the International Financial Reporting Standards (IFRS).

The CBRC does regular, extensive, and in-depth reviews of asset quality and the provisioning system. Major audit firms audit the majority of listed banks. The regulatory system has encouraged robust provisioning and requires capital buffers to be held as part of a firm's equity. Traded market risk in the Chinese banking system is generally low. China's implementation of the capital adequacy framework, which is a key component of the prudential regime, has generally been conservative. The result is that Chinese banks uniformly have capital ratios above the Basel minimums. The quality of bank capital is also strong and is composed primarily of high-quality core capital, in keeping with the current focus on capital quality in international discussions. The CBRC has required banks to hold more capital and higher provisions as a safeguard against a possible deterioration in loan quality following the rapid loan growth of recent years.

Risk management systems in Chinese banks are evolving. The CBRC has encouraged banks to improve their risk management systems in conjunction with their efforts to deliver on the government's economic and social objectives. Following its mandate, and as a result of observed and potential deficiencies in risk management practices, the CBRC has introduced a range of prudential measures, including more stringent credit risk management of loans to local government platforms and real estate lending. Most major banks have developed risk management systems for each of the major individual risks they face, although the systems are of mixed quality.

An extensive approval regime spanning products, activities, and businesses underlies the supervisory framework. China defines the permissible activities of banks and operates an extensive bank licensing and approval process. Considerable resources are devoted to approving the licensing of new institutions, new branches or sub-branches of existing institutions, new products, and changes in ownership. Fit and proper criteria apply not only to board members and senior management but also extend to other positions in banks. The use of the term "bank" is appropriately controlled and shell banks are not permitted. Minimum capital requirements to start a new bank are based on the type of bank and are in line with or higher than international norms. The CBRC implements an appropriate approval process for changes in ownership and major acquisitions. Investments by banks, including in overseas branches, require approval as part of the general approval system.

Innovation has lagged in Chinese banks, perhaps an unavoidable consequence of the comprehensive regulatory regime and the absence of market pressures to produce high earnings faced by banks with extensive public shareholders. Banks are generally prohibited from investing in nonbank activities, although in the recent past exceptions have been permitted for investment in financial leasing and asset management. Bank-insurance and bank-securities cross-investments have not been allowed until recently, with four cross-ownership pilots currently under way. In those cases the CBRC imposes firewalls between the banks and the other entity. Among other considerations, there are also explicit provisions that these pilots must earn at least average industry returns or they are to be dissolved.

Overall, consolidated supervision within the banking system is effective and the CBRC has developed a wide network of formal and informal home-host information sharing arrangements and has used these effectively as both a home and host.

MAJOR SUPERVISORY CHALLENGES THAT NEED TO BE ADDRESSED

Compared to the more advanced economies, the Chinese banking system undertakes more conventional banking business and is exposed to less complexity. As markets further open and China's banks expand, complexity and risks will increase. Both supervisors and banks must evolve in the short term to be ready to meet those challenges.

Although the framework of laws and guidance is generally of high quality and modeled on international standards, much of the framework guidance is relatively recent and untested. Experience is still being gained in its application in the local context. A period of settling in is required for effectiveness to be enhanced, for banks that are not advanced to catch up, and for the CBRC to ensure that all banks have risk management systems commensurate with the risks they are assuming. Supervisory capacity to effectively evaluate the risk management capacity of banks is also developing, but it typically takes years to build a critical mass of experienced supervisors.

The funding and governance of the CBRC raises the risk of potential constraints to its ability to build its capacity and effectiveness. This in turn could hamper its ability to provide world-class supervision, particularly as Chinese banks become more complex and innovative and expand abroad. The role and authority of the State Council vis-à-vis the CBRC needs to be clarified and refined to ensure that the CBRC has the ability to take decisions free from any political interference. While the CBRC reports that no interference has occurred since its creation, the existing arrangements do not comply with international best practice and could be problematic in the future.

A related challenge facing supervisors is responding to the predominant role of the state in the financial system, both in day-to-day operations and in crafting their policy framework. While heavy state involvement in the banking system may contribute to perceptions that the state provides a financial backstop for the banks (which may in turn promote financial stability), it can also override soundness concerns, contribute to the misallocation of bank credit, and lead banks to be less responsive to supervisory advice that may conflict with advice from state officials. This potential conflict between safety and soundness objectives versus other objectives exists in many countries but may be more acute in China because of the predominant reliance on the banking system to achieve economic and social goals. Credit intermediation is thwarted to the extent that lending to SOEs and local governments squeezes out the fledgling private sector. More than one-third of bank assets continue to be in exposures to the government or central bank, and even more if local government-related vehicles are taken into account.

The focus of the major commercial banks in making large infrastructure loans and extending credit to SOEs has led to a shortfall in bank lending to the private sector and households. The state has sought to address this problem by setting policy lending goals for banks to increase financial access to underserved segments such as small businesses. Implementing this policy has been left to the bank supervisors, given their extensive knowledge of the banking systems and their regular interaction with the banks during their examinations. But this is an example of one distortion leading to another, and the growth of the large underground banking system suggests that the banks are unable to fully meet the credit needs of the private sector and households.

Together with the differently aligned incentives promoted by bank ownership by the state, banks have reduced incentives to focus on developing risk management. The new risk governance, measurement, and management systems have not been tested under stress and some areas for material improvement are clearly evident. Board-approved strategies are often too focused on target loan growth in various sectors and regulatory-determined key performance indicators rather than on targeted risk measures linked to the banks' own risk systems.

Comprehensive, enterprise-wide risk management that takes account of interactions between risks in measuring, managing, and stress testing, and that relates capital to risk, is at an early stage in many banks. For these banks, the priority is to ensure that a sound risk management framework is fully in place, imbedded in their culture and group-wide operations, and sustainable. While much of banking in China is deposit-taking and lending, the Chinese lending market is complex by virtue of its scope and diversity, and banks are getting into new areas of lending and other activities. The quality and sophistication of risk management needs to be commensurate with these realities.

As evidenced in the approach to credit risk management, there is an intense focus by all parties in the system on minimizing the level of NPLs. This is understandable given the serious bad loan experience in the early part of the decade. But this may divert attention away from other early, forward-looking measures of credit risk that need to be addressed. It also runs the risk that by making the level of NPLs a key performance indicator, NPLs will be written off or restructured regardless of cost, to the detriment of banks developing more robust risk cultures and enjoying long-term profitability.

Market risks may increase as market liberalization occurs. Exchange rate liberalization will increase foreign exchange risk for banks and their customers. Risk management tools, information technology, and the data infrastructure to support the tools are generally commensurate with the current level of risk, but the level of sophistication will need to increase over time as liberalization continues.

The relative newness of the supervisory methodology means that supervisory assessments are not as forward-looking as they need to be. Heavy reliance on a few basic simple ratios, though advantageous from the perspective of implementation, should not be permitted to discourage more judgment-based assessments of inherent risk and the quality of banks' risk management and governance. Optimally, the benefits of simple basic indictors would be maintained, supplemented by banks' compliance with CBRC guidance to develop more sophisticated supervisory approaches. This would encourage more of a risk culture in banks and should reduce the risk that banks will rely excessively on regulatory compliance rather than their own risk assessments.

The CBRC has the authority and has demonstrated a willingness to act to resolve nonviable institutions. Dealing with problem banks has been on the basis of "going-concern" solutions, and the capability to close an institution may need to be enhanced going forward.

Consolidated supervision of banks and their direct subsidiaries and branches on the mainland or offshore is of high quality. However, existing laws may permit more complex structures, and presently there is not a framework for consolidated supervision of financial conglomerates. The PBC is developing a proposal to have a lead supervisor in charge of multisector conglomerates. As the Chinese system evolves toward a system of less state ownership and more private ownership, it will be important that supervisory capacity be enhanced to be able to deal with more complex ownership structures. The mixed conglomerate structure that has proven itself to be difficult to regulate in other markets is beginning to take root in China. A system of effectively supervising these entities is a challenge, and current legal authority needs to be amended to facilitate conglomerate supervision—for example, the laws do not allow supervisory review of beneficial ownership or indirect changes of control. Other rules that also involve potentially more complex bank ownership structures (e.g., related-party rules) should also be reviewed to ensure that they are sufficiently comprehensive.

Reliance by one supervisor on the work of other supervisory agencies in examining mixed corporate groups (bank/insurance/securities pilots) has not always worked well in practice globally and will need to be carefully monitored and considered as the PBC develops its framework for consolidated supervision of conglomerates.

RECOMMENDATIONS

Given the environment in China, which is slowly evolving to a more market-oriented configuration, and the desire to accommodate the G20 international regulatory reform agenda, which is moving rapidly to conclusion, what should the Chinese supervisors aim for? The Chinese system already has some of the features that are now deemed desirable for supervisors, such as intensive and intrusive supervision. But there are other features that make it difficult to achieve the tenets of good supervision. Although it is likely is that the economy will be dominated by SOEs in the foreseeable future, households and the private sector may play an increasingly important role. Therefore, over the medium term, the authorities should aim for a supervisory system that promotes development of a financial system that can meet the varied needs of Chinese savers and borrowers of all sizes, both state and private. It is assumed that the Chinese financial system will continue to be comprised of both private and state-owned commercial banks and state-run policy banks.

The first objective should be to *foster increased transparency*, which will enable market discipline and government accountability to play a role in supplementing supervisory efforts. The CBRC already collects a lot of data from institutions, but disclosure both by banks and the CBRC could be significantly enhanced through quarterly release of at least aggregate data together with key financial ratios and peer group indicators. The CBRC has also developed a strong analytical capacity and should take on the task of providing both information and analysis on a regular basis. Continued attention will need to be given to the development of the private accounting and audit profession in China to ensure that financial statements are professionally prepared and audited. The CBRC should be empowered to reject and rescind the appointment of an external auditor who is deemed unfit to perform a reliable and independent audit.

The second objective should be to place greater emphasis on *improving the governance and management of banks*. The state will likely continue to play a major role in the sector via ownership, and the supervisors should aim to strengthen the ability of the boards of banks to provide strong strategic guidance and better understand and then articulate meaningful policies for risk tolerance and appetite. This will require supervisory involvement that goes beyond the fit and proper regime to the laying out of stronger expectations of the role of both supervisors and banks' management and boards. Further developing plans for continuing board education (as has been successfully done in some other countries in the region) will be helpful.

The third objective should be to gradually *relax the prescriptive and approval-based regime*. Bank management needs to be held more accountable for setting the strategic direction of the bank and for maintaining robust balance sheets and prudent risk levels. The CBRC needs to place less reliance on rules, punishment, and prohibition and gradually shift toward placing more reliance on the principles underlying the approaches that it expects banks to follow. Weaning banks off their dependence on the sanctity and safety of state ownership and their lending to state-determined priority sectors and projects is a necessary first step to building the risk management capacity of banks. This is easier said than done, especially given the lessons of the global financial crisis. Some of the advanced economies had clearly gone too far in relying on banks' own risk management systems. So what is needed is a balance between the two approaches.

The fourth objective should be to *enhance supervisory effectiveness by developing a strong cadre of bank supervisors* across all segments of the banking system. While there have been impressive gains in quality, there is a need to develop greater numbers of skilled and trained banking supervisors across the system.

China has both global and domestic systemically important banks as well as thousands of small banks, and though the supervisory focus has been on the former, much more attention may need to be placed on midsize and smaller banks to ensure that they upgrade their risk management and governance performance.

The fifth objective should be to *strengthen both the mechanisms and the actual coordination and cooperation among supervisors* in the system. As of now, the State Council has played the key role in bringing the supervisors together, but as the system moves to greater integration across the different sectors, the introduction of more cross-sector products, and the rise of conglomerate businesses, coordination among the different sector supervisors will have to become a way of life and transcend the turf issues that prevail in most countries. This should also be the case for interagency coordination with the PBC, which has a key role to play in the macroprudential agenda.

The sixth objective should be for China to play a *greater role in the international standard-setting process* by providing inputs based on its own experience to reinforce the impetus in ongoing international discussions of the value of simple approaches. While several emerging market economies have become members of international policy setting fora such as the Basel Committee and the Financial Stability Board, the discussions continue to be dominated by the experiences of the more advanced economies. In searching for longer-term solutions to the problems exposed by the crisis, the inputs that could be provided by China and other emerging market economies could make an important contribution to shaping the reform agenda.

The seventh and probably the most important objective should be to *retain both the willingness and ability of supervisors to play an intrusive role in the operations of banks and to be skeptical and pose the right questions to bank management,* while at the same time not substituting supervisory judgment in areas that are more appropriately left to bank management. This requires a delicate balancing act by supervisors.

CONCLUSIONS

Despite being an ancient country, China has a relatively young financial supervisory system. Given the tremendous growth of its economy, it has the ability to deal with issues of resources and capacity that have plagued other countries. It has used a policy of gradualism, for example, to temper the effects of opening up to foreign bank entry. This has allowed supervisors to keep pace with their more complex products and activities. Both the PBC and CBRC are widely respected inside and outside of China. The CBRC, in particular, has demonstrated its willingness to act in pursuit of its safety and soundness mandate. It needs to continue to work on developing a plan to enhance its capacity and expertise and to ensure that progress made so far is sustainable. Accomplishing this objective requires the continued support of the government. Enhanced vigilance is required by banks and the regulatory community to keep risks under control in China's financial system.

In many ways, the strength of bank regulation to date lies in the deliberately simple, conservative approach taken, often relying on specific prudential ratios that banks must meet. The challenge going forward is that this approach, by itself, will not be sufficient as markets and banks evolve. The CBRC is well governed within the constraints it faces and has steadily and materially increased its transparency. There is a need for more forward resource planning and an urgent government-supported strategy for material upgrading and retention of experienced supervisors, especially those with specialist skills. In its evolution, the government should aim to meet the Western model halfway, retaining some of the elements of its current regime, including the focus on simplicity and conservatism, while at the same time embracing the lessons that came out of the crisis regarding the importance of holding management accountable for building an effective and forward-looking risk management capacity.

CHAPTER 10

Strengthening Macroprudential Management

CHANGNENG XUAN

In recent years, the People's Bank of China (PBC) and other relevant agencies have striven to deepen financial reforms, strengthen financial risk monitoring and assessment, and establish systems to prevent systemic risk and facilitate orderly resolutions. The aim is to ensure a stable operating environment for China's financial system, taking into account domestic economic realities and keeping in step with the global regulatory reform agenda. A high priority has been placed on strengthening the overall macroprudential framework and improving mechanisms to maintain financial stability.

ROLE OF THE PEOPLE'S BANK OF CHINA IN MONITORING AND MANAGING SYSTEMIC RISK

The *Law of the People's Republic of China on the People's Bank of China*, amended in 2003, entrusts the PBC with the important responsibility of "preventing and defusing systemic risk and maintaining financial stability." To perform this statutory function the PBC has taken several steps toward monitoring and preventing systemic risks.

Progress toward a monitoring framework started in 2005, when the PBC began to publish its annual *Financial Stability Report*.[1] The report has gradually helped establish a monitoring and assessment framework covering the macroeconomic environment, financial markets, banking, securities, and insurance sectors. The framework also reports on the financial condition of the government, the corporate sectors and households, and the financial market infrastructure. The PBC has adopted analytical techniques that combine quantitative and qualitative financial stability risk indicators. Since 2010, regular use has also been made of stress testing to bolster quantitative risk analysis.

Drawing on the lessons of the 2008 global financial crisis, the PBC has strengthened the monitoring of correlations between the macro economy and the financial system, as well as the domestic and cross-border interconnectedness

---

[1]The 2011 edition of the report is available at www.pbc.gov.cn/image_public/UserFiles/english/upload/File/China%20Financial%20Stability%20Report%202011.pdf.

of the financial system. Particular attention is being paid to potential cross-sectoral risks and cross-market financial products, systemically important financial institutions, and shadow banking operations. Using data from the interbank payment and settlement system, a financial network structure model has been built to capture interconnectedness among financial institutions and to dynamically analyze the liquidity risk transmission process among those institutions (primarily banks).

To institutionalize its stress-testing framework, the PBC has established a dedicated stress-testing team and initiated annual stress testing of 17 commercial banks. This includes stress testing of credit risk sensitivity and the macroeconomic scenario. The stress-test results show that, at present, the banking system has relatively high asset quality and capital adequacy, and relatively strong resilience to macroeconomic shocks.

At the regional level, the branches of the PBC have initiated onsite assessments of financial institutions, including in areas such as corporate governance, internal controls, primary operating risks, and contagion risk. This is facilitating an early identification of risks, liquidity stresses, and deterioration in asset quality.

China's shadow banking system is relatively small and straightforward. The use and retailing of any derivative-type products is relatively rare. The PBC and its branches are continually monitoring risks from the shadow banking system. Steps are under way to collect data on a more regular basis and to develop a regulatory framework that would guide the healthy development of the shadow banking system in China in terms of wealth management products and entrusted loans, financial guarantee companies, pawn shops, private equity funds, and private lending.

Since 2009, the PBC, in collaboration with 11 other governmental agencies, has been subject to a comprehensive assessment of China's financial stability by the International Monetary Fund and the World Bank. In 2011, their Financial Sector Assessment Program (FSAP) report affirmed the enormous accomplishments of China's financial development in recent years. However, it urged China to continue to deepen financial reforms, accelerate the development of financial markets, strengthen the financial stability and crisis management framework, and improve the effectiveness of financial regulation.

MANAGING SYSTEMIC RISK

After the Asian financial crisis in 1997, there was commentary that China's large commercial banks were in a state of "technical bankruptcy." Since 2003, the PBC and the relevant agencies have resolutely promoted the joint-stock reform of large commercial banks. Accordingly, four steps have been undertaken and completed: writing off losses, stripping off nonperforming assets, using foreign exchange reserves to inject capital, and completing initial public offerings of the large commercial banks.

Through the reforms, the large commercial banks have gradually standardized corporate governance structures and continually improved internal control levels and product innovation capabilities. Profitability has grown relatively quickly and the value preservation of state-owned capital has improved. The success in the reform of large commercial banks has further propelled and encouraged the reform and development of "intermediate" financial institutions such as joint-stock and urban commercial banks. This has helped improve the competitiveness of the banking sector in China.

For over a decade, China has successfully handled several financial risk events. The PBC has cooperated closely with the relevant agencies and local governments, adopting a variety of methods and policy measures, including mergers, restructuring, and bankruptcies, to effectively limit the systemic spread of financial risk.

A comprehensive overhaul of the trust industry included bankruptcy liquidation of the noted Guangdong International Trust and Investment Corporation, and restructuring and consolidation of all trust and investment companies engaged in illegal operations, facing a payment crisis, or unable to repay maturing debts. Through this overhaul, the number of trust and investment companies was reduced from over 200 to a few dozen. A similar approach was taken to cleaning up urban credit cooperatives and commercial banks. A comprehensive overhaul of securities companies has also been initiated, with 31 high-risk securities companies, including Southern Securities, shut down or declared bankrupt, and nine securities companies, including Galaxy Securities and China Securities, restructured. Market reforms have also been used to dispose of "DeLong Group" risk, which primarily involved production and financing risks.

The China Securities Investor Protection Fund and the China Insurance Protection Fund were established in August 2005 and September 2008, respectively, marking the establishment of a safety net for investors and policyholders. Since their formation, the two entities have participated in the resolution of weak securities and insurance companies. This has played an important role in maintaining social stability and in protecting the interests of investors.

FURTHER ADVANCES

China's long-term economic outlook remains positive. However, there remain various financial imbalances and the issue of uncoordinated development and growth of the financial sector. Uncertainties also remain regarding the external sector. Macroprudential management thus needs further strengthening, and methods for systemic risk monitoring need to be improved. Some of these areas that need closer attention are discussed below.

A Framework for Macroprudential Management with Countercyclical Controls

In 2011, the PBC introduced a mechanism for the dynamic adjustments to differentiated reserve requirements, which is used in combination with routine monetary policy tools such as open-market operations, reserve requirement ratios, and interest rates. Dynamic adjustments to differentiated reserve requirements are based on the scale of social financing, the degree of divergence between bank credit and major socioeconomic development objectives, and the effect on the overall divergence of specific financial institutions. It takes into account such factors as the specific financial institution's systemic importance and implementation of national credit policies. Relevant parameters may be adjusted quarterly to facilitate more targeted mobilization of excess liquidity so as to guide reasonable and stable extension of credit by financial institutions.

The core elements of the mechanism draw on two basic concepts of Basel III: countercyclical capital buffers and capital surcharge for systemically important financial institutions. The mechanism for the dynamically adjusted differentiated reserve requirement ratio can be expressed as a transparent, formulaic requirement that uses a flexible mechanism that strengthens risk prevention capabilities by increasing capital levels and improving asset quality. This reflects the requirements of macroeconomic management while achieving the purpose of preventing the accumulation of cyclical systemic risk and leaving room for market-based competition. Over the past years, the results of implementing this reserve requirement ratio have proven to be effective, and inflation has been notably restrained. This macroprudential policy is still at an exploratory stage and this framework will be further refined following the implementation of Basel III in China.

Analytical Methods for Monitoring Systemically Important Financial Institutions

Under this category comes the interplay between the financial sector and the real economy, making stress testing a routine financial stability tool, and establishing sound monitoring and assessment systems for the shadow banking system. This includes complying with international standards and norms, paying close attention to the assessment framework for domestic systemically important financial institutions, raising regulatory standards, refining orderly risk disposition and liquidation arrangements, strengthening shareholder and creditor assumption of liability for risk, and preventing the "too-big-to-fail" risk of financial institutions. For financial holding companies that have developed rather quickly and have become too big or too complex to fail, the PBC is instituting regulations, capital requirements, good corporate governance standards, limits on related-party transactions, and lower concentration risk. The overall goal is to reduce the probability and cost of bailouts.

Establishing a Deposit Insurance System

The global financial crisis reinforced the relevance of a well-designed deposit insurance system. A total of 47 countries used deposit insurance policies to prevent and defuse financial risk, protect depositor interests, and withstand the financial crisis. In June 2009, the International Association of Deposit Insurers and the Basel Committee on Banking Supervision jointly published *Core Principles for*

Effective Deposit Insurance Systems.[2] The principles were soon incorporated into the 12 core international financial standards by the Financial Stability Board.

The experiences of the United States and Europe demonstrate that outcomes of handling financial crises vary depending to a large degree on the design of the deposit insurance mechanism. Since 2008, nearly 400 banks have faced problems in the United States, but owing to timely and effective handling by the deposit insurance system the numerous bank failures did not trigger public panic, and stability was preserved in the banking system as a whole. The *Dodd-Frank Wall Street Reform and Consumer Protection Act* in the United States further authorized deposit insurance institutions to perform orderly liquidation of the risks of systemically important financial institutions.

China also attaches importance to depositor protection and has explicitly defined the objectives and requirements. At present, China's macroeconomic environment remains stable, and the primary financial and regulatory indicators of China's banking industry are largely healthy. The financial condition of rural credit cooperatives and other small institutions has improved substantially after reform and with policy support. All of these are advantageous conditions for the establishment of a deposit insurance system. In recent years, the PBC in concert with the relevant departments has studied the establishment of such a system. Drawing on the general requirements of international standards and the experiences of other countries, China should establish a properly funded deposit insurance system as rapidly as possible that makes insurance mandatory, employs differentiated premium rates, involves limited payments, and facilitates early correction of problem banks and risk disposition.

---

[2] The document is available at www.iadi.org/cms/secure/docs/JWGDI%20CBRG%20core%20 principles_18_June.pdf.

CHAPTER 11

Capital Markets and Financial Stability

SHUQING GUO

As a result of years of efforts, China's capital markets have grown in size and capacity. They are playing an increasingly important role in supporting national economic and social development. By the end of September 2012, there were 2,489 listed companies on China's stock markets with a combined RMB 21.39 trillion (US\$3.37 trillion) in terms of market capitalization, the third highest worldwide. The outstanding amount of bonds under custody reached approximately RMB 23.06 trillion (US\$3.64 trillion) (Appendix Table 11.1), also ranking third worldwide after the United States and Japan. The volume of commodity futures traded in China has been ranked as the highest in the world for two consecutive years (Appendix Table 11.2).

THE CAPITAL MARKET SETTING

The market framework in China currently includes equity, bond, and futures derivatives markets, which are described in turn below.

Equity market: Having established a multilayered institutional framework consisting of the Main Board, Small and Medium-Sized Enterprise Board, Growth Enterprise Board (GEB), and Stock Transfer Agent System, the Chinese equity market is now helping meet the basic equity financing needs of different economic constituents.

Bond market: The bond market offers a wide range of instruments, including Treasury bonds, local government bonds, central bank bills, corporate bonds, foreign bonds, short-term financing notes, asset-backed bonds, medium-term notes, and collective bonds for trading in interbank markets and exchange-traded markets. Table 11.1 shows the combined volumes issued and traded in the first half of 2012.

Futures derivatives market: Based on the vibrant growth of commodity futures, which has enabled China to be ranked number one in terms of combined trading volume, the financial derivatives market has started to grow. There are currently 28 commodity futures products in China. At present, the only financial futures product listed for trading, however, is the CSI 300 Index Futures, which has become one of the most actively traded futures products (Table 11.2). In addition, China is in the process of studying the possibility of launching T-bond futures.

TABLE 11.1

Combined Market Capitalization by Market
(In hundreds of millions of renminbi)

Market	Amount
Main boards (Small and Medium-Sized Enterprise Board included)	205,563.71
Growth Enterprise Board	8,383.66
Stock Transfer Agent System	342.85

Source: China Securities Regulatory Commission.
Note: Data valid as of September 28, 2012.

TABLE 11.2

Various Service Providers in the Capital Markets, end-August 2012

Service Provider	Number	Asset Size (in hundreds of millions of renminbi)
Securities companies	114	16,434.11
Futures firms	161	429.43
Fund management companies	73	31,136.21
Securities investment advisors	88	NA
Custodian banks	18	NA
Securities rating agencies	6	NA

Source: China Securities Regulatory Commission.
Note: Assets of fund management companies refer to assets under management; NA=not applicable.

TABLE 11.3

A-Shares Held by Foreign Shareholders, end-2011
(In hundreds of millions of shares and renminbi)

Shareholder	Number of Shares	Market Capital	Percent of A-Share Market Capital
Qualified Foreign Institutional Investors	168.86	1,777.68	0.83
Overseas shareholders	298.74	3,520.43	1.65
Joint ventures and wholly foreign-owned enterprises	117.64	843.12	0.39
Total	585.24	6,141.23	2.87

Source: China Securities Regulatory Commission.

There has been steady progress in the opening up of the capital market. By the end of August 2012, 1,024 China-concept companies were listed on foreign exchanges; 174 domestic companies were listed abroad, raising US$184.021 billion; 181 foreign firms were granted Qualified Foreign Institutional Investor (QFII) status; and 32 fund management companies obtained Qualified Domestic Institutional Investor (QDII) status and 67 QDII fund products were approved. By the end of 2011, foreign shareholders had taken up 2.87 percent of the aggregate market capitalization in the A-shares market valued at RMB 614.124 billion in total (Table 11.3).

Supervision of the capital markets has become multifaceted, with a regulatory and supervisory framework that covers markets, investors, fund managers, financial products, and service providers.

Guidelines for Market Development

Through a series of carefully crafted reforms, China's capital markets have blazed a unique trail of development consistent with both market principles and growth imperatives. The reforms have included the following:

- *Market-based approach.* The policy intent is to create the right incentives for market entities with adequate checks and balances in place. Capital market reforms aim at developing a market-based mechanism in securities and futures markets with information disclosure rules at its core.

- *Rule of law.* A wide spectrum of rules and regulations has been implemented. These cover areas such as market making, new products, investment and financing, mergers and acquisitions and restructuring, asset management, supervision, and enforcement. A legal system is in place to allow securities contracts to be written and enforced.

- *Principle of transparency.* Strong emphasis has been given to accountability standards for listed companies, securities firms, and fund management firms. Several initiatives have been undertaken to make information relating to legislation, investigation and enforcement, routine supervision, and granting of administrative licenses publically available. A market integrity record database is currently under development.

- *International reach.* The process of Chinese companies "going global" and the Chinese market attracting foreign investment has been accelerated. This has further opened up China's capital markets.

Role of Capital Markets in Economic Development

To push economic reform forward, China has promoted the shareholding system, established the basic framework for modern corporate governance, and increased reliance on market-oriented capital allocation systems. New investment and financing channels have been fostered and banks are no longer the only source of financing. This is forcing financial institutions, including banks, to upgrade their business models and competitiveness, thus improving the overall resilience of China's financial system.

To support sustainable economic development, China's capital markets offer a viable intermediation channel to transform savings into investments. This has helped support the rapid development of infrastructure, pillar industries, and high-tech sectors. In order to encourage innovation, capital markets in China today provide a platform for new firms to grow. This is helping private capital formation, including venture capital and private equity funds, so as to boost capital generation and capital preservation within China. Considerable attention is also being given to promoting public awareness about capital market concepts, securities contracts, enforcement, transparency, and market integrity.

CURRENT ISSUES IN CHINA'S CAPITAL MARKETS

Despite the progress outlined above, China's capital markets face several complex challenges. The markets still lack depth and are unable to fully meet the needs of the real sector as China transitions away from a fully planned state system into a market-based system.

Small Share of Capital Markets in the Financial System

China's economy remains highly dependent on indirect modes of financing. Direct financing via equities and bonds is still relatively small. Of the overall financing of the economy in 2011, loan and acceptance bills accounted for 86 percent, while equity and bond financing made up only 14 percent (Figure 11.1). In terms of financial assets, as of end-2011, outstanding bank loans made up

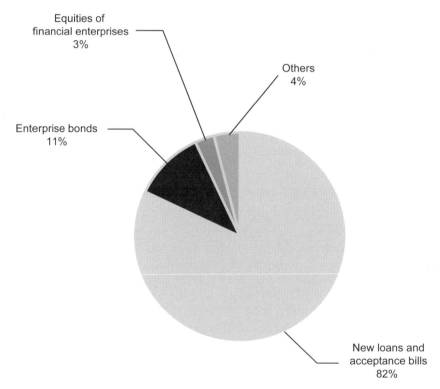

Source: China Securities Regulatory Commission.

Figure 11.1 Breakdown of Overall Funding Provided to Real Economy in 2011
(In percent)

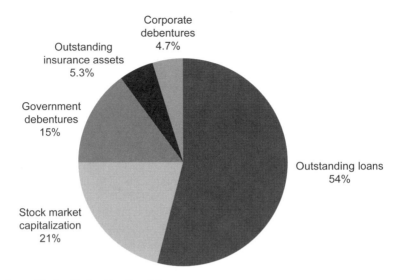

Source: China Securities Regulatory Commission.

Figure 11.2   Breakdown of Financial Assets as of end-2011
(In percent)

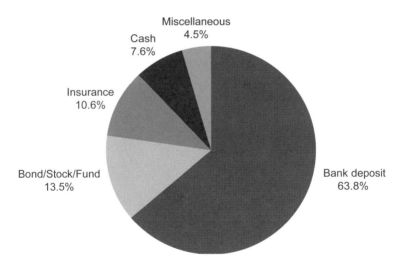

Source: China Securities Regulatory Commission.

Figure 11.3   Breakdown of the Financial Assets Owned by Chinese Residents as of end-2010
(In percent)

54 percent, while aggregate market capitalization and outstanding bonds accounted for only 26 percent, numbers significantly lower than those in most developed markets (Figure 11.2).

With respect to financial investments by individuals, bank deposits accounted for 64 percent, while investments in bonds, equities, and funds made up less than

14 percent (Figure 11.3). In contrast, residents in developed markets place almost 70 percent of their assets in capital market instruments. China's financial system thus remains dominated by commercial banks, which gives an obvious advantage to large enterprises and government-related companies and limits access for small and medium-sized enterprises (SMEs), microenterprises, and new ventures.

Concerns over the Internal Structure of Capital Markets

Several structural imbalances exist in China's capital markets that require policy attention. First, the development of the bond market is lagging. In September 2012, the combined stock market capitalization reached RMB 21.39 trillion and outstanding bonds under custody stood at around RMB 23.06 trillion (Figure 11.4). However, in most mature markets the bond market generally exceeds the stock market in volume. Furthermore, in China, government debentures, including T-bonds, local government bonds, central bank bills, and bank debentures, account for the majority of the bond market. For instance, as of end-2011, government debentures accounted for 76 percent of total trading volume of the bond market, while corporate debentures constituted only 24 percent.

Second, China's equity market is not yet deep enough to cater to diverse demands. In markets such as the United States, there are main boards (New York Stock Exchange) that serve large and medium-sized enterprises, and boards like the NASDAQ, which target small and medium-sized high-tech companies. There are also the over-the-counter (OTC) markets such as the OTC Bulletin Board and the Pink Sheet Market, and the Gray Market on an even lower level. However, China's markets consist only of the Main Board, SME Board, GEB, Stock Transfer Agent System, and regional equity trading markets, which are far from adequate for China's financing needs, especially in the SME and microenterprise sector (Figure 11.5).

The futures and derivatives markets are also underdeveloped, with insufficient investment and risk management controls. Compared with the mature markets, China's derivatives markets have a lot of room for improvement. Although China has the world's largest trading volume in commodity futures, it has only 28 futures products—similar to the numbers of futures products in the United States in the 1950s. Moreover, price discovery in China is not effective enough for the development of reliable benchmarks and hedging products.

A fourth factor pertains to the imbalanced investor base. In China, professional institutional investors in A-share markets account for 15.4 percent of total market capitalization, while the percentage in mature markets can be as high as 70 percent. Individual investors in A-share markets are not sophisticated enough to trade rationally. While they hold 26.4 percent of total market capitalization they contribute 85 percent of the trading volume (Figures 11.6 and 11.7).

Finally, fund raisers are dominated by large and medium-sized enterprises, which constitute the large majority of listed companies in China. Listing thresholds are still very high, even at the GEB, making it almost impossible for small businesses and microenterprises to list. According to China's definition of SMEs,

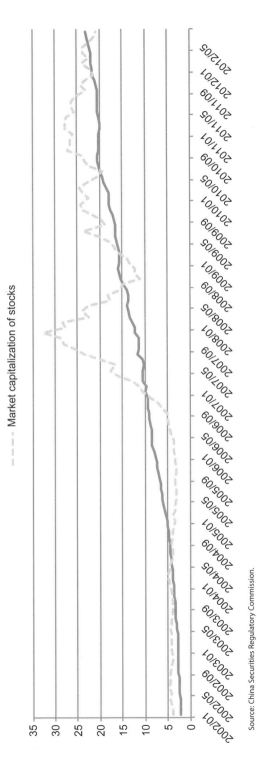

Source: China Securities Regulatory Commission.

Figure 11.4 Market Capitalization of Stocks and Bonds
(In trillions of renminbi)

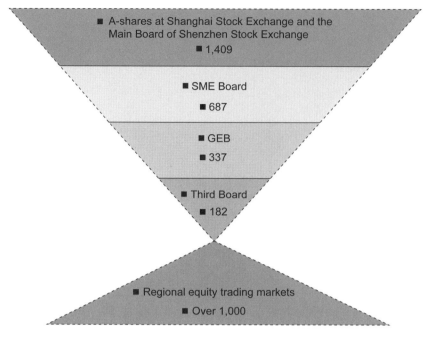

Source: China Securities Regulatory Commission.
Note: Amounts are as of December 31, 2011. GEB = Growth Enterprise Board; SME = small and medium-sized enterprises.

Figure 11.5 Equity Market in China
(Numbers of companies listed on the respective markets)

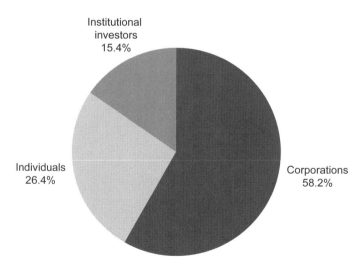

Source: China Securities Regulatory Commission.

Figure 11.6 Breakdown of Shareholders in the A-Share Markets as of end-2011
(In percent)

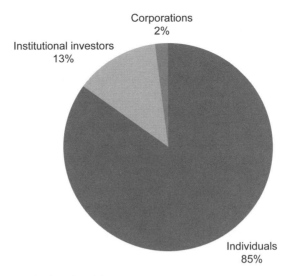

Corporations
2%

Institutional investors
13%

Individuals
85%

Source: China Securities Regulatory Commission.

Figure 11.7   Breakdown of Transactions in the A-Share Markets by Investor Category, 2011
(In percent)

of the 2,400 listed companies, less than 400 issuers are from the SME and microenterprise sector. Given that there are over 12 million SMEs in China, this level of capital market access remains narrow.

RECENT REFORM IN CHINA'S CAPITAL MARKETS

It has become imperative to solve the structural imbalance in China's capital markets. This is crucial to help accelerate structural adjustment and industrial transformation. A multipronged approach is needed to adjust the market structure and widen and deepen the domestic capital markets.

The first priority is to increase the share of direct financing. Bank-based financing can meet only certain specific types of financing needs. The capital markets, however, are capable of meeting a much wider range of investment and financing needs with diversified risk profiles.

The second priority relates to establishing multilayered capital markets. Apart from the equities markets, China is seeking to develop a properly developed bond market. The aim is to unify the supervisory standards for bond issuance and place emphasis on the development of corporate bonds, as is being done in the pilot program for SME private placement bonds. Furthermore, by reforming the stock issuance and delisting systems, China is encouraging listed companies to pay higher dividends and enhance their corporate governance. The OTC market is also growing and the plan is to establish such a market under a unified national supervisory system. This will help guide the healthy development of the

TABLE 11.4

Capital Market Priorities and Reform Measures

Key Reforms to Balance the Development of Different Markets		Reform Measures Already Implemented or Being Considered
Indirect financing	→ Direct financing	• General objectives of the reform
Exchange markets	→ Over-the-counter markets	• The New Third Board • Regional over-the-counter equity trading markets
Equity financing	→ Bond financing	• Small and medium-sized enterprises' private placement bonds • Unified supervisory standards on bond issuance • Linkage between interbank markets and exchange markets
Public offering	→ Private placement	• Small and medium-sized enterprises' private placement bonds • Equity trading markets for nonpublic offerings • Privately placed securities investment funds and price-earnings ratios brought under supervision • Investor suitability arrangements
Domestic capital markets	→ International capital markets	• More enterprises listed overseas • Foreign enterprises allowed to list in China
Financing of large and medium-sized enterprises	→ Financing of small and medium-sized enterprises and microenterprises	• Small and medium-sized enterprises' private placement bonds • Over-the-counter markets • Private equity/Venture capital
Individual investors	→ Institutional investors	• Gradually introducing corporate pension funds, social security fund, housing providence fund, and public pension funds, etc., as equity investors • Expanding the scope of fund investment and developing wealth management business • Relaxing the thresholds of QFII qualification
Domestic investors	→ Overseas investors	• Increased number of QFIIs
Commodities	→ Derivatives	• Silver futures, crude oil futures, T-bond futures • Stock index futures, stock options and swaps
No investor suitability arrangements	→ With investor suitability arrangements	• CSRC establishing Investor Protection Bureau • Investor suitability arrangements

Source: China Securities Regulatory Commission.
Note: CSRC = China Securities Regulatory Commission; QFII = Qualified Foreign Institutional Investor.

regional equities trading markets. In addition, more financial derivative products are being introduced. China has listed silver futures for trading and is conducting research on the launch of crude oil futures and T-bond futures. Meanwhile, plans are afoot to launch stock index options, stock options, and swaps.

Promoting institutional investors is yet another priority. The China Securities Regulatory Commission (CSRC) is devoted to serving and developing institutional investors. On the basis of fund management business, the scope of investment will be enlarged to nurture the wealth management industry, offering a broader spectrum of wealth management services to investors onshore. Entry barriers relating to professional institutional investors from overseas are being removed. The goal is to have a fair and efficient platform for investment by corporate pension funds, social security funds, housing providence funds, public pension funds, and wealth management schemes managed by insurance companies, trust companies, and banks.

Priority is also being placed on offering differentiated investment and financing instruments. China's capital markets are currently focused on publicly offered products. In the future, efforts will also be made to push for the development of privately offered markets. Such markets can provide more investment opportunities to institutional investors with higher risk tolerance, and they can also create financing channels for high-risk fund raisers. These measures will speed up the financing process and lower the overall financing cost. Of course, in developing a privately offered market and derivatives markets, the investor suitability principle has to be adopted. The CSRC has carried out a number of experiments in this regard with the stock index futures and the GEB market. The CSRC has also recently founded an Investor Protection Bureau to secure investor interests (Table 11.4).

IMPACT OF CHINA'S CAPITAL MARKETS ON FINANCIAL STABILITY

The stock market constitutes the major market segment in China, while other markets remain small in scale. China's individual investors are not mature enough, and many of them tend to speculate and flip stocks. Meanwhile, the A-share market in China lacks a short-selling mechanism and hedging tools and is therefore more vulnerable to market instability and dramatic price swings. Moreover, financial services firms in the capital markets also see wide fluctuation in profitability, which affects overall development of the financial industry.

Nevertheless, systemic risks in the capital markets remain relatively low for several reasons:

- *Low leverage ratios.* This is true for the leverage ratios of both service providers and investors. Securities firms have a leverage ratio of 1.4, which is one-tenth that of their counterparts in Europe and the United States. According to available statistics, the outstanding stock purchased through securities lending is only RMB 55.8 billion, with an average guarantee rate of 2.81.

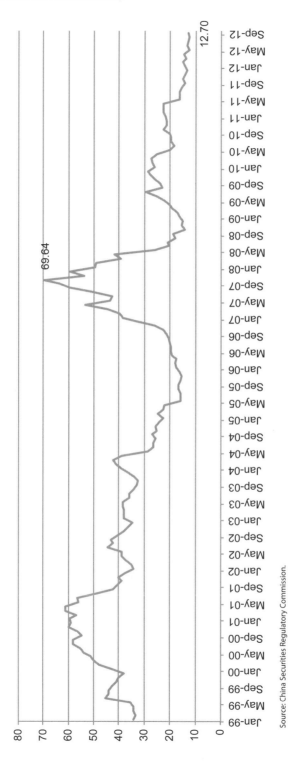

Source: China Securities Regulatory Commission.

Figure 11.8 Month-end Average Price-Earnings Ratio of Shanghai Stock Exchange

- *Segregation of investment and commercial banking.* In China, investment banking services and other capital market services are separated from the services of commercial banks. Banks are not allowed to operate across sectors. Securities firms are allowed to operate businesses limited to the capital markets, and there is no direct contagion risk between capital markets and commercial banks.

- *Low overall valuation of the A-share market.* Over the past 10 years, the average price-earnings ratio of A-share markets has dropped from 50–60 to 11. As of end-September 2012, the price-earnings ratio of the Shanghai Composite Index stood at 11.25, while the S&P 500 Index, DAX, and Nikkei 225 Index had ratios of 14.67, 13.84, and 21.80, respectively. Compared with other markets around the world, and taking into account the long-term growth rate of China, the current valuation of A-share markets remains quite low. In fact, its valuation has already hit a historical low, not only far below its peak in 2007 but also lower than the two troughs witnessed in the aftermath of the financial crisis in October 2008 or prior to the nontradable shares reform in May 2005 (Figure 11.8). The risk of a dramatic decline over the medium term has thus declined.

- *Stronger capital market supervision.* An overhaul of the securities industry was launched in 2004 with the closing of 31 securities firms. Since then, the CSRC has strengthened its supervision over securities firms and different capital market segments. With overall risks in the capital markets running low, now is an opportune time to push for reforms. It is true that financial innovation may bring new risks, but an in-depth reform of the capital markets would require a higher risk tolerance and a better balance between market innovation and more intensive market surveillance to prevent systemic risks.

While it is true that the capital markets in China now have certain negative effects on the stability of the overall financial system, the reason does not lie in the inherent risks of the capital markets but rather in the fact that China's capital markets are thin and underdeveloped. As a channel for direct financing, these markets provide a platform that can lower the cost of funding and diversify risks within the financial system. Proper capital market development will help reduce risk concentration, help the country alleviate the negative impact of the financial crisis, and improve the resilience of China's financial system.

APPENDIX TABLE 11.1

Bonds under Custody in China's Bonds Markets in August 2012
(In hundreds of millions of renminbi)

Bond type	Amount under Custody	Bond Type	Amount under Custody
Government bonds	78,107	Collective bills	161.0
Central bank bills	16,130	Foreign bonds	40.0
Financial bonds	86,994	Corporate bonds	4,331.9
Government-backed bonds	2,940	Convertible bonds	1,218.2
Enterprise bonds	20,496	Warrant bonds	796.2
Short-term financing notes	10,775	Small and medium-sized enterprises' private placement bonds	31.3
Asset-backed securities	82		
Medium-term notes	22,395	Total	244,497.6

Source: China Securities Regulatory Commission, *Monthly Statistics of China's Securities Markets* (Issue 8, 2012).

APPENDIX TABLE 11.2

Trading in China's Futures Derivatives Markets, 2011

Commodity Futures		Financial Futures	
Trading volume (10,000 lots)	Turnover (hundreds of millions of renminbi)	Trading volume (10,000 lots)	Turnover (hundreds of millions of renminbi)
100,372.56	937,503.89	5,041.19	437,658.55

Source: China Securities Regulatory Commission, *Monthly Statistics of China's Securities Markets* (Issue 6, 2012).

PART IV

Outlook for the Future

China's Road to Sustainable Growth and Financial Stability: A Systemic Perspective

ANDREW SHENG AND GENG XIAO[1]

As China becomes a major player in the global economy, what are the key reform issues that would deliver systemic stability with growth in the financial sector? Finance is a key factor in support of real sector growth, but its fragilities can also upset growth. As the Chinese economy integrates more closely with the global economy, the capacity to deliver long-term, sustainable, and inclusive growth will require a careful sequencing of reforms in both the real and financial sectors that provide both internal and external balance. A systemic approach is necessary, since it is increasingly apparent that there are endogenous and exogenous factors accounting for systemic instability, requiring careful calibration of macro, micro, and institutional policies to enable the system as a whole to be more resilient to systemic shocks.

China's market-oriented reform began in 1978 with a unique economic reform approach that was graphically characterized by the phrase "birds in a cage" coined by Chen Yun, the mastermind of China's economic planning system from the 1950s to the 1980s. According to Chen Yun, market-oriented reform meant allowing the birds (firms and households) to fly freely in a socialist market economy that is limited by the expanding cage (the bounded resources defined by planning). This gradual "expanding the cage" philosophy has served the Chinese leadership well over the last three decades in its searching and experimenting in terms of macroeconomic and financial stability, while progressively opening and liberalizing the Chinese economy to the world.

There is a practical logic to this philosophy, which was shaped by the reality that China is a continental economy with limited natural resources and, prior to opening up, little access to foreign exchange. With self-sufficiency as a guiding principle, China has been fiscally and financially prudent while bold in the execution of real sector opening and institutional innovation.

Progress in the process of opening has been impressive, as shown by the establishment of strong macroeconomic management and financial and regulatory institutions with modern instruments and staffed by professionals. China's economic

---

[1] The authors are grateful to Louis Kjius and Sean Quirk for helpful comments.

management team has delivered both growth and stability, creating the second-largest economy in the world. But realistically, even these achievements may not be good enough to deal with the ever-rising complexity and scale of the challenges at the technological, social, and global levels. As stated by Premier Wen Jiabao, China is faced with the risks of an "unbalanced, unstable, and uncoordinated economy" emerging in an unbalanced, uncoordinated, and systemically fragile global environment. Since China is a globally large and systemically important economy, its reform is really about maintaining national stability in the context of contributing to the systemic stability of the global economy. Thus, maintaining China's stability contributes significantly to global stability.

Throughout China's long history of macro and financial cycles, there has been a persistent feature that, translated from Chinese, means that when the central government exercises tighter control, the economy stops, but when control is relaxed, the system falls into chaos. In other words, Chinese macro control relies more on the "left hand" (quantitative and administrative tools such as reserve requirement ratios, credit quotas, and policy directives), rather than the "right hand" (market-oriented tools such as interest rates, exchange rates, market-driven prices, etc.).

Due to the country's top-down administrative and institutional structure, Chinese policymakers have much richer experience and stronger implementation capacity in using the "left hand" rather than the "right hand" to manage macroeconomic conditions. But there are inherent risks in this imbalanced and uneven two-handed approach. At this juncture, a systemic, global-local and business-relevant perspective is essential for Chinese policymakers to understand options in rebalancing toward an even-handed approach to the country's macroeconomic management. As China's economy becomes more integrated with the global market economy, a balanced two-handed toolbox is necessary to manage systemic trade-offs between efficiency, stability, innovation, and resource constraints. Complexity arises because China needs to simultaneously and dynamically maintain and balance economic, financial, social, ecological, and global stability.

The first challenge in assessing China's options is to ensure relevancy to the real economy. The underlying structural transformation in the real economy within a global context has produced rising productivity, derived from integrating China into the global markets, which is the most important driver of rapid growth. This rapid rise in productivity has led to a convergence in real income, purchasing power, living standards, and general price levels between China and the advanced economies, shown most clearly in the increase of China's per capita GDP from about $300 in 1978 to $4,428 in 2012.

This productivity growth was basically facilitated through a stable political environment, prudent fiscal and monetary policies, and an opening up to a favorable external environment. But even as absolute poverty has been reduced, income and wealth disparities, growing resource demands, pollution, corruption, and rising middle-class social expectations are bringing new challenges to managing stability in a dynamically changing landscape.

CHINA'S TRAJECTORY TOWARD CONVERGENCE WITH ADVANCED COUNTRIES

Productivity catch-up is largely a secular, real-sector issue. However, maintaining macroeconomic stability along the convergence path remains important, and this includes managing volatility in key prices in the economy—wages, consumer prices, asset prices, and the exchange rate. At the same time, there is a need to manage the balance-sheet effect of such changes in prices, since sharp volatility in asset prices may have an impact on the solvency of the household and corporate sectors and also the capacity of fiscal authorities to manage the economy.

China's growth model over the last 30 years depended on cheap labor. This cannot be sustained once the Lewis turning point has been reached, that is, the point at which rural surplus labor disappears and real wages begin to increase. Moreover, under the Twelfth Five-Year Plan, China intends to increase minimum wages by up to 13 percent per annum.

At the same time, real estate prices have risen substantially in the last 20 years, which will sooner or later feed into higher rents and demand for higher wages, as well as add to cost-push factors. The Balassa-Samuelson theorem suggests that rapid productivity growth in the tradable sector leads to higher wages across the economy, including in the nontradable sector, even though productivity growth there is very limited. Furthermore, upward pressures on real estate prices are amplified by the generous credit flows to state-owned enterprises (SOEs) and local governments at low interest rates. In other words, China will inevitably face a period of higher "structural cost-push" inflation.

Indeed, financial sector arrangements and distortions are a major reason behind the structural misallocation of resources. In China, banks lend excessively to SOEs and local governments and insufficiently to small and medium-sized enterprises (SMEs) and the household sector. It means that SMEs have to pay excessively high real rates to borrow on the informal market while the low deposit rate in the formal banking sector leads to financial repression and fuels speculation in real estate. Hence, current banking sector credit policies are the root of the so-called shadow banking problem in China, as the much higher informal market interest rates in places like Wenzhou are creating opportunities for arbitrage between high real lending rates for SMEs and low deposit rates in the formal banking sector through "creative" wealth management products that may create new risks to the healthy development of Chinese banking and stock markets.

Since real estate prices can significantly affect the collateral and solvency of the banking system, China needs to develop more efficient and robust financial institutions by liberalizing interest rates, so that there is less room for leveraged speculation in the asset markets through low interest rates.

The low interest rates for SOE and local government projects as compared to the prevailing high informal market interest rates have long-term systemic consequences. Keeping them in place would mean that SOEs and local governments would continue their investment-driven business model, which may lead to problems of financial viability. Local governments tend to open up new land and offer it as subsidies to investors, thus distorting foreign direct investment (FDI) flows. This explains why inward FDI is still rising even as China is trying to increase outward FDI.

Deepening capital markets to balance the dominance of the banking system is critical to achieving systemic stability. For example, the low interest rate regime in China encourages distortive behavior in the stock market, as companies invest in low-return projects and then rush into the initial public offering (IPO) markets to raise funds in bubbly markets. This crowds out high-return projects. Moreover, due to the limited access of private and foreign companies to IPOs in the A-share market, the most competitive and profitable companies in China are not well represented in China's stock markets. The European experience has also shown that the maturity mismatch of allowing long-term sovereign debt to be funded by banks that rely on wholesale funding can lead to systemic instability.

China's macro policy mix since 2005 has been a careful trade-off between controlling inflation, maintaining growth, and managing export cycles. It consists of a low target inflation rate of 3 to 4 percent, a low and stable interest rate of around 3 to 3.5 percent for one-year deposits, gradual and steady renminbi appreciation of 3 to 5 percent per year, and controls on bank lending through frequent adjustment of the reserve requirement ratio, ranging from a low of 9 percent in early 2007 to a high of 21.5 percent in mid-2011.

The above policy mix set was clearly calibrated with an eye on global macro conditions and policies such as zero interest rate policies in the advanced countries. China's policymakers did not raise interest rates in the face of domestic inflation, clearly concerned about hot money inflows if interest rates were much higher in China than abroad.

Furthermore, China has started to allow the renminbi to appreciate gradually at a rate of 3 to 5 percent per year since 2005. This contributed to the reduction of the current account surplus from the peak of about 10 percent of GDP in 2007 to 3 percent in 2011.

Nevertheless, there were two effects from this set of policy choices. The first was that it contributed to the accumulation of large foreign exchange reserves. While current account surpluses were the main driver behind this accumulation, financial capital inflows have at times also been large, as investors rushed into renminbi assets, speculating on renminbi appreciation as well as gains on investments in China's real estate. The second effect was leveraged speculation on real estate, funded through borrowing from Chinese banks at very low interest rates, especially for those who could get access to bank credit. This led to a socially unstable redistribution from poor depositors to rich mortgage borrowers.

In order to maintain system stability in the medium term, the Chinese authorities must not only strengthen the institutional infrastructure and the range and effectiveness of policy tools but also seek to rebalance access to credit by the private sector and introduce competition across different sectors and jurisdictions, which are currently supervised in vertical silos by different ministries. In order to improve the use of market-based tools, China would have to liberalize interest rates and remove impediments to price discovery by lowering barriers to entry, creating futures and options markets, and improving the transparency of market activities and regulatory processes.

For example, to improve the credit discipline of local governments, there should be transparency on disclosure of financial conditions of municipalities and all local government debt vehicles on a timely basis. Greater transparency regarding financial conditions and interest rates paid by SMEs would also enhance credit discipline in the private sector, allowing market forces to better price risks. Improvements in the SME funding market would bring down the usurious rates currently observed in the unofficial credit market, such as those in Wenzhou.

To summarize, microregulatory policies can only work if macroeconomic prices reflect credit and market risks and the distribution of financial resources across sectors is broadly in balance. Given the interactions and interdependence of macroeconomic conditions between China and the global economy, for Chinese policies to achieve systemic stability requires both a big-picture appreciation of transformations in the real and financial sectors at the global and local levels as well as an understanding of specific microfragilities and their institutional causes. In the medium term, global rebalancing will continue as advanced markets adjust to slower growth to repair their balance sheets, and as emerging markets seek capital to finance their urbanization and green and inclusive growth.

To maintain productivity growth, economic efficiency, and social fairness, China needs to rationalize its financial markets by ensuring that the price of capital (real interest rate) is consistent with its scarcity and value in the real sector. This means that China may have to maintain positive real interest rates over time and a real effective exchange rate that is consistent with its rapid growth in total factor productivity. Chinese concerns about systemic stability must be understood in the context of building a more balanced toolbox of market and administrative tools that "fits" the stages of development of the real and financial sectors. Channeling the pattern of growth toward a larger role for consumption and services requires an array of reforms. In the financial sector, it is essential to reward aging savers positive real interest rates so that they have income to spend. Increasing social inclusivity would require removing financial repression and paying labor a fair share of total factor income, while exercising discipline on the efficiency of investment. To achieve these objectives, it is essential for China's policymakers to adopt a systemic, global-local, and business-relevant approach to study and deal with its macroeconomic management challenges.

CHAPTER 13

Delivering Financial Stability in China

Joseph Yam

When commenting on financial reform in China, Premier Wen Jiabao has often emphasized the philosophy of "gradualism, controllability, and the ability to take the initiative." Like many other sound bites of leaders in China, this philosophy has been reduced to a slogan to the extent that the underlying important messages have become fuzzy with the passage of time. Against the continued international chorus of politically inspired calls for financial liberalization—for example, freeing up the exchange rate and opening up the capital account—it seems necessary to reemphasize the philosophy in any professional discussion of financial reform in China.

The risk of departing from the premier's philosophy of financial reform for China is, of course, financial instability, which the severe financial crises of the past two decades have demonstrated can be debilitating to emerging as well as developed economies. With globalization and an abundance of liquidity, financial markets have become rather potent. They can wreak havoc on open economies, big or small, sometimes indiscriminately, playing on the slightest of aberrations in public policies in an almost predatory manner, and justifying such action as a manifestation of valuable market discipline in a free market environment.

There is little doubt that market freedom in finance ensures the efficient allocation of financial resources. In the socialist market economy of China, where the involvement of the state in finance is high relative to other jurisdictions, particularly developed capitalist ones, the case for allowing the market to play a bigger and freer role in finance is clear. But in moving in this direction, China needs always to remind itself of the theoretical assumptions behind the efficient market and be alert to the possibility that, in the real world, these assumptions do not always hold true. In finance, we have observed time and again that Adam Smith's invisible hand cannot always be relied upon to transmute individual acts of selfishness into desirable collective outcomes for all. In finance in the real world, there are factors limiting the mobility of the invisible hand. They include information problems, herding behavior, market imperfections such as monopoly or oligopoly power, market globalization while regulation remains domestic, incentive distortions, derivative products (or the tail that wags the dog), greed, fear, stupidity, criminality, leverage, speculative bubbles, irrational exuberance, uncertainty, manipulative and predatory behavior, policy blunders, the political influence of self-interested groups . . . the list could go on yet further.

An important function of the market is price discovery. It is precisely in this important function that financial markets have exhibited repeated tendencies to fail. Greed and manipulative behavior often produce volatility in financial markets that is so pronounced as to undermine the viability of financial institutions and therefore the stability of the financial system. In the major foreign exchange markets, for example, less than 5 percent of turnover is represented by the foreign exchange needs arising from real economic activity, such as trade and foreign direct investment. The other more than 95 percent is represented by position taking, largely of a speculative nature but presented as necessary market-making to provide liquidity. But instead of accurate price discovery to facilitate those important real economic activities, there is sharp volatility and frequent exchange rate overshooting, undermining financial stability. One can clearly question the need for the over 95 percent of turnover unrelated to real economic activity, other than serving to provide employment for the large number of well-remunerated foreign exchange traders and the (unsustainable) profits they make for the financial institutions where they work.

Thus, it is necessary in reforming the regulatory framework for the financial system in China as well as in other jurisdictions to place great emphasis on arrangements that allow the potency of financial markets to be harnessed in the public interest, delivering stability, integrity, diversity, and efficiency in financial intermediation that is so important for promoting economic growth and development. For example, with regard to renminbi convertibility, if this approach involves a mechanism for seeking and giving approvals, and for providing information for activities to be appropriately monitored, China should not shy away from it simply because it is not the norm for most of the rest of the world. The reform agenda for the rest of the world, against the backdrop of the ongoing financial crisis, is also a matter of harnessing the potency of financial markets, which have caused chaos with market freedom, through tighter regulation. There is ground in between to be explored.

Another philosophical issue in financial reform that China as well as other jurisdictions should recognize is the inherent conflict between the private interests of financial intermediaries in maximizing profits and bonuses, on the one hand, and the public interest of efficient financial intermediation, on the other. Put simply, the greater the profits and bonuses of the financial intermediaries (the higher the intermediation cost), the lower the efficiency of financial intermediation, with investors and depositors getting a lower rate of return and the fund raisers incurring a higher cost of money. Naturally, the financial intermediaries seek to manage, or rather hide, this conflict through innovative arrangements that, at least for a while, promise higher rates of investment return and lower costs of funds, even to those who are not creditworthy—financial innovation that enhances financial efficiency. For that, the intermediaries became even more highly remunerated.

It would be difficult to argue that financial innovation does not enhance financial efficiency. Credit risk transfer through securitization enhances financial efficiency, until it creates the incentive in the financial system that erodes credit standards. When that happens, financial innovation becomes a form of intertemporal transfer of the intermediation spread from the future (widening of the spread) to the present (narrowing of the spread) that gives the impression of increasing financial efficiency alongside (the contradictory) rising profitability of the financial intermediaries. Unfamiliar risks to financial stability build up in the process and culminate in financial crises that are inevitably manifested in a sharp widening of the intermediation spread. In turn, investors find themselves losing money and fund raisers not being able to raise funds.

Thus, for China, which still has a rather rudimentary financial system, there is a need for great caution when it embraces financial innovation as a means to enhance much-needed financial efficiency. Those in the financial industry would argue that it is not for bureaucrats to try to outsmart financial markets by, for example, predetermining the boundaries for financial innovation by administrative means. But at a time when the financial systems of developed markets are struggling to go back to the basics, it is well justified for the financial authorities in China to be proactively involved in assessing the risks associated with innovative financial arrangements and ensuring that prudent risk management mechanisms, both within financial institutions and in the financial system as a whole, are a precondition to their introduction.

Financial authorities should simply say no to financial proposals that they find difficult to understand, notwithstanding whatever good track record or sound theoretical arguments are presented in support of these proposals. If the financial authorities in the United States had been courageous enough to say no to subprime mortgages and insist on the securitization of mortgages only with conservative loan-to-value ratios, the ongoing financial crisis of the century could well have been avoided. In the same vein, financial authorities should also just say no to financial arrangements that, in their opinion after having surveyed the domestic circumstances, do nothing to promote the fundamental function of financial intermediation, however fashionable such arrangements might be in other financial systems. "Others have it" is never a good enough reason for the introduction of innovative financial products—witness the damage to the global financial system caused by collateralized debt obligations and credit default swaps.

In this regard, China should be alert to the political reality that financial intermediaries, given that they control where money comes from and where it goes, have a strong political lobby, a phenomenon that is perhaps more pronounced in the developed markets in Europe and the United States than in China. This has led in the developed markets to inadequate powers and tools in legal frameworks for financial authorities to exercise prudential supervision of financial institutions and regulation of financial market behavior. Within the framework of the socialist market economy of China, this seems less of a problem.

Furthermore, the policy transmission mechanism in China seems a lot more efficient in terms of producing desirable results. However, as China progresses further on its path of financial reform and liberalization, it is inevitable that some of the levers currently available, effective as they may be, will be lost, thus eroding China's ability to deliver financial stability. It is not easy to strike the right balance in this delicate development. One strategy may be to retain many of the powers and tools that are considered essential, but to enhance transparency and accountability when financial authorities exercise them. With globalization and an abundance of international liquidity, financial liberalization is a risky process. It would be prudent for China to keep as much as possible of the financial armory that has served it so well in the past.

For the financial authorities to deliver financial stability in the complex external and domestic environment confronting China is clearly a challenging task. There is a need for the right incentive system to attract the necessary talent from the financial industry (which is increasingly run on a commercial basis and given autonomy in determining the remuneration for its employees) as well as from overseas. This is an issue that extends to the much wider dimension concerning the incentive system in the labor market of the socialist market economy of China. There has, nevertheless, been some labor mobility between the financial regulators and the financial industry, although it has been less market-oriented than desired. The preference is for financial talent to move from the public sector to the private sector and for the reverse, particularly at the senior levels, to be mandated by the state, an arrangement that arguably undermines regulatory effectiveness. Although this practice has not, hitherto, led to any apparent supervisory or regulatory failings of a systemic dimension, there is doubt as to whether the current arrangement will continue to be as effective as it has been as finance in China gains in sophistication. It seems desirable for the financial authorities to be given financial autonomy and for the necessary financial resources to be derived from the financial industry through appropriate financial levies.

One specific way of achieving this may be for the People's Bank of China (PBC), as the central bank, to be given financial autonomy, allowing it to keep the profits from the issue of currency notes and charge a service fee for the management of foreign reserves. It may be that there is significant surplus that could go toward funding part of the budgets for the three regulatory commissions as the PBC's contribution to financial stability, thus lessening the impact of levies to be charged by the three commissions overseeing the financial industry.

The maintenance of financial stability is not an academic issue, hence the nonacademic approach of this short chapter. It is a difficult task, but it can be made easier to achieve by creating a culture among financial system stakeholders that continuously reminds them of the basic function of such a system, which is to support the economy, rather than to provide a playground for making money. Many financial markets are basically zero-sum games. Consistently trading profits year after year for financial institutions or traders can only be possible if they possess technical skills that are superior to others, have access to inside information, and are persistently lucky. None of these hold true in the long run. In the short term, unsustainable profits and bonuses allow distorted incentives to creep in, leading many to forget the purpose of their existence and behave in a manner that eventually undermines financial stability. There is a need for a cultural revolution in finance.

CHAPTER 14

The Impact of Financial Liberalization on China's Financial Sector

JUN MA AND HUI MIAO

The growing consensus in China that it should internationalize its currency—driven by a mix of national pride, external demand, and perceived economic benefits for the Chinese economy—is beginning to serve as a commitment device for pushing forward other financial reforms. This is because financial liberalization—including interest rate liberalization, exchange rate flexibility, capital account liberalization, and opening up of the financial industry—is a precondition for a meaningful internationalization of the renminbi.

Of course, there are other important rationales in addition to internationalization of the renminbi for financial liberalization, as outlined in the paragraphs below.

First, China is facing structural headwinds such as the erosion of demographic dividends that will inevitably lead to a moderation of economic growth. It is thus becoming increasingly urgent for China to look for alternative sources of growth. Financial liberalization (especially interest rate liberalization) will help improve the efficiency of resource allocation and mitigate the downward pressure on growth potential.

Second, an open financial system is essential for developing China's international financial centers such as Shanghai. The financial services sector is viewed as the next growth driver by several other major cities in China.

Third, existing controls on foreign exchange conversion and cross-border flows, as well as interest rate controls, are becoming increasingly difficult to enforce given rapid financial innovations. For example, the massive growth of informal lending activities has become a source of concern of late. Trust loans and other wealth management products have significantly destabilized the deposit base and undermined the effectiveness of monetary policy.

Finally, political backlash against big banks is gaining popular support, as banks are often viewed as making too much profit but not providing enough credit to small and medium-sized enterprises (SMEs). In March 2012, Premier Wen Jiabao authorized a pilot financial liberalization reform program in Wenzhou permitting the establishment of smaller financial institutions.

This chapter discusses the implications of the financial liberalization program for China's financial companies, with an expectation that the proposed reform process will be largely completed over the next three to five years.

NONBANK FINANCING WILL GAIN ITS MARKET SHARE

Financial liberalization will gradually reshape the structure of China's financial system and open a range of new business opportunities. A major change is for the financing structure to move away from a bank-dominated indirect financing model toward greater use of nonbank direct financing. These nonbank financing or direct financing options include bond issuance, equity financing (public and private), and trust loans. Based on Japan's liberalization experience in the 1980s, the share of bank lending in domestic financing will likely shrink while direct financing and overseas lending/borrowing will increase.

China's corporate debt financing has been growing below its full potential, owing to eight key constraints: (1) debt financing limits that restrict the scale of corporate debt financing; (2) inefficiencies in primary debt market pricing mechanisms; (3) the quality and standing of domestic credit rating firms; (4) further modernization of the current legal framework; (5) low secondary market liquidity; (6) the shallowness of the domestic bond market investor base; (7) continuation of investment restrictions on domestic institutional investors' market risk exposure; and (8) the nascent state of the domestic credit derivatives market.

Going forward, regulators can be expected to launch policy initiatives to address these constraints, and therefore corporate debt financing will grow at a much faster pace than bank lending. Specifically, we forecast the size of the credit market to grow fourfold over the next five years to RMB 20 trillion. This

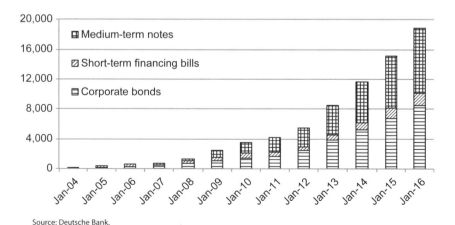

Source: Deutsche Bank.

Figure 14.1 Forecast of China's Credit Market
(Outstanding amount in billions of renminbi)

TABLE 14.1

Financial Intermediation Structure (In percent)				
	China 2011	Japan 1965–74	Japan 1975–84	Japan 1985–90
Bank loans	79	70	55	48
Equity	3	5	4	10
Bonds	10	15	28	10
Offshore borrowing	5	3	3	5
Overseas lending	2	8	11	28

Sources: Bank of Japan; CEIC; China State Administration of Foreign Exchange; and Deutsche Bank.

outlook is consistent with Japan's experience—bond issuance as a percentage share of total financing almost doubled during Japan's financial liberalization in the 1970s and 1980s.

The acceleration in credit market growth will reinforce the substitution effect between debt financing and bank loans. Therefore, medium-to-long-term loans could gradually become a less significant driver for new lending growth in the coming years. Moreover, regarding the asset composition of commercial banks, substituting loans with corporate bond holdings implies a narrowing interest rate margin. This could tip the balance of commercial bank lending toward SMEs, which would improve capital allocation to less-privileged sectors over the medium term. In addition, the expansion of the bond market can be expected to improve brokers' earnings from corporate bond underwriting revenues (Figure 14.1).

In addition to the rapid growth of the bond market, equity initial public offerings (IPOs) could double in the coming years, as the China Securities Regulatory Commission (CSRC) is planning to replace the approval process with a "registration process" (Table 14.1).

BANKS' NET INTEREST MARGINS WILL CONTRACT, BUT A FURTHER DOWNSIDE MAY BE LIMITED

A major concern for Chinese banks during the liberalization process is that interest rate deregulation will lead to a contraction in their net interest margin (NIM) and a slower pace of deposit/lending growth. First, with the gradual removal of deposit and lending rate restrictions, banks will be encouraged to bid more aggressively (by raising deposit rates and cutting lending rates) for deposits and loans. Second, some large corporates that have been the banks' most profitable clients will likely switch to bond financing due to lower funding costs. This will also increase the pressure for banks to cut lending rates. Depositors will also be attracted by the liquidity and attractive yields offered by bond funds, thus forcing banks to raise deposit rates. Third, banks will face relatively high regulatory costs (a high reserve requirement ratio and tax burden) compared to their offshore competitors in Hong Kong SAR or Singapore and thus might lose some clients to offshore financial centers.

While the NIM will narrow, the key question is by how much is it likely to fall during the liberalization process. An IMF staff study shows that China's deposit rates will likely rise by 30 basis points following interest rate liberalization (Feyzioglu, Porter, and Takats, 2009). Deutsche Bank analysts estimate that the NIM might contract by 37 basis points if deposit rates converge to short-term interbank rates with similar maturities. Of course, the initial monetary condition also matters. If the regulated deposit rates are close to the interbank rates with similar maturities, the overall deposit rates may not change much after deregulation. A general conclusion could thus be that if macro conditions are well under control—that is, consumer price index inflation is modest, real interest rates are positive, and interbank rates are broadly in line with deposit rates—then the impact of deposit rate deregulation on the NIM can be within a 20–30 basis point range.

In June 2012, the People's Bank of China (PBC) expanded the floating range of deposit and lending rates. Lending rates are now allowed to be priced at or above 0.8 times the benchmark rates (previously the lower bound was 0.9 times) and deposit rate ceilings are set at 1.1 times the benchmark rates (previously the ceilings were the benchmark rates). Immediately after the deregulation, all large banks raised their one-year deposit rate to 3.5 percent (7.7 percent above the new benchmark rate), while many smaller banks raised their one-year deposit rate to 3.575 percent (1.1 times the benchmark). The NIM of the banking system contracted immediately by about 10 basis points.

Given that the deposit and lending rates of large banks are no longer constrained by the lower or upper bounds, this implies that the rates at most banks are close to their equilibrium rates. Even if the floating ranges for interest rates are expanded further, the average lending and deposit rates may not change significantly from their current levels. Therefore, the most difficult phase of interest rate liberalization is perhaps now behind us and a large one-off NIM contraction has already occurred and is likely to not repeat itself going forward.

There are several other reasons to believe that further downside risks to the banking system's NIM may be limited. First, the NIM of Chinese banks does not appear excessive when compared to global peers. It is normal for foreign banks to maintain a 2 to 3 percent NIM regardless of the stage of financial development and capital account openness (Table 14.2).

Second, after the June 2012 reform, the ceilings on three-year and five-year deposit rates were already close to or even higher than the lower bounds for three-year and five-year lending rates. This means that although the scope for extreme margin contraction is already provided under the current policy, excessive margin compression is unlikely.

Third, the Chinese banking system is dominated by five banks that account for nearly 50 percent of outstanding loans and deposits. These banks will likely retain their rate-setting influence in the banking market. In Hong Kong, for example, retail banking business was dominated by three major banks. Following the removal of the interest rate agreement in the early 2000s, there was

TABLE 14.2

Comparison of Bank Net Interest Margins in the Asia Pacific Region
(In percent)

	2008	2009	2010	2011
China	3	2.3	2.4	2.6
Hong Kong SAR	2	1.7	1.6	1.5
India	3.3	3.4	3.3	3.5
Indonesia	8	9.5	10.6	9.5
Malaysia	2.3	2.4	2.3	2.2
Philippines	3.7	3.9	3.6	3.5
Singapore	2.2	2.2	2	1.8
South Korea	3	2.6	2.8	2.6
Taiwan Province of China	1.9	1.4	1.4	
Thailand			5.7	5.9
Australia	2	2.2	2.3	2.3

Source: Deutsche Bank.

no significant hike of deposit rates, as the large banks continued to set the key rates while the smaller banks followed.

Finally, the deposit mix matters in China. Demand deposits account for 40 percent of total deposits, and interest-rate-sensitive corporate time deposits are only 17 percent of total deposits. Demand deposits are much less sensitive to changes in interest rates than corporate time deposits.

BANKS' INCOMES FROM FEES WILL RISE RAPIDLY

Despite the challenges posed by interest rate and capital account liberalization, banks will also benefit from new business opportunities. First, Chinese banks are already the dominant players in the interbank bond market. The booming bond and foreign exchange businesses will bring in extra fee and trading incomes. Currently, daily renminbi-related foreign exchange spot trading volume is only US$30 billion, compared to U.S. dollar daily foreign exchange trading volume of US$4 trillion. Once the renminbi assumes a floating character without capital account restrictions, the hedging and trading demand will significantly pick up. Renminbi trading revenue could rise by as much as 50-fold to 5 percent of total bank income over the medium term. Current fee income from trading foreign exchange is only about 0.3 percent of Chinese banks' total revenue. As a comparison, major global banks such as HSBC derived 4 to 5 percent of income from foreign exchange trading in 2011. Among Chinese banks, the Bank of China, given that it has a 30 percent market share of foreign exchange trading, should benefit the most from the surge in foreign exchange trading due to capital account liberalization.

Other trading and fee incomes from selling interest rate and derivative products will also rise. During financial liberalization in Japan in the 1970s, foreign exchange transaction volume (spot and swap) rose 500-fold, from US$12 billion in 1970 to US$6 trillion in 1990, and bond market volume rose sixfold from JPY 29 trillion in 1975 to JPY 184 trillion in 1991. Total bond market transactions increased from JPY 56 trillion in 1980 to JPY 534 trillion in 1991, an increase of 9.5 times.

As the process of liberalization unfolds and the capital account opens further, Chinese banks will be able to sell many more global financial products to domestic clients, and provide more services to international clients (such as custody and bond trading services for Qualified Foreign Institutional Investor clients). Chinese banks are also currently involved in the distribution of mutual funds offered by Qualified Domestic Institutional Investor (QDII) managers. Given the limited size of QDII operations, the potential for distributing more global mutual fund products to Chinese clients is sizable. Finally, Chinese banks can also benefit from the overseas expansion of Chinese companies by providing trade finance, merger and acquisition (M&A), and global treasury services.

GLOBAL EXPANSION IS A DOUBLE-EDGED SWORD

Despite the fact that China is the second-largest economy in the world, Chinese banks have had a very limited presence to date in major financial centers. Some Chinese banks will follow the overseas expansion of Chinese companies and find new business abroad. Some others may seek a stronger presence in major markets to serve local clients.

Of course, the overseas expansion is also risky given the lack of experience of Chinese financial institutions in global markets. In the 1970s, Japanese banks became major players in other financial centers, with the number of offshore offices rising from 139 to 327 and offshore assets jumping from JPY 25 trillion (in 1980) to JPY 127 trillion (in 1991). Overseas lending by Japanese banks also rose from JPY 10.9 trillion in 1980 to JPY 73.5 trillion in 1991. Simultaneously, foreign banks also expanded their businesses in Japan. Not all Japanese overseas investments were successful, with some suffering from serious losses in the U.S. property markets and others incurring trading losses due to poor risk management.

Given the Japanese experience, foreign borrowers can also be expected to be more active in China. Panda bonds will likely take off together with the Dim Sum bond market. Again, for historical perspective, between 1980 and 1991, the outstanding amount of Samurai bonds rose from JPY 1.8 trillion to JPY 6.2 trillion, and euro-yen from JPY 200 billion to JPY 18.1 trillion (Figure 14.2).

Given the limited experience and significant cultural differences between Chinese and foreign institutions, the chance of success for large-scale M&As by Chinese banks is not high. It would be prudent for Chinese financial firms to pursue organic growth initially, with a focus of serving Chinese companies going abroad. In addition, they need to be sensitive to returns on equity for business expansion, rather than base decisions solely on a concept that certain geographic regions will have attractive growth potential. Finally, Chinese banks should also

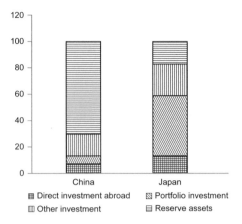

Sources: China's State Administration of Foreign Exchanges; and Japan's Ministry of Finance.

Figure 14.2 Composition of International Investment Position
(In percent)

leverage Hong Kong as the place to test the waters before they venture further away from their turf.

BROKERAGE AND ASSET MANAGEMENT SECTORS WILL BENEFIT

Securities brokers in China currently engage mostly in domestic equity underwriting and trading business, but their international business is very limited. Brokers will benefit from financial liberalization in at least two ways. First, local brokers will benefit from Chinese investing abroad. Currently, the private sector (including Chinese households and private corporates) has about 1 percent of assets offshore. Most of China's overseas assets are held by public sector entities such as the State Administration of Foreign Exchange in the form of foreign exchange reserves (US$3.3 trillion). In Japan, by comparison, US$7.3 trillion of overseas assets are mostly held by portfolio investments (US$3.4 trillion). So the pent-up demand for Chinese investors to invest in overseas equities and bonds could be huge. This will create significant business opportunities for local brokers in terms of commissions for trading foreign financial products and facilitating cross-border M&A businesses.

Second, foreign investments in Chinese bond and equity markets will also increase substantially. Currently, foreign ownership in Chinese bonds and the A-share equity market is only 1 percent of the market cap or outstanding amount. Compared to other emerging market countries, which on average have a foreign participation rate of 26 percent for equity markets and 13 percent for bond markets, the room for growing foreign portfolio investments into China is easily a

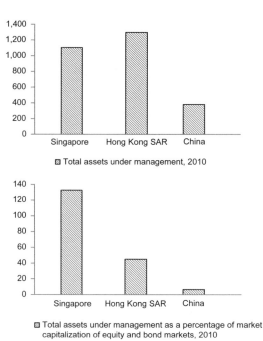

Source: Deutsche Bank.

Figure 14.3 China's Underdeveloped Asset Management Industry
(Top panel in billions of U.S. dollars; bottom panel in percent)

fivefold increase in the coming five years. Portfolio inflows will also increase trading commissions for local brokers.

In addition to benefits for brokers, asset management companies should also see a significant increase in assets under management (AUM) as private investors invest more in overseas securities markets and a wider range of liquid domestic products become available. Currently, total AUM by China's asset management industry are only about RMB 2.5 trillion, a third of that in Hong Kong. As a comparison, total deposits in China reached RMB 87 trillion by the end of 2011. In developed countries, the ratio of AUM to deposits tends to range from 100 to 200 percent, compared to China's 3 percent (Figure 14.3).

INSURANCE WILL LIKELY SEE IMPROVED RETURNS ON INVESTMENT

The impact of interest rate liberalization on insurance companies is negative in the short term but positive over the long term. Insurance companies have been mainly selling savings and investment policies, so low and regulated deposit rates have provided advantages to them. But in a liberalized interest rate environment in which deposit rates tend to rise, these insurance products will become less attractive. Their savings products will face direct competition from bank deposits, bond funds, and other wealth management products. This is the negative impact that insurance companies are experiencing right now.

On the other hand, higher deposit rates tend to benefit insurance companies by boosting their asset returns, given that the majority of insurance premiums are invested in bonds and deposits. This positive impact on insurance companies' investment returns will be realized in the longer term, as the impact mainly benefits new investments made by insurance companies.

LIBERALIZATION MEASURES WILL BENEFIT BANKS BASED IN HONG KONG

As discussed earlier, capital account liberalization will be the most important next step toward internationalization of the renminbi. Once the capital account is open, there will be multiple channels through which renminbi liquidity can flow to the offshore market, including Hong Kong. These include individuals' and corporates' remittances of renminbi to the offshore market, the ability of Hong Kong and foreign residents to more freely convert foreign currencies to the renminbi in the offshore market, and a higher multiplier effect due to more active offshore renminbi lending (partly due to free remittance of renminbi into and out of China). The offshore market will likely continue to grow rapidly during and after the opening of China's capital account.

On July 1, 2012, Chinese President Hu Jintao visited Hong Kong to attend the celebration of the 15th anniversary of Hong Kong's return to China's sovereignty. During his visit, the Chinese government announced additional liberalization measures that could boost CNH liquidity, CNH trading, and Dim Sum bond issuance on the renminbi offshore market.[1] The Bank of China (Hong Kong) (BOC), which has more than half of renminbi deposits in the Hong Kong market, will likely see a significant upside to its renminbi lending, bond issuance and trading, renminbi foreign exchange conversion, and other renminbi-related businesses. For example, outstanding Dim Sum bonds can be expected to rise from the current RMB 230 billion to RMB 1.5 trillion in 2015. BOC (HK) will be the biggest beneficiary from the growth of the renminbi offshore market.

REFERENCE

Feyzioglu, Tarhan, Nathan Porter, and Elod Takats, 2009, "Interest Rate Liberalization in China," IMF Working Paper 09/171 (Washington: International Monetary Fund).

---

[1]The acronym CNH is used to represent offshore renminbi.

CHAPTER 15

This Time Is Different: The Domestic Financial Impact of Global Rebalancing

VICTOR SHIH

In 1998, the Chinese financial system faced a severe challenge. The region was in financial turmoil, and the wave of bankruptcies of state-owned enterprises (SOEs) in the 1990s had produced official nonperforming loan (NPL) ratios of over 25 percent. Yet, the Chinese leadership brought China through the difficulties with sweeping financial reform that revolved around the centralization of the "Big Four" state banks and the disposal of NPLs in asset management companies (AMCs). The result was stunning success that ended with the successful listing of all of China's major state banks.

Today, China faces a much more benign but nonetheless challenging environment. External demand has remained stagnant and official NPL ratios remain at historically low levels, although the pool of illiquid assets on the banks' balance sheets may well be large. Yet, China now has a smaller cushion with which to buffer a significant worsening of the financial balance sheets. The main reason is that trade surplus and foreign exchange flows no longer infuse the banking system with large new deposits, which in the past allowed the banks to comfortably roll over illiquid assets while still financing new economic activities. Also, off-balance-sheet financial activities make up a much larger share of total credit than was the case in 1998. Going forward, the central bank will need to be much more aggressive in releasing sufficient liquidity into the economy, especially if significant financial reforms are carried out simultaneously. Over time, Chinese firms must learn to reduce their demand for capital inputs.

FINANCIAL RESTRUCTURING IN THE LATE 1990s

The administration of Zhu Rongji devised a set of sweeping changes to reduce NPLs in the late 1990s because existing policy on write-offs only resolved a tiny fraction of the estimated RMB 3.3 trillion in NPLs (37 percent of 2000 GDP). In October 1997, the Central Committee and the State Council jointly issued the *Notice Concerning Deepening Financial Reform, Rectifying Financial Order, and Preventing Financial Risk* (*Guanyu Shenhua Jinrong Gaige, Zhengdun Jinrong Zhixu, Fangfan Jinrong Fengxian De Tongzhi*). Local branches of the state banks and of the People's Bank of China (PBC) were removed from the local party committees' jurisdiction and placed under the newly formed Central Finance Work Committee. The central government also closed hundreds of locally controlled trust and investment companies and underground banks (Zhu, 1998). To ensure compliance with these stunning announcements, Zhu, who was slated to become premier in the spring of 1998, chaired an emergency Central Finance Conference in November 1997 with the main theme of "preventing financial risk" (*fangfan jinrong fengxian*).[1]

A crafty politician, Zhu offered provinces in western China, as well as large state-owned enterprises, additional financial support in exchange for their agreement with his plans to centralize the banking system and institute sweeping changes to the banks' internal credit approval process. Zhu also set harsh targets to lower the ratio of NPLs and ordered state banks to implement systems of responsibility such that managers who authorized loans could be punished with wage reductions and employment termination (Zhu, 1998). PBC governor Dai Xianglong further specified this policy by ordering the Big Four banks to lower their NPL ratios by 2 to 4 percent annually depending on the quality of their portfolios (Editorial Committee of the Great Reference of Economics, 2001).

To resolve the enormous NPL problem at the time, the four AMCs—Xinda, Changcheng, Huarong, and Dongfang—assumed the NPLs from the China Construction Bank (CCB), Agricultural Bank of China (ABC), Industrial and Commercial Bank of China (ICBC), and Bank of China (BOC), respectively (the People's Bank of China, Ministry of Finance, and China Securities Regulations Commission, 2000). In essence, the four AMCs issued RMB 1.4 trillion in financial bonds to the state banks and used the funds to purchase RMB 1.4 trillion in NPLs from the Big Four state banks at face value.[2] A few years after the NPLs were offloaded from the major state banks, the central government transferred US$45 billion from China's foreign exchange reserve to the CCB and the BOC in preparation for their listings, followed by an additional US$30 billion, half from the foreign exchange reserve and the other half from the Treasury, to recapitalize the ICBC. Finally, the ABC received a whopping US$40 billion for its recapitalization. Central Huijin, which was capitalized by resources from China's foreign exchange reserve, injected an additional US$45 billion in the Everbright Bank and two policy banks. With a much-reduced NPL burden and a bolstered capital base, China's major banks listed in Hong Kong SAR and Shanghai in succession throughout the 2000s.

The sweeping financial reform of the late 1990s has become the foundation of the world's confidence in China's ability to deal with potential banking crises. With a great deal of control over the banks and the largest foreign exchange

---

[1] The routine Central Financial Conference had already taken place in January 1997.

[2] "At face value" means at the original amount of the loan plus accrued interest. In a market economy, private asset management companies by definition never purchase a NPL at face value because of its high risk profile.

reserves in the world, surely China can repeat its actions in the late 1990s to rescue the banks.

CHALLENGES TO CHINA'S BANKS TODAY

In many ways, conditions today are significantly more benign for China than in the late 1990s. For one, China's economy is much bigger today, making it more resilient to external and internal economic shocks. Even in 2008, China had the third-largest economy in the world behind only the United States and Japan, but today China has become the second-largest economy in the world. With a current GDP of US$8.24 trillion, few external crises can have a catastrophic impact on China. Also, China now has the world's largest foreign exchange reserves at US$3.2 trillion, making the country's currency seemingly impregnable to speculative attacks. Finally, the banking reform of the late 1990s left its mark, as banks in China today generally are much more professional than they were in the mid-1990s. Since the late 1990s, reducing NPL ratios has become an obsession with Chinese banks, and as a result banks in China now have some of the lowest NPL ratios in the world (Figure 15.1).

Despite these great advantages, some worrisome trends have also emerged for China's banking sector. First and foremost, the banking recapitalization a decade ago was too successful, in a sense. When the world financial crisis descended on China in 2008, Chinese banks were so well capitalized and had so much liquidity that they could boost lending by over 30 percent in one year. After 2009, Chinese banks' balance sheets continued to grow at a rapid clip such that bank assets, when one takes into account assets in the shadow banking sector, are now approaching 300 percent of GDP. Figure 15.2 shows that whereas China's GDP in 2011 was RMB 47 trillion, assets in the formal banking sector totaled RMB 115 trillion, and bank assets continued to grow to RMB 125 trillion by end-July 2012. Meanwhile, Fitch Ratings (2012) estimates that wealth management products, which also provide credit, totaled RMB 10 trillion as of mid-2012. In 1998, repairing a hypothetical 50 percent NPL ratio meant finding resources equivalent to 50 percent of GDP. Today, if 50 percent of bank assets were to become nonperforming, the write-down would be close to 150 percent of GDP. Even a nonperforming asset ratio of 20 percent translates to a nearly 60 percent of GDP write-down.

Also, in a way, China was lucky in the late 1990s because it was on the verge of entering the most spectacular period of current account surplus the world had ever seen. When money flowed into China from the current account surplus, foreign direct investment (FDI), or hot money inflows, the recipients of dollars sold them to their banks in return for renminbi. When banks ran short on renminbi, they had to sell their dollar holdings to the PBC, which printed high-power money to purchase banks' foreign exchange sales. Thus, indirectly, the creation of high-power money by the PBC allowed foreign exchange earners to increase their renminbi deposits while exchange rates remained at roughly the same level. At their height in early 2008, net foreign exchange inflows over a

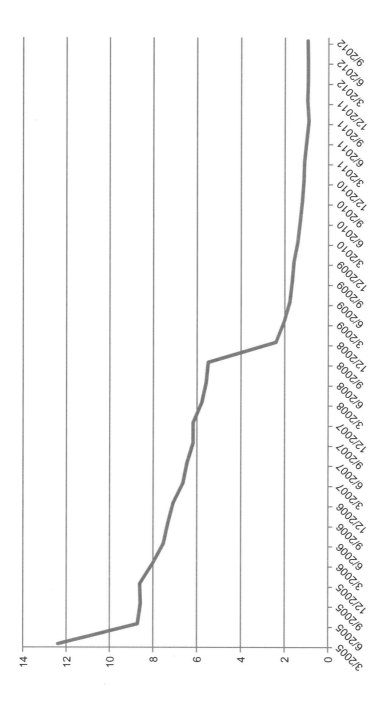

Source: CEIC.

Figure 15.1 Commercial Bank Nonperforming Loan Ratio
(In percent)

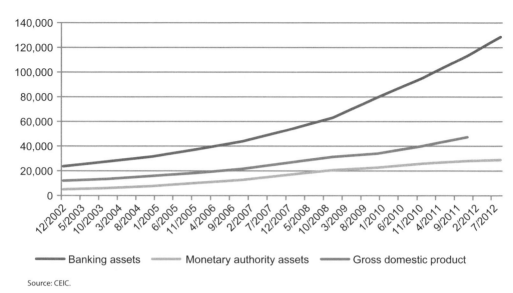

Banking assets ——— Monetary authority assets ——— Gross domestic product

Source: CEIC.

Figure 15.2 GDP, Central Bank Assets, and Bank Assets
(In billions of renminbi)

12-month period increased deposits by 7 percent of bank assets (Figure 15.3). The trade surplus increased deposits by 3.5 percent of bank assets over a 12-month period in 2007–08. Even as late as mid-2011, net foreign exchange inflows still increased deposits equivalent to 3.5 percent of bank assets over a 12-month period. Into 2012, however, these inflows only brought in a tiny amount of new liquidity. By July 2012, net foreign exchange inflows only brought in deposits equivalent to 0.5 percent of bank assets over a 12-month period. In sum, easy money creation from net foreign exchange inflows has become a thing of the past.

The enormous size of China's banking system and the end of easy liquidity from foreign exchange inflows have enormous implications for China's monetary policy going forward. First and foremost, without active PBC intervention to increase money supply, the pace of lending will slow to a level that is detrimental to the targeted growth rate of 7.5 percent. To be sure, since the beginning of the year, the PBC has continued to redeem PBC sterilization bills and to lower reserve requirement ratios to release high-power money into the economy (Figure 15.4). However, in combination with weak external demand, industrial output and fixed-asset investment have both slowed substantially from previous years. Growth in 2012 will be more modest than in the previous years. Without the PBC's short-term facilities in the form of reverse repos, growth likely would be even slower. This stands in sharp contrast to the situation in the 2003–08 period, when the PBC only had to guard against inflation because banks had plenty of liquidity with which to lend to firms. Today, the PBC needs to be ever more vigilant against liquidity shortages in the interbank markets and intervene in a timely matter to prevent spikes in interbank rates.

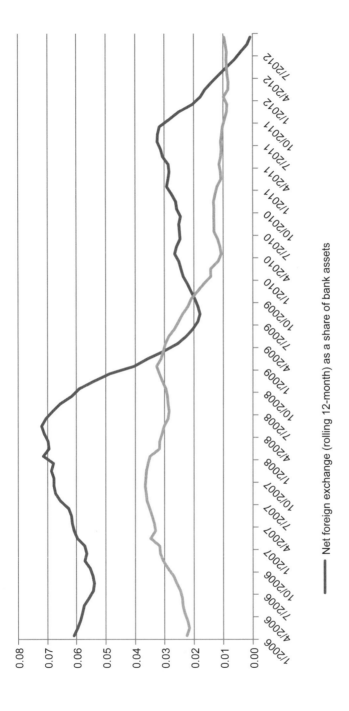

Source: CEIC.

Figure 15.3 Trade Surplus and Net Foreign Exchange Inflows (12-month rolling) as a Share of Total Bank Assets
(*In percent*)

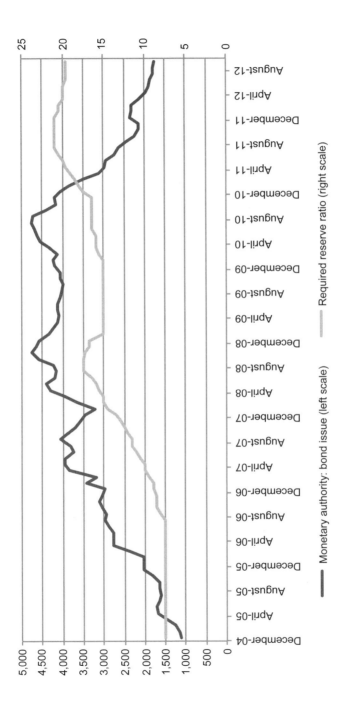

Figure 15.4 The People's Bank of China Bills Outstanding
(Billions of renminbi, LHS; reserve requirement ratio, RHS)

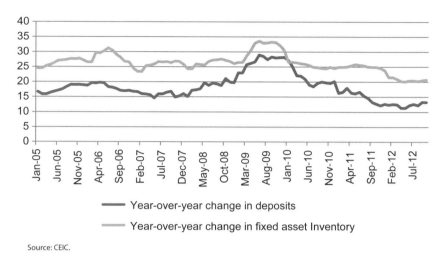

Year-over-year change in deposits

Year-over-year change in fixed asset Inventory

Source: CEIC.

Figure 15.5 Percent Increases in Fixed-Asset Investment and Deposits *(Year over year)*

For firms in China, the era of easy credit from the banks is over. As bank deposit growth slowed sharply after 2011, the real cost of capital for firms also rose, despite rate cuts by the PBC (Figure 15.5). Smaller firms have a hard time borrowing from the banks, forcing them to borrow from trust companies and underground banks at much higher rates. Even larger real estate firms have had to borrow from trust companies, which raise money by issuing trust products paying high yields. Figure 15.5 reveals that the gap between the rate of investment growth and the rate of deposit growth is diverging, which is not sustainable. If the rate of deposit growth continues to slow due to low foreign exchange inflows, firms in China will need to slow the pace of investment. In the long term, this will contribute to economic rebalancing in China. However, in the short and medium term, this may cause painful changes in industries that are used to easy liquidity from the banks.

Fortunately for China, the PBC still has multiple weapons with which to ease this process of slowing investment by firms. First, as seen in Figure 15.4, China continues to have some of the highest reserve requirement ratios in the world and can lower those requirements to pump long-term liquidity into the banking system. Second, the PBC can redeem the RMB 1.8 trillion or so in sterilization bonds, which it has done at a relatively fast pace in recent months. Finally, the PBC can provide short-term liquidity via reverse repos. However, because reverse repos mainly provide 7-day or 14-day liquidity, banks are reluctant to provide long-term liquidity to firms, fearing that PBC inaction would force them to borrow at a high cost in the interbank market. With the end of easy liquidity, the PBC must find a way to provide banks with long-term expectations of sufficient liquidity that does not signal reckless easing. The PBC may be wary that aggressive reserve requirement ratio cuts may give rise to another investment mania.

However, the slowdown in inflows itself should credibly signal to firms the limit of PBC easing.

In the medium term, the greater challenge for the PBC and the financial regulators, as well as China's planning authorities, is to slowly adjust the economy away from capital-intensive investment toward a more consumption-driven growth model. As Yifu Lin and others have noted, distortions in the form of taxes and subsidies need to be removed over time to reduce incentives to engage in a capital-intensive pattern of investment (Lin and Li, 2009). Distressed assets in the banking system will increase, and the authorities need to anticipate this and deal with the rising pool of distressed assets in an orderly fashion. Perhaps the greatest challenge going forward is the political opposition from capital-intensive industries against any adjustment policies.

REFERENCES

Editorial Committee of the Great Reference of Economics, 2001, *"Guoyou Yinhang Shangshi Sannian Zhinei Meixi"* ("There Will Not Be Much for State Banks IPO within Three Years)," *Jingji Da Cankao (The Great Reference of Economics)*, No. 4.

Fitch Ratings, 2012, "Chinese Banks: Wealth Management Risks Climb as Small Banks Accelerate Issuance," July 27. www.fitchratings.com.cn.

Lin, Yifu, and Feiyue Li, 2009, "Development Strategy, Viability, and Economic Distortions in Developing Countries," World Bank Policy Research Working Paper No 4906 (Washington: World Bank).

The People's Bank of China, Ministry of Finance, and China Securities Regulations Commission, 2000, *"Guanyu Zujian Zhongguo Xinda Zichan Guanli Gongsi De Yijian"* ("Opinion Concerning the Formation of Xinda Asset Management Company"), in *Lun Zhongguo Buliang Zhaiquan Zhaiwu De Huajie (On the Dissolution of Bad Debt and Bad Debt Obligations in China)*, ed. by Xiangyang Zhan (Beijing: China Financial Publisher).

Zhu, Rongji, 1998, *"Shenhua Jinrong Gaige; Fangfan Jinrong Fengxian; Kaichuang Jinrong Gongzuo Xin Jumian"* ("Deepening Financial Reform, Preventing Financial Risks, and Creating a New Phase for Financial Work"), in *Xin Shiqi Jingji Tizhi Gaige Zhongyao Wenxian Xuanbian* ("A Selection of Important Documents for Economic Structural Reform in the New Period"), ed. by Document Research Center of the CCP Central Committee (Beijing: Central Document Publisher).

CHAPTER 16

The Renminbi's Prospects as a Global Reserve Currency

ESWAR PRASAD AND LEI YE[1]

Popular discussions about the prospects of China's currency—the renminbi—range from the view that it is on the threshold of becoming the dominant global reserve currency to the concern that rapid capital account opening poses serious risks for China. A number of recent academic studies have pointed to the renminbi's rising importance in the international monetary system, although these studies are divided on its prospects of becoming a dominant global reserve currency (Eichengreen, 2011b; Frankel, 2011; Subramanian 2011; and Yu, 2012).

This issue has broader ramifications, as the rise of China's economy and its currency have implications for global macroeconomic and financial stability. Among the currencies of the world's five largest economies, the renminbi is the only one that is not a reserve currency. Even though its economy has neither a flexible exchange rate nor an open capital account, the Chinese government has recently taken a number of steps to increase international use of the renminbi. Given China's rising shares of global GDP and trade, these steps are gaining traction and portend a rising role for the renminbi in global trade and finance.

The popular debate often conflates three related but distinct aspects of the renminbi's role in the global monetary system:

- *Internationalization:* use of the renminbi in denominating and settling cross-border trade and financial transactions, that is, its use as an international medium of exchange.

- *Capital account convertibility:* the country's level of restrictions on inflows and outflows of financial capital. A fully open capital account has no restrictions.

- *Reserve currency:* whether the renminbi is held by foreign central banks as protection against balance of payments crises.

A currency's international usage and its convertibility are different concepts, and neither one is a necessary or sufficient condition for the other. Both conditions have to be met, however, for a currency to become a reserve currency. We consider these aspects in turn.

---

[1] This article is based on the study by the authors entitled "The Renminbi's Role in the Global Monetary System," published in February 2012 by The Brookings Institution.

China is promoting the international use of its currency by:

- Permitting the settlement of trade transactions with the renminbi;
- Easing restrictions on cross-border remittances of the renminbi for settlement;
- Allowing the issuance of renminbi-denominated bonds ("Dim Sum bonds") in Hong Kong SAR and by foreigners on the mainland;
- Permitting selected banks to offer offshore renminbi deposit accounts; and
- Setting up local currency bilateral swap lines with other central banks.

The trajectory is steep in each of these categories but the amounts are still modest. Trade settlement occurs mostly on the import side; Dim Sum bonds remain narrow in scope in terms of industry (primarily banking and financial institutions) and geography of issuance (primarily mainland China); and bilateral swap lines are not always drawn upon. Nevertheless, a big advantage for China is that Hong Kong provides an effective platform for launching these measures in an experimental manner without full capital account opening. Having said that, these developments could soon hit their limits unless China's capital account becomes more open.

The renminbi is also starting to appear in the reserve portfolios of some emerging market as well as advanced economy central banks. The bilateral currency pact that China and Japan agreed upon in December 2011 is an interesting example of how China is attempting to reduce its dependence on the dollar, while other countries, especially in the Asian region, appear eager to participate in such agreements because they see advantages to tighter trade and financial links with China. These shifts, which are more symbolic than substantive at present, will develop critical mass over time and have the potential to start transforming the global monetary system.

The renminbi's prospects as a reserve currency will be influenced by the following criteria:

- *Economic size.* A country's size and its shares of global trade and finance are important but not crucial determinants of its currency's status as a reserve currency. China now accounts for 10 percent of world GDP (15 percent if measured by purchasing power parity rather than market exchange rates) and 9 percent of world trade. In 2011, it is estimated to have accounted for about one-quarter of world GDP growth.
- *Open capital account.* The currency must be easily tradable in global financial markets with no restrictions on capital flows. China is gradually and selectively easing restrictions on both inflows and outflows. The capital account has become increasingly open in de facto terms, but extensive capital controls still prevail (Prasad and Wei, 2007; Prasad and Ye, 2012).
- *Flexible exchange rate.* Reserve currencies generally trade freely at market-determined exchange rates. It is worth emphasizing that an open capital account is not synonymous with a freely floating exchange rate. China still

has a tightly managed exchange rate, which will become increasingly hard to manage as the capital account becomes more open.

- *Financial market development.* A country must have broad, deep, and liquid financial markets so that international investors will have access to a wide array of financial assets denominated in its currency. China has relatively shallow and underdeveloped government and corporate bond markets. Many other securities and derivatives markets are in their nascent stages.

- *Macroeconomic policies.* Investors in a country's sovereign assets must have faith in its commitment to low inflation and sustainable levels of public debt. China has a lower ratio of explicit public debt to GDP than most major reserve currency economies and has maintained moderate inflation in recent years.

There are no ironclad rules about the relative importance of the factors listed above or trade-offs between them. For instance, the Swiss franc is a global reserve currency even though Switzerland's shares of global GDP and trade are quite modest. Moreover, the euro zone, Japan, and the United States have large and rising public debt burdens, which raises questions about their macroeconomic stability but has not (yet) affected their currencies' status as reserve currencies. Some analysts have in fact extrapolated from the U.S. experience to argue that China must run large current account deficits if it wants to provide reserve assets to the rest of the world. But this is neither a necessary nor sufficient condition for attaining reserve currency status. Some major reserve currency economies, including the euro area and Japan, have run current account surpluses or at least a balanced current account for a long time.

Financial market development in the home country is one of the crucial determinants of a currency's international status.[2] Historically, each reserve currency has attained that status under unique circumstances and spurred by different motivations. But in all cases foreign investors have been able to buy high-quality assets, typically government and corporate bonds, denominated in the country's currency.

The relevant aspects of financial market development are the following:

- *Breadth:* the availability of a broad range of financial instruments, including markets for hedging risk;

- *Depth:* a large volume of financial instruments in specific markets; and

- *Liquidity:* a high level of turnover (trading volume).

Without a sufficiently large debt market, the renminbi cannot be credibly used in international transactions. If there is insufficient liquidity in markets for renminbi-denominated assets, the currency will not be attractive to foreign investors. Other central banks and large institutional investors will demand

---

[2]For example, the strengthening of the U.S. financial market relative to that of the United Kingdom was a critical factor that contributed to the rise of the U.S. dollar's reserve currency status (Eichengreen, 2011a).

renminbi-denominated government and corporate debt as "safe" assets for their portfolios. At the same time, both importers and exporters may be concerned about greater exchange rate volatility resulting from an open capital account if they do not have access to derivatives markets to hedge foreign exchange risk.

A key determinant of the U.S. dollar's status as the dominant global reserve currency can be traced to its financial markets, which remain unmatched in their breadth, the range of financial instruments available to foreign investors, the amounts of each such instrument, and the volumes of trading in those instruments. Paradoxically, for want of other safe assets, the high and rising level of U.S. government debt is cementing the role of the dollar as the dominant reserve currency. This safety could well be a chimera if the U.S. debt position becomes unsustainable.

In addressing the reserve currency criteria vis-à-vis the renminbi, China faces two major challenges:

- Sequencing of capital account opening with other policies, such as exchange rate flexibility and financial market development, to improve the cost/benefit trade-off; and

- Financial market development and strengthening the banking system, that is, developing deep and liquid government and corporate bond markets as well as foreign exchange spot and derivative markets.

China's ability to meet these challenges will determine the balance and sustainability of its economic development as well as the renminbi's role in the global monetary system. For example, liberalizing outflows could deliver collateral benefits, such as a broader range of saving instruments for households, and alleviate pressures to further accumulate foreign exchange reserves. Liberalizing inflows could help develop and deepen China's financial markets. Taken together, such measures can help catalyze progress toward China's objective of making Shanghai an international financial center and allow rebalancing of growth. However, a more open capital account can hurt financial stability and constrain monetary policy in the absence of a more flexible exchange rate and financial system reforms (Lardy and Douglass 2011; Prasad, Rumbaugh, and Wang 2005).

Thus far, commercial policies designed to increase the offshore use of the renminbi have been the centerpiece of China's currency internationalization process. Although this has been effective in promoting the renminbi's global role without risking the potential deleterious effects of capital account liberalization, the full potential of the Chinese currency's international use cannot be realized without more active onshore development.

Given its size and economic clout, China is adopting a unique approach, which we refer to as "capital account liberalization with Chinese characteristics." As with virtually all other major reforms, China is striking out on its own path to a more open capital account. This is likely to involve removing explicit controls even while attempting to exercise soft control over inflows and outflows through administrative and other measures. The medium-term objective, which will likely be achieved in the next five years, is an open capital account but with numerous administrative controls and regulations still in place.[3] This will allow the renminbi to play an increasingly significant role in global trade and finance, but in a manner that allows the government to retain some control over capital flows.

Although China's rapidly growing size and dynamism are enormous advantages that will help promote the international use of its currency, its low level of financial market development is a major constraint on the likelihood of the renminbi attaining reserve currency status. Moreover, in the absence of an open capital account and free convertibility of the currency, it is unlikely that the renminbi will become a prominent reserve currency, let alone challenge the dollar's dominance. However, on the basis of the anticipated pace of reforms, the renminbi will become a competitive reserve currency within the next decade, eroding but not displacing the dollar's dominance.

Even with only gradual financial market development, the renminbi can be expected to be included in the basket of currencies that constitute the IMF's Special Drawing Rights (SDR) basket within the next five years. The IMF needs China a lot more than China needs the IMF, and the prospect of the renminbi's inclusion in the SDR basket could be seen as a way for the IMF—and the international community that it represents—to exercise leverage over China in internalizing the global repercussions of its domestic policies.

The Chinese government's approach to policies that promote the renminbi's use as an international currency is inherently linked to domestic macroeconomic objectives and financial market development. The impact of the renminbi on the global monetary system and whether it contributes to greater global financial stability depends on the manner and speed with which China opens up its capital account and develops its financial markets, what other policy changes are put in place to support this process, and what the implications are for China's own growth and stability.

The big question now is whether China's government will use the goal of making the renminbi a global currency to catalyze momentum on a broad agenda of domestic policy reforms that are required to support this goal. Ultimately, the path of China's growth and its role in the global economy will depend on those policy choices.

REFERENCES

Eichengreen, Barry, 2011a, *"Exorbitant Privilege: The Rise and Fall of the Dollar and the Future of the International Monetary System* (New York: Oxford University Press).

———, 2011b, "The Renminbi as an International Currency" (unpublished; University of California, Berkeley).

Frankel, Jeffrey, 2011, "Historical Precedents for the Internationalization of the RMB," paper prepared for workshop sponsored by the Council on Foreign Relations and China Development Research Foundation, Beijing, November 1.

---

[3]Yam (2011) has referred to such a system as "full capital account convertibility."

Lardy, Nicholas, and Patrick Douglass, 2011, "Capital Account Liberalization and the Role of the Renminbi," Working Paper 11–6 (Washington: Peterson Institute for International Economics).

Prasad, Eswar, Thomas Rumbaugh, and Qing Wang, 2005, "Putting the Cart before the Horse? Capital Account Liberalization and Exchange Rate Flexibility in China," IMF Policy Discussion Paper 05/1 (Washington: International Monetary Fund).

Prasad, Eswar, and Shang-Jin Wei, 2007, "China's Approach to Capital Inflows: Patterns and Possible Explanations," in *Capital Controls and Capital Flows in Emerging Economies: Policies, Practices, and Consequences*, ed. by Sebastian Edwards (Chicago: University of Chicago Press for the National Bureau of Economic Research).

Prasad, Eswar, and Lei Ye, 2012, "The Renminbi's Role in the Global Monetary System," Brookings Institution Report, February (Washington: Brookings Institution). www.brookings.edu/~/media/research/files/reports/2012/2/renminbi%20monetary%20system%20prasad/02_renminbi_monetary_system_prasad.pdf.

Subramanian, Arvind, 2011, "Renminbi Rules: The Conditional Imminence of the Reserve Currency Transition," Working Paper 11–14 (Washington: Peterson Institute for International Economics).

Yam, Joseph, 2011, "A Safe Approach to Convertibility for the Renminbi," Working Paper 5 (Hong Kong: Institute for Global Economics and Finance, Chinese University of Hong Kong).

Yu, Yongding, 2012, "Revisiting the Internationalization of the Yuan," ADBI Working Paper 366 (Manila: Asian Development Bank Institute).

Afterword

Two years after the successful completion of China's first assessment under the Financial Sector Assessment Program (FSAP), the International Monetary Fund (IMF) has arranged for publication of this collection of writings on *China's Road to Greater Financial Stability: Some Policy Perspectives*. I would like to express my gratitude to the IMF and the experts who have contributed to this book. I hope that the book will enhance everyone's understanding of the challenges of the reform process, as well as the planned development of China's financial industry that will play a positive role in further improving the robustness of the country's financial system.

After the Asian financial crisis, the IMF and the World Bank jointly introduced the FSAP to provide a comprehensive and objective assessment of the robustness of member-country financial systems, reduce the possibility that financial crises would occur, and promote financial reform and development. The current global financial crisis has further underscored the importance of financial stability assessment work. The G20 leaders have committed themselves twice, at their summits in Washington and London, to the need to undergo assessments under the FSAP. China launched its FSAP assessment in August 2009. After careful planning and diligent work on the part of the People's Bank of China (PBC), other concerned departments, and the China FSAP team, the assessment was completed in November 2011. The assessment was a comprehensive "physical exam" of China's financial system and its financial stability framework from a global perspective. It affirmed China's accomplishments with respect to financial reform and developing and maintaining financial stability. The assessment, however, also identified potential risks to China's financial system and proposed several noteworthy ideas pertinent to the country's financial development.

This book is grounded in the context of taking China's financial industry reform and development as the point of departure, with the focus on the country's financial stability policies, challenges, and approaches. Based on an analysis of the potential risks China's financial industry faces, the book proposes financial stability policy measures that China should adopt as it moves forward.

The Chinese government has consistently attached great importance to financial stability. As early as 1997, when the crisis erupted in Asia, the Chinese authorities recognized that deepening reforms and strengthening financial regulation were important foundations for preventing and managing systemic risk. Since 1997, we have earnestly learned from the lessons of the crisis. We have comprehensively overhauled the financial system and disposed of a group of local and problematic small and medium-sized financial institutions, effectively eliminating hidden risks that had accumulated in the financial system over its history. In particular, since 2003, we have resolutely upheld an overall path of reform and development to promote stability, seized strategic opportunities to promote stable and relatively rapid growth of the Chinese economy, and decisively advanced and completed a series of major financial reforms.

Through the "quartet" program of writing off capital that was in fact already lost, stripping and disposing of nonperforming assets, using foreign reserves to effect capital infusions, and completing domestic and foreign initial public offerings, the major commercial banks have undergone historic changes. Their financial condition has improved dramatically, corporate governance has been continuously upgraded, risk tolerance levels have been markedly improved, and overall performance continues to improve. This laid a strong microfoundation for the financial industry's response to the global financial crisis in 2008, and afforded the financial system the ability to provide ample credit support and financial services for economic recovery.

At the same time, we persisted with market reforms, developing the bond market and encouraging and supporting product and systems innovation that conformed to market-based principles to improve the resource allocation function. We have also attached importance to upgrading and implementing international standards for financial system health, implementing the Basel Capital Accords, placing special emphasis on capital adequacy ratios and capital quality, and substantially increasing disclosure requirements as well as accounting and external audit standards.

Since 2005, the PBC has also published an annual *China Financial Stability Report* that comprehensively monitors and assesses the resilience of the financial system.[1] All these efforts, in concert with the work of other financial regulatory agencies, have continually strengthened China's ability for timely monitoring and evaluation of financial system risk.

Since 2008, in the headwinds of a once-in-a-century global financial crisis, the authorities have decisively implemented aggressive fiscal policies and moderately loose monetary policy, which smoothed the path for the Chinese economy toward stabilization and recovery. Thereafter, targeting new situations and issues that arose as a consequence of China's economic advancement, we have prudently made use of instruments such as interest rates, foreign exchange rates, deposit reserve rates, and open-market operations to promote reasonable growth in money and credit, adjust and optimize credit structures, and maintain steady and relatively rapid economic growth.

Starting in 2010, we actively established countercyclical macroprudential policy tools and implemented a dynamic differential reserve requirement measure with respect to certain banks that had relatively rapid credit growth and were systemically important. This has allowed us to limit excessive growth in credit and reduce inflation, with some positive results. The deep and unpredictable spillovers from the financial crisis continue to surface even today, and the

---

[1] The 2011 edition of the report is available at www.pbc.gov.cn/image_public/UserFiles/english /upload/File/China%20Financial%20Stability%20Report%202011.pdf.

global economic slowdown, monetary easing, and crisis-related fiscal measures in certain major economies have increased the difficulty and complexity for China to manage its financial system. Managing inflationary expectations and cross-border capital flows, for example, poses an ongoing challenge. We will carefully consider these factors in the policy framework and respond appropriately.

As this book suggests, certain potential risks and challenges remain in China's financial industry and must be resolved. We must perfect the countercyclical macroprudential policy framework and better balance the relationships between promoting economic growth, maintaining price stability, and preventing financial risk. We must establish a broader crisis management framework; improve systemic risk monitoring, assessment, and early warning systems; strengthen financial regulation; and address regulatory gaps and inadequacies. And we must establish systems that are more market-oriented, improve liquidity management, strengthen corporate governance of financial institutions, and expand financial markets and financial services.

Most of these have already been expressly stated in China's Twelfth Five-Year Plan. They were further emphasized at the National Financial Work Conference and the Central Economic Work Conference in late 2012. This demonstrates that the recommendations of the China FSAP team are essentially consistent with China's overall path to advance financial reform and maintain financial stability. As a developing country and an economy in transition, while drawing on international experiences and practices, we will comprehensively, systematically, and methodically press ahead with reforms that are suitable to China's particular circumstances and consistent with the characteristics of the domestic financial industry.

China's financial industry today stands at a new historic starting point. Against a backdrop of continued deepening of economic and financial globalization and integration, China has new strategic opportunities to expand domestic demand, improve innovation capacity, and promote a transformation of its economic growth pattern. Further deepening of reform, and opening up and development of China's financial industry, are critically important to promoting stable and sustainable development in China and even in the global economy.

In accordance with the requirements of the Twelfth Five-Year Plan, we will continue to accelerate reforms in focus areas and accelerate the establishment of a multilevel financial market system that is globally competitive and resilient to systemic risk. We will continue to implement sound monetary policy, strengthen the flexibility of monetary operations, steadily promote interest rate and foreign exchange rate liberalization, and gradually achieve renminbi capital account convertibility.

In particular, in light of the lessons of the global financial crisis, we will firmly ensure that finance serves the real economy, and prevent financial activities from deviating from the demands of the real sector. To this end, we must promote rational distribution of various financial services, expand financial support to weak areas, actively expand domestic demand, safely guide urbanization, maintain reasonable social financing, enlarge the coverage of financial services in the real economy, and diversify financing channels. This approach will help reduce the financing costs of economic development, markedly increase the level of financial services to the real economy, and establish a sound and modern financial system that promotes macroeconomic stability and supports economic growth and development.

The deeper impact of the global financial crisis is not over yet. The legacy of the crisis will last for a while. All countries need to strengthen policy coordination and cooperation. We are grateful for the tireless efforts of the IMF to promote international financial system reform and global financial governance, and we are grateful as well for everyone's concern and support for China's financial industry. As always, China will implement international financial standards and norms and deepen bilateral and multilateral economic and financial policy dialogue and coordination, while also continuing to strengthen cooperation with the IMF to jointly promote financial stability, economic prosperity, and sustainable growth in China and the world.

Zhou Xiaochuan
Governor
The People's Bank of China

Index